Praise for Lost Fire Lookout Hikes and Histories

I couldn't stop reading! *Lost Fire Lookout Hikes and Histories: Olympic Peninsula and Willapa Hills* is a must-have for anyone interested in fire lookouts, Washington state history and/or hiking. The book combines interesting historic facts with detailed driving directions and trail descriptions.

—Tammy McLeod, creator of *Fire Lookouts of the West Coloring Book*

Author Leslie Romer not only gives the necessary information needed to visit the "lost" lookouts of Washington's Olympics and Willapa Hills, she has painstakingly researched and updated lookout histories. I am placing my copy of *Lost Fire Lookout Hikes and Histories: Olympic Peninsula and Willapa Hills* on the shelf next to my well-worn copy of Kresek's magnum opus, *Fire Lookouts of the Pacific Northwest*. That's where it belongs.

—Keith Lundy Hoofnagle, Former Olympic Fire Lookout and National Park Service Ranger

When it comes to exploring the hills, doing the research and having knowledgeable contacts, Leslie leads the pack. This long-needed guide from her many site visits provides everything you need to have a wonderful fire lookout experience, even if the lookout building is long gone. The guidebook lays out the history, access and route in excellent detail, prompting the reader to want to go out and explore them.

—Eric Willhite, Peakbagger and Fire Lookout Blogger

Leslie Romer performs a major feat of archival research, as well as years of footwork, to come up with this wonderful new contribution to the Northwest's great-outdoors bookshelf. She spells out exactly how to follow in her footsteps, and she fleshes out the experience with details of both the present plant life and the past—in words and in exhumed photos.

—Daniel Mathews, author of *Cascadia Revealed: A Guide to the Plants, Animals and Geology of the Pacific Northwest Mountains*

This is a magnificent book, written by an experienced hiker and environmentalist. She has specialized in hiking to old fire lookout sites and has now visited more than 500 sites, most of them in Washington state. The book contains extensive overviews of 65 lookout sites in Washington's coastal region, providing historic background as well as practical information and detailed route maps.

—Bragi Ragnarsson, Professional Hiking Guide, Reykjavik, Iceland

Part hiking guide and part history book, Leslie Romer's *Lost Fire Lookout Hikes and Histories* is a richly detailed account of the long forgotten fire lookouts that once dotted the Olympic Peninsula and Willapa Hills. Romer, a backcountry enthusiast, adeptly guides the reader to the lookouts on trails just waiting to be explored.

—John Dodge, author of A Deadly Wind: The 1962 Columbus Day Storm

It is delightful . . . Leslie Romer makes a difference—inspiring a search for our history while exploring our beautiful world. May her readers follow her footsteps and find their own paths.

—Molly Erickson, US Forest Service, Retired (44 years)

LOST FIRE LOOKOUT HIKES AND HISTORIES

OLYMPIC PENINSULA AND WILLAPA HILLS

LESLIE ROMER

Sidekick Press
Bellingham, Washington

Copyright © 2021 Leslie Romer

Individual writers, artists, illustrators, and photographers retain all rights to their work, unless they have other agreements with previous publishers.

All rights reserved. No part of this publication may be reproduced, distributed, or transmitted in any form or by any means, including photocopying, recording, or other electronic or mechanical methods, without the prior written permission of the publisher, except in the case of brief quotations embodied in critical reviews and certain other noncommercial uses permitted by copyright law. For permission requests, write to the publisher at the address below "Attention: Permissions Coordinator."

Publisher's Note: Portions of this work are memoir. Interactions with other individuals are as the author remembers them.

Sidekick Press
2950 Newmarket Street
Suite 101-329
Bellingham, Washington 98226
www.sidekickpress.com

Lost Fire Lookout Hikes and Histories: Olympic Peninsula and Willapa Hills
ISBN 978-1-7369351-0-1
LCCN 2021918256

Cartographer: Martha Bostwick
Cover photograph: Kloshe Naniche replica cabin, 2003 (Leslie Romer).
Uncredited photographs in the text are by the author.

Cover Design: Elke Barter at elkebarter.com

All varieties of travel in unfamiliar territory include potential dangers. Readers of this book are responsible for their own actions and safety. The publisher and author are not responsible for the safety of the users of the information included here.

Dedicated to Henry Romer, my partner in life—
and in many adventures.

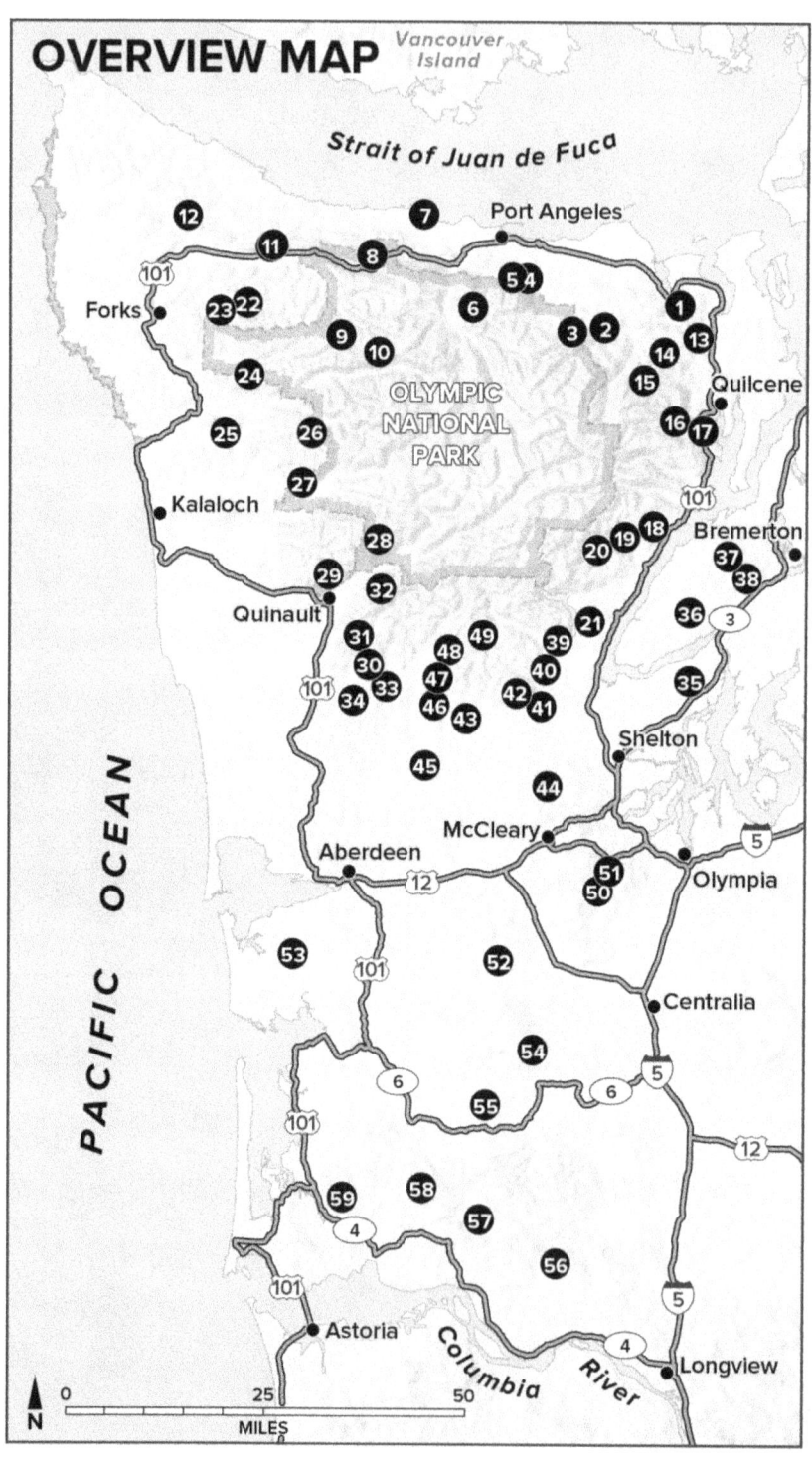

CONTENTS

Introduction 1
Overview History of the Fire Lookouts in Washington's
   Coastal Region 1
Know Where You Are Hiking 3
Federal Lands: Olympic National Park and Olympic
   National Forest 3
State Forestlands 5
Private Forestlands 5
Safety 6
Safety Essentials 7
Another Perspective 8
Animals, Plants, and Water 9
Hike Summary Tables 11

OLYMPIC PENINSULA NORTH 17
1. Blyn Lookout 18
2. Ned Hill Lookout 22
3. Blue Mountain Lookout 26
4. Mount Pleasant Lookout 30
5. Foothills Lookout 34
6. Hurricane Hill Lookout 38
7. Striped Peak Lookout 42
8. Pyramid Mountain Lookout 47
9. Sol Duc Lookout 52
10. Bogachiel Peak Lookout 57
11. Kloshe Nanich and North Point Lookouts 65
12. Ellis Lookout 71

OLYMPIC PENINSULA EAST 77
13. Skidder Hill Lookout 78
14. Mount Zion Lookout 83
15. Mount Townsend Lookout 88
16. Big Quilcene Lookout 94
17. Mount Walker Lookouts 97
18. Webb Mountain Lookouts 101
19. Hamma Hamma Guard Station Lookout 109
20. Jefferson Ridge Lookout 114
21. Dow Mountain Lookout 119

OLYMPIC PENINSULA WEST 125
22. Hyas Lookout 126
23. Crowsnest Lookout 130
24. Geodetic Hill Lookout 134
25. Mount Octopus Lookout 140
26. Owl Mountain Lookouts 144
27. Kloochman Rock Lookout 150
28. Finley Peak Lookout 156
29. Higley Peak Lookout 162
30. Humptulips Ridge Lookout 165
31. Chester Ridge Lookout 170
32. Colonel Bob Lookout 173
33. Humptulips Auxiliary Lookout 177
34. Twin Peak Lookout 182

KITSAP PENINSULA 187
35. Mason Lake Lookout 188
36. Tahuya Lookout 192
37. Green Mountain Lookout 197
38. Gold Mountain Lookouts 203

OLYMPIC PENINSULA SOUTH 209
39. Dennie Ahl Lookout 210
40. Grisdale Hill Lookout 214
41. Simpson Lookout 219
42. South Mountain Lookout 224
43. Kelly Lookout 229
44. Lost Lake Lookout 234
45. Mobray Lookout 239
46. Drake Lookout 242
47. Weatherwax Lookout 247
48. Anderson Butte Lookout 252
49. Dusk Point Lookout and Neby Lookout Tree 259

WILLAPA HILLS 265
50. Capitol Peak Lookout 266
51. Rock Candy Mountain Lookout 271
52. Byles Lookout 276
53. Johns River Lookout 281
54. Doty Lookout 286
55. Squally Jim and Walville Peak Lookouts 290
56. Incline Lookout 297

57. Blaney Mountain Lookout 301
58. Hull Creek Lookout 306
59. Cowan Lookout 311

Appendix One: Fire Lookout Sites No Longer Accessible 317
Appendix Two: Sekiu Fire Lookout at the Forks Timber
    Museum 319
Glossary and Abbreviations 321
Acknowledgments 323
Bibliography 326
About the Author 328
Author's Note 329
Index 330

INTRODUCTION

Overview History of the Fire Lookouts in Washington's Coastal Region

This book includes the hike routes and histories for sixty-six fire lookout sites in Washington's coastal region still accessible today. The hikes range from one-half mile to twenty-one miles, flat to steep, easy to challenging, and coastline to mountaintop. If you are looking for a new place to hike, you can find it here.

There are very few lookout buildings still standing in this region. With the historical information and hike directions in this book, you can visit the sites and restore the buildings in your mind. Three-fourths of these hike routes are published here for the first time. If you like solitude in the woods, trailheads without competitive parking, and untrammeled paths, you can find them among these hikes.

Early in the twentieth century, forest managers with foresight began to realize America's forests and wood supply would not last forever. Loggers had worked their way across the continent, and were harvesting giant trees close to the Pacific Ocean. Major forest fires occurred in the Pacific Northwest, even on the often rain-drenched Olympic Peninsula. Just as the value of early forest fire detection was recognized in other areas, the early forest managers in this region recognized the potential value of forest fire lookouts.

Early fire lookout stations appeared as mountain peak cabins, hilltop towers with small viewing platforms, and trees with ladders and seats on top. The first fire lookout on the Olympic Peninsula was the cedar shake-covered Finley Peak lookout cabin, built by the US Forest Service on a ridge north of Lake Quinault in 1916. A little white clapboard building with a cupola called Kloshe Nanich was perched above the Sol Duc River Valley in 1919, a joint effort of state, federal, and private cooperation. Close to ninety fire watch stations were staffed during fire seasons in Washington's coastal region between Finley Peak Lookout's first fire season and the 1960s.

Almost from the start of lookout construction in Washington state, aerial fire patrols were considered a potential alternative to stationary fire lookouts. The economics of air patrols gained support in the 1960s, and both federal and state forestry agencies changed their fire management policies during that decade. Most of the fire lookout buildings in Western Washington were closed and either abandoned or demolished by 1970. The roads and trails that led to those summit towers and cabins were abandoned or decommissioned. Nature was left to take its course.

This guide for hiking to historic fire lookout sites in coastal Washington is based on my exploration of the magnificent public and private forestlands in this region of the Pacific Northwest. After experiencing hiking trails from New Zealand to Iceland and a variety of places in between, I am happy to admit a preference for my home region. While we have many beautiful options for hiking, I have found exploration of the routes to old fire lookouts the most satisfying. Each offers not only its own combination of panoramic views, plant life, wildlife, and water features, but its own unique history as well.

As visitors to currently unrecognized historical sites, each of us has an opportunity to learn from the remnants of the fire lookout buildings and their surroundings. We also have a responsibility to leave artifacts where we find them. Photographs provide much better records of our visits than scraps of wood, glass, or metal. A collection of lookout site detritus in your home will have little meaning—while it could help paint an historical scene for another visitor—if it stays in place.

Fire watch stations needed good visibility in all directions, so they were located above the surrounding countryside, often on freshly logged hilltops. As a result, almost all lookout hikes involve elevation gain, and all provide panoramic perspectives, either at the summit or along the way.

Many of the hiking routes in this collection rely on the forest roads lookout staff drove to get to their workstations, if roads were available.

On private tree farms and state forestlands, most of those roads are still drivable partway to their destinations—many with a locked gate that ensures hiking at least part of the distance. In the Olympic National Forest and Olympic National Park (separate authorities with different expectations), most fire lookout sites are now reached by trail. Among the hikes in this collection, the routes on these federal lands are the best known, most popular, and most likely to require a pass or fee for entrance.

Know Where You Are Hiking

Have you ever arrived at a trailhead and discovered that some kind of pass is required, and you cannot buy it there? The hikes in this book are found in national parks, national forests, state forests, and on private tree farms. All Olympic National Park lookout hikes, some Olympic National Forest hikes, and many of the hikes on state forestlands require the appropriate pass for entrance. The owners of private forestlands do not require permits or payment for hiking the routes included in this collection, but each forestland management company has its own rules, posted on signs beside its property gates. There are other differences in the policies of these land management systems you should be aware of, as well.

Federal Lands: Olympic National Park and Olympic National Forest

Generally speaking, the landscapes in the federal parks and forests represent the highest conservation values available in the hiking world. The hike routes are more likely to be on trails than the routes on state or private lands, and the highest elevations are found here.

ANNUAL PASSES

Annual passes offer the best deal for visiting the Olympic National Park, and Olympic National Forest trailheads, where services are

provided. They additionally permit entrance for pass holders and their vehicle passengers into most other federal recreation lands.
- For national forests in Washington and Oregon, obtain a $30 annual Northwest Forest Pass.
- For national parks and federal recreation lands, obtain an $80 annual America the Beautiful Interagency Pass.
- For seniors (62 years and older) visiting national parks and federal recreation lands, obtain a $20 annual or $80 lifetime Interagency Senior Pass.
- For active military personnel and their families: free annual passes to federal lands are available.

SHORT TERM PASSES
- A $5 one-day pass is available on the internet for a visit to a trailhead in a national forest where services are provided (such as a restroom).
- A $30 seven-day pass is available for a private vehicle and its passengers for entry to the Olympic National Park.

ROADS
Despite the revenues from the interagency pass programs begun in 2017, these jurisdictions receive only enough funding to maintain their major roads and most popular trails. The numbering system for national forest roads identifies the traffic anticipated on each road by the number of digits in its road number.
- Two-digit roads, such as Forest Road (FR) 22, the Donkey Creek Road, are principal roads in the Olympic National Forest. They are usually paved roads, intended for use by passenger vehicles.
- Four-digit roads, the next level of road quality, are partly paved and partly gravel. FR 2206, which leads to Pete's Creek campground and trailhead, is an example.
- Three-digit roads are not usually maintained for passenger vehicles in the Olympic National Forest.

PETS
- Controlled pets are welcome on most national forest trails; leashes are sometimes required.
- Fully trained service animals are allowed on national park trails.
- Companion animals and pets are not allowed on national park trails.
- Companion animals and pets on leashes are often allowed in parking lots and visitor center areas in national parks.

Check the Olympic National Park and Forest websites for the latest guidance: https://nps.gov/olym/planyourvisit/basicinfo.htm for Olympic National Park and https://fs.usda.gov/main/olympic/home for Olympic National Forest.

State Forestlands

The Washington State Department of Natural Resources (DNR) manages twelve million acres of land statewide. Most of this land is available for recreational use. Areas named state forests almost always include recreational facilities, such as campgrounds, picnic areas, and trails. Most named state forests have signs requiring a state Discover Pass for parking. An annual pass is $30; a day pass is $10. The Discover Pass also offers entry to Washington State parks and Washington Fish and Wildlife lands. Other state forestlands do not currently have such signs, but may in the future.

Hikes to fire lookout sites located in state forests usually include some travel on gravel roads. Trails in named state forests are often shared with mountain bikes and horses, and occasionally, with motor bikes. The forest roads included here as hike routes are lightly traveled by motorized vehicles.

Private Forestlands

While a high percentage of private tree farms in this state now require purchase of recreational permits more costly than the annual state and federal passes, several timberland owners are notable as exceptions to this trend. Their plantations may have locked gates, but non-motorized recreation is welcome for day use. This is true for Hancock Timber Management and Campbell Global in the coastal region, and most of the Green Diamond Resource Company lands on the Olympic Peninsula. If recreational users respect the tree farms' access rules, it is likely these policies will continue.

The most important rule on private forestland is to avoid areas with active logging—this means to give tree harvest activities a wide berth; don't merely stop and wait for them to let you pass. Equally important is staying out of the way of logging trucks. If you see any signs of active logging, be prepared to yield a forest road to their vehicles. Your use of the route assumes you understand your status as a guest. Many private lands have been closed to recreational access, at least partly because of the inappropriate behavior of guests.

Hike routes on private forestland are almost always on gravel roads, ending at a dead end or logging landing, or finishing with a partially overgrown byway that leads in a short distance to an opening in the forest that may—or may not—contain artifacts.

Safety

In her 2017 book, *Found: A Life in Mountain Rescue,* Bree Loewen mentions that "Seattle Mountain Rescue volunteers do, on average, 135 rescues per year."[1] That is more than one rescue every three days! Please read this section with the intention of avoiding participation in these statistics.

When I was a trail crew volunteer with the Washington Trails Association, their priorities always impressed me: 1) Be safe; 2) Have fun; and 3) Get some work done.[2] That's what I hope you will do while hiking to lost lookouts—except the work part, of course. Some of these hikes are on well-known, well-maintained trails. Others are on forest roads occasionally used by logging trucks and other high-clearance

---

[1] Bree Loewen, *Found, a Life in Mountain Rescue* (Seattle, Mountaineer Books, 2017), 45.
[2] *WTA Trail Work Guide*; https://www.wta.org/get-involved/volunteer/about-trail-work/trail-work-guide.

vehicles. Many are on little used trails or decommissioned roads—which are not likely to be maintained. A good number of these hikes start on a well-defined route that evolves into an adventure hike as you progress.[3] If an adventure is indicated, leave the trailhead well-prepared for more than a short walk in a park. When you hike beyond the popular trails in national parks and forests or state forest recreation areas, you may not see another human from the time you leave your car until you return to a major highway on the way home.

Safety Essentials

- Tell someone where you are going, and, if you change your mind, text them an update while you still have a phone signal. Hike with a partner, especially if you haven't done a lot of hiking. The solo hikers I know have decades of experience and often carry electronic signaling devices for emergency messaging. I recommend them to solo hikers.
- Understand the navigational information in the hike description. Carry a detailed map with you. Either paper or electronic will do, as long as you are experienced with your device and confident it can maintain its signal and won't run out of battery power before you return.
- Even on shorter hikes, take enough food and water with you for a long day in the woods.
- Take more clothes than you imagine you might need. These hikes are in Washington's coastal region, and the weather can quickly change to cold and wet. Rain pants and jacket, gloves and a winter cap are never out of season in the Olympics and Willapa Hills.
- Carry a light and fire-starting tools on all hikes. I have a headlamp and matches in my pack. Others prefer a flashlight and lighter.
- Add an emergency shelter to the bottom layer. They come in small, lightweight packages and you may never need one. If you do, it could be a lifesaver.

---

[3] Check for adventure hikes in the *Hike Summary Table*.

- Carry a first aid kit equipped with your personal remedies for common ailments (aspirin, ibuprofen, Tums, Pepto-Bismol, insect repellent, After Bite, Benadryl, whatever). Take adhesive bandages (such as Band-Aids) in several sizes, a bandana for a sling and other uses, and whatever you have heard your hiking friends say they never intend to leave home without. It may be a knee brace, self-stick elastic bandages, or a clotting pad. My personal favorite is the 3.5"×4.5" *Pocket Guide to Emergency First Aid*. I have had repeated training, but am sure if an emergency occurs in the wilderness, reviewing the key steps to assessing and treating each condition will improve both the patient's and my confidence.

Another Perspective

My husband, Henry Romer, completed the "100 Peaks of Mount Rainier" in 2018. He says the two critical safety issues in wilderness are where you place your feet, and navigation. Every year, some well-known hiker misplaces a step and disappears. Even if you are only out of sight of your companions briefly, it may take a long time to find you. I have several friends who were luckier. They stepped in a hidden hole, or off the edge of the trail, and only sprained an ankle or strained a knee. How long and painful their return to the trailhead was depended on the strength of the rest of their party and how far they had to go.

Navigation is critical for hiking in the wilderness and the less popular areas of our forests. It is okay to rely on another member of your party to navigate if you stay together. Your expert friend may say it is easy to find the campsite; you can go at your own pace. Many forests have networks of trails and roads that can easily become confusing. If you are not carrying your own map or confident in the one you have, stick to your leader.

Most people carry phones into the forest these days. The mapping programs available can be excellent, but electronic resources have their own problems. Does yours run without mobile data? How long will it track your location without running down the battery? While it is possible to recharge your phone deep in a wilderness, that too requires additional specialized equipment.

I carry both a smartphone and a Global Positioning System (GPS). The GPS is battery-powered, and I carry spares. I can load information about my intended routes in the GPS before I leave home and accurately track and measure my trips wherever I travel. Despite the value I place on my GPS, I do recognize that GPS coordinates will not take me to an absolutely precise location. A GPS is typically accurate to a 5-meter (16.4-foot) radius under a clear sky.

When going somewhere for the first time, I also carry one or more paper maps. One map covers the approach route, while another provides the hike plan and sometimes alternatives. Comparing the GPS track with the anticipated route on paper is extremely important for arriving at a desired destination. Even straight lines can look very different on the landscape than on maps or even aerial photographs.

Animals, Plants, and Water

Should you worry about wildlife in the Olympics? Ninety-nine percent of the time there is nothing to worry about, but it is always safer to keep your distance. Don't assume a seemingly placid animal will wait patiently while you take the perfect photo. Any animal with teeth, big feet, or even little horns can cause a fatal injury. The bears in coastal Washington state are all black bears; they and cougars are usually shy. If they don't move away from you, retreat noisily. Mountain goats are being removed from the Olympic Range, but there will always be some, and even a placidly grazing goat may change its mind and charge. Smaller animals may look cute, but their slowness may be caused by an illness that could infect you, and your children, too.

It is important to carry enough water for the conditions. Only drink water that has been treated, unless you bring it from home. A lightweight water filter or purification treatment will make clear, flowing water safe to drink. Information on water safety options is readily available on the internet. Avoiding abdominal flu or giardia is well worth the effort.

Do not eat plants unless you are really confident you know what they are. Follow the simple red, white, and blue rule for berries in the Pacific Northwest: You can always eat blue, sometimes eat red, and never eat white. Once you get to know the berries, you can snack on them along the trail or take some home. Mushrooms range from safe and delicious to attractive and deadly poisonous. Study books, take classes, or ask friends who collect regularly, but be absolutely sure you know which are safe before picking or tasting any.

Some vegetation can sting as fiercely as a vicious insect. Two plants to become familiar with are devil's club and nettles. The spines on the tall devil's club stems can cause an inflammation from each contact. Touching a few fine needles on nettle leaves may leave only a brief tingling, but extended exposure can cause multi-day discomfort. Remove the big devil's club needles from your skin, then apply Benadryl cream. Benadryl cream or tablets also help with nettle stings that don't fade away promptly. These remedies have worked for me. Herbal treatments work for some people but I have not found them reliable. Carry medications that work for you every time.

Hiking to new places is great fun, but only if you return safely!

HIKE SUMMARY TABLES

Difficulty rating:	
1	Easy: Up to 4 miles roundtrip and up to 500 feet elevation gain.
2	Moderate: 4-8 miles roundtrip and up to 1200 feet elevation gain.
3	Hearty: More than 8 miles roundtrip or 1200 feet elevation gain.
4	Strenuous: More than 8 miles roundtrip or 2000 feet elevation gain.
5	Challenging: Beyond strenuous
🏠	Identifies a hiking route with a standing lookout.
🚶	Identifies a backpacking route.
Adventure: The route of an adventure hike includes a section of abandoned roads or trails that are not adequately, if ever, maintained.	

Olympic Peninsula North

Hike #	Name	Distance (RT in Miles)	High Point	Elevation Gain	Difficulty	Season	Wildflowers	Kid-Friendly	Adventure
1	Blyn	5.5	1966'	1100'	2	Apr-Nov	●	●	
2	Ned Hill Lookout 🏠	2.2	3460'	900'	2	May-Nov	●	●	
3	Blue Mountain Lookout	0.5	6007'	170'	1	Jun-Oct		●	
4	Mount Pleasant Lookout	5.0	2636'	1400'	3	Mar-Nov	●	●	
5	Foothills	1.2	2270'	450'	1	All Year		●	●
6	Hurricane Hill	3.2	5757'	650'	2	Jun-Oct	●	●	
7	Striped Peak	6.5	998'	1500'	3	All Year	●	●	
8	Pyramid Mountain 🏠	7.5	3100'	2400'	4	Apr-Nov	●		●
9	Sol Duc	9.5	4375'	2200'	4	Jun-Oct	●		●
10	Bogachiel Peak 🚶	16.5	5474'	3500'	5	Jul-Oct	●		
11	Kloshe Nanich and North Point 🏠	9.2	3340'	2730'	4	Jun-Oct	●		
12	Ellis	7.2	2338'	1450'	3	Apr-Oct	●		

Olympic Peninsula East

Hike #	Name	Distance (RT in Miles)	High Point	Elevation Gain	Difficulty	Season	Wildflowers	Kid-Friendly	Adventure
13	Skidder Hill	10.5	2125'	1500'	3	All Year			●
14	Mount Zion	3.5	4278'	1350'	3	Late Apr-Nov	●	●	
15	Mount Townsend	6.1 / 9.0 / 10.6	6212' / 6280' / 6280'	2200' / 2900' / 3500'	4	Jun-Oct	●		
16	Big Quilcene	5.0	3235'	1000'	2	Jun-Oct		●	
17	Mount Walker (2)	5.0	2802'	2000'	3	All Year	●		
18	Webb Mountain (2)	4.3 –7.8	2775'	615'-1440'	3	Apr-Dec	●		●
19	Hamma Hamma 🏠	2.0	655'	235'	1	All Year	●	●	
20	Jefferson Ridge	6.6	3850'	2750'	4	Jun-Nov			●
21	Dow Mountain	7.0	2514'	1700'	3	All Year		●	

Olympic Peninsula West

Hike #	Name	Distance (RT in Miles)	High Point	Elevation Gain	Difficulty	Season	Wildflowers	Kid-Friendly	Adventure
22	Hyas	2.6	3077'	750'	3	Apr-Oct	●		●
23	Crowsnest	1.25	2020'	180'	1	Apr-Oct		●	●
24	Geodetic Hill	6.0	3018'	1000'	3	Apr-Nov			●
25	Mount Octopus	5.0	2444'	800'	1	May-Oct	●	●	
26	Owl Mountain (2)	4.5	3484'	700'	4	Jun-Aug	●		●
27	Kloochman Rock	1.3+	3356'	800'	4	Late May-Aug			●
28	Finley Peak 🚶	21.0	3421'	4950'	5	Jul-Oct	●		●
29	Higley Peak	1.0	3025'	250'	1	May-Oct	●	●	●
30	Humptulips Ridge	4.0	1760'	1000'	4	Mar-Dec			●
31	Chester Ridge	2.5	1384'	500'	1	Mar-Dec			

Olympic Peninsula West (continued)

Hike #	Name	Distance (RT in Miles)	High Point	Elevation Gain	Difficulty	Season	Wildflowers	Kid-Friendly	Adventure
32	Colonel Bob	8.2	4492'	3450'	5	Jul-Sept	●		
33	Humptulips Auxiliary	6.0	1690'	350'	1	All Year		●	
34	Twin Peak	8.0	1340'	1250'	4	All Year			●

Kitsap Peninsula

Hike #	Name	Distance (RT in Miles)	High Point	Elevation Gain	Difficulty	Season	Wildflowers	Kid-Friendly	Adventure
35	Mason Lake	2.8	362'	400'	1	All Year		●	
36	Tahuya	6.5	443'	260'	2	All Year	●	●	
37	Green Mountain	7.4	1639'	1200'	2	All Year			
38	Gold Mountain (2)	8.0	1761'	1600'	3	All Year	●		●

Olympic Peninsula South

Hike #	Name	Distance (RT in Miles)	High Point	Elevation Gain	Difficulty	Season	Wildflowers	Kid-Friendly	Adventure
39	Dennie Ahl	3.0	2004'	450'	1	All Year		●	
40	Grisdale Hill	4.0	1511'	800'	2	All Year		●	
41	Simpson	3.6	1240'	950'	2	Oct-Dec		●	●
42	South Mountain	8.0	3040'	2450'	4	Oct-Dec			
43	Kelly	1.6	880'	330'	1	All Year		●	
44	Lost Lake	5.2	860'	530'	1	All Year		●	
45	Mobray	0.5	656'	50'	1	All Year		●	
46	Drake	8.0	1443'	750'	2	All Year			
47	Weatherwax	8.0	2640'	1950'	3	May-Nov			

Olympic Peninsula South (continued)

Hike #	Name	Distance (RT in Miles)	High Point	Elevation Gain	Difficulty	Season	Wildflowers	Kid-Friendly	Adventure
48	Anderson Butte	7.0	3358'	2300'	5	Jun-Nov	●		●
49	Dusk Point and Neby Lookout Tree (2)	6.7	3240'	1200'	2	Apr-Oct	●	●	●

Willapa Hills

Hike #	Name	Distance (RT in Miles)	High Point	Elevation Gain	Difficulty	Season	Wildflowers	Kid-Friendly	Adventure
50	Capitol Peak	8.2	2658'	1850'	3	Apr-Nov		●	
51	Rock Candy Mountain	6.5	2364'	1800'	3	All Year Best: Apr			
52	Byles	9.0	970'	1000'	2	All Year	●	●	●
53	Johns River	3.0+	410'	300'	1	All Year		●	
54	Doty	6.0	2081'	950'	3	Apr-Nov	●		●
55	Squally Jim and Walville (2)	6.0	2417'	1300'	3	All Year	●	●	●
56	Incline	7.8	2291'	1250'	3	Apr-Nov			
57	Blaney Mountain	2.5+	2546'	350'	2	Apr-Nov	●		●
58	Hull Creek	4.0	2042'	1050'	2	Apr-Nov	●		
59	Cowan	6.5	1940'	1500'	3	Apr-Nov			●

MAP LEGEND

(5)	Interstate highway	→	Direction of travel
(2)	US highway	——	Main trail
(530)	State route	········	Alternate or other trail
1230	Forest road		
≍	Bridge	-----	Crosscountry route
▲	Campsite or campground	═══	Paved road
⊢⊣	Gate or barrier	⊥⊥⊥⊥	Gravel road, traveled
L	Lookout site	⊤⊤⊤⊤	Gravel road, not traveled
🏠	Lookout, standing	— — — ·	Abandoned road
P	Parking	— — · ·	Abandoned road, not traveled
•	Point of interest	▭	Park or forest area
TH	Trailhead	•——•	Transmission line

OLYMPIC PENINSULA NORTH

Hikes accessible from US Highway 101
from its junction with State Route 20 at Discovery Bay
to its junction with State Route 113 at Sappho.

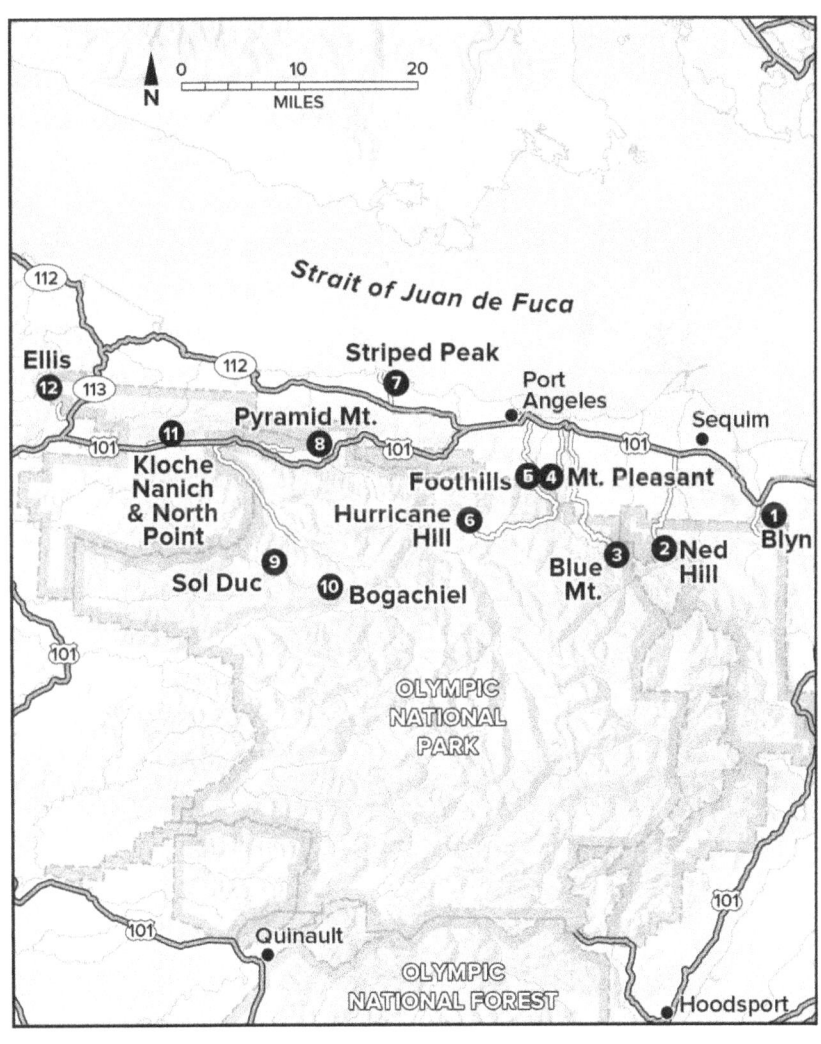

1. BLYN LOOKOUT

RT Distance: 5.5 miles
High Point: 1966 feet
Elevation Gain: 1100 feet
Season: Apr–Nov
No pass or permit is required.

History

Blyn, the small, nineteenth-century community on the south end of Sequim Bay, was named for Matthew Blinn, an early mill owner.[1] The Civilian Conservation Corps (CCC) built the first fire lookout tower in the area, a few miles south of the town. The CCC was the Depression-era employment program that contributed many interesting structures in parks and forests across the United States. In 1933, they built a ninety-foot pole tower with an 8×8-foot viewing station on top, plus a ground cabin for staff housing during fire season. A narrow ladder provided the only access to the platform.[2] A violent October 1934 windstorm blew the cabin against the tower, tearing the cabin to pieces and damaging the pole tower. It was all repaired the next year.[3] The Aircraft Warning Service replaced the station's ladder with stairs in 1942, intending to make the assignment more accessible to women who volunteered for the war effort.[4]

Blyn Lookout tower 1930s. US Forest Service photograph found in National Archives, Seattle. Courtesy of Ron Kemnow.

In 1959, the Department of Natural Resources replaced the very tall structure with a live-in cabin on a forty-foot tower. Olga Hughett, a Port Townsend mother and grandmother, who served as lookout at Blyn for fourteen summers, was working there at the time. Hughett, who retired in 1964, climbed the tall tower until her mid-fifties, and probably

---

[1] James W. Phillips, *Washington State Place Names*, 16.
[2] J. R. Rooney, *Frontier Legacy*, 41.
[3] Washington Forest Fire Association, *Twenty-seventh Annual Report*, 1934, 15.
[4] Ira Spring and Byron Fish, *Lookouts: Firewatchers of the Cascades and Olympics*, 94.

appreciated having her workspace and lodging eventually combined under one roof. The multitalented Hughett wrote freelance articles for the local newspaper, edited a monthly newsletter for Department of Natural Resources fire lookout staff, and later served on the board of the Jefferson County Historical Society. Two years after she left the lookout job, her granddaughter, Karen Ronning, accepted the assignment on Blyn Lookout—after being trained by Hughett.[5]

The cabin was removed from its aerie in the 1970s and transported to another location for use as a vacation home.[6] The fire lookout's outhouse remained upright at the lookout site into the twenty-first century, before settling into the landscape.

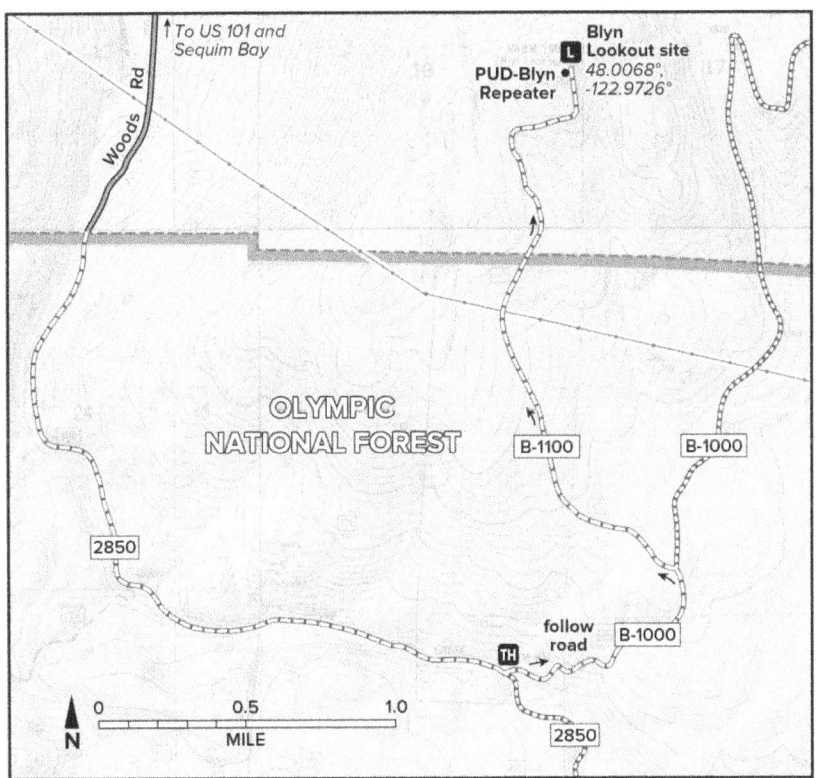

---

[5] Olga Hughett, "Eleven Lookouts Watch for fires in Jefferson County," *Port Townsend Leader*, August 2, 1962, 7; article in *Port Angeles Evening News*, October 5, 1966, quoted in https://washingtonlookouts.weebly.com/blyn.html.
[6] Ray Kresek, *Fire Lookouts of the Northwest; Revised Lookout Inventory*, 2015, 22. (hereafter cited in notes as Kresek, *2015*).

Hike Summary

This is a road hike in state forest, winding through dense woods high above Sequim Bay. Enjoy a few long views on the way up and down. An interesting array of artifacts—including a hidden benchmark, footing blocks from both the towers that stood on the hilltop, and an outhouse in the woods—await the persevering hiker.

Getting There

- From US Highway 101 at the south end of Sequim Bay, turn south on Woods Road between mileposts 271 and 272.
- The road is paved for 1.6 miles. There it enters the Olympic National Forest with only a small *Stop Wildfires* sign to suggest the boundary. Woods Road becomes Forest Road (FR) 2850 on maps and runs close to the eastern bank of Jimmycomelately Creek until the road rounds a curve and turns eastward. There, Snow Creek takes over as the tumbling water beside the road.
- At 4.2 miles from US Highway 101, a side road continues straight, while the National Forest road curves to the right and southward. The straight road is state FR B-1000, marked with a small sign: *PUD Blyn Repeater*. Park on the state forest road and start your hike here.

Hiking Route

This hike passes through a healthy forest of conifers and deciduous trees, with a variety of small shrubs in its understory. There are many Douglas firs, western hemlocks, big leaf maples, and alders along the way, highlighted with cedars near marshy, damp areas. Salal and red huckleberry are common along the roadside, with rhododendrons appearing often at higher elevations.

Maps identify the initial road as B-1000. Hike 0.8 mile on this lane, then take a left at a Y onto B-1100. Signs along the route mark the turns needed to reach the *PUD Blyn Repeater*, one of the communication towers occupying the lookout site. At 1.5 miles, cross under high voltage power lines in a cleared area. The elevation here is 1750 feet. In another 0.25 mile, keep left at the fork.

At 2.4 miles, turn right for the last segment of the hike. There are still curves in the path ahead, but no more side roads requiring directional decisions. Parcels harvested since 2010 allow long views to the northeast.

At the summit, two towers inside chain-link fences catch the eye. To the right, six or more footing blocks sit visible in the short grass. A quick examination reveals an age difference between two sets of blocks. Apparently the two towers on the site had overlapping footprints. Records of a 1966 site visit by National Coast and Geodetic Survey staff indicate the US Army Corps of Engineers survey marker stamped *Blyn* was found in good condition 12 feet east of the center of the contemporary tower. The US Coast and Geodetic Survey report noted that its original location had been under the center of the original lookout tower on the site.[7] Not finding this benchmark during my last visit, I have to think it is well hidden in the neighboring foliage.

The remains of the outhouse are sheltered by tree cover, as well. The sagging remnants of the once classic wooden structure may be found slightly downhill, on the north side of the Blyn Hill summit. Enjoy your exploration.

---

[7] US National Geodetic Survey, "Data Sheet PID TR1738 BLYN LO"; https://www.ngs.noaa.gov/cgi-bin/ds_mark.prl?PidBox=TR1738.

2. NED HILL LOOKOUT

RT Distance: 2.2 miles
High Point: 3460 feet
Elevation Gain: 900 feet
Season: May-Nov
No pass or permit is required.

History

According to the inventories of historical fire lookouts published in the 1980s, the unique Ned Hill fire lookout tower was built on a high bluff overlooking the Slab Camp Creek Valley in 1933.[1] Confirming its age, the tower's railing appears in a 1935 US Forest Service panoramic photograph taken from the site.[2] The pictured railing looks quite similar to those on the current fragile tree platform. Unlike any other standing fire watch station in Washington, this twenty-foot structure is supported by two rooted trees and several poles, two straight and a couple serving as diagonal braces. Smaller logs serve as flooring for the viewing platform.

"During the 1930s, fire guards stationed on Slab Camp Creek southeast of Ned Hill went up to the platform to look over the Gray Wolf River Valley and the slopes of Maynard and Mount Baldy. Blue Mountain (site of the Deer Park ski area then) was four miles directly west; to the north he could see the Strait of Juan de Fuca."[3]

In 1936, the Forest Service considered the site for a more substantial lookout structure. Ranger Robert H. Mealey visited the station and completed a fire lookout site evaluation form: "I recommend this point highly. It is almost ideal. A road can easily be built

The Ned Hill Lookout 2017.

---

[1] Spring and Fish, 198; Kresek, *Fire Lookouts of the Northwest*, 1998, 115 (hereafter cited in notes as Kresek, *1998*).
[2] Osborne photographs and documentation accessed in 2018 at http://iamwho.com/cdv2/Wa/olympic/olym140/site.htm.
[3] Spring and Fish, 102-103.

to the summit. It gives excellent coverage on high hazard areas, it is low and hence below the fog, and, altogether, is practically ideal from all standpoints."[4]

According to the trailhead billboard, Jim Halvorson, a retired recreation ranger, restored the trail, improved the parking, built trailside benches, and kept the old tower intact in the 1990s. More recently, another volunteer, Jim Sanderson, has worked to maintain these facilities for visitors.

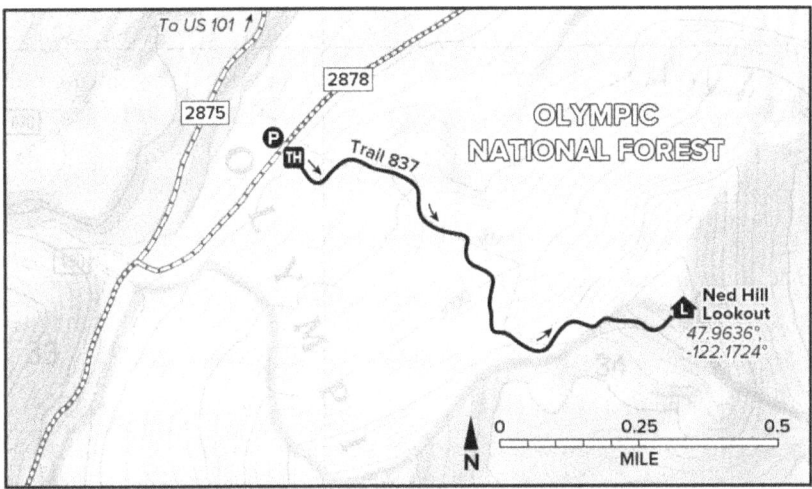

Hike Summary

This is a short, shady hike on a nice trail with rhododendrons brightening the way to the barely standing lookout tower. The route zigzags up to ridge views, with benches at the end of each of four steep stretches.

Getting There

- Drive US Highway 101 between Sequim and Port Angeles.
- At milepost 262, turn south on the Taylor Cutoff Road.
- At 2.6 miles, follow the roadway to the right as it becomes the Lost Mountain Road.

---

[4] Robert H. Mealey, [Fire Lookout Site Evaluation] "Ned Hill," 2; July 23, 1936; Document 18-15, National Archives in Seattle.

- At 5.2 miles, turn left on well-maintained gravel Forest Road (FR) 2870, at a sign for Slab Camp.
- At 6.1 miles, follow the right branch, FR 2875.
- At 9.7 miles from US Highway 101, turn left on FR 2878, which usually lacks a visible sign. FR 2875 ends at this road junction at the trailhead for Slab Camp.
- Drive 0.6 mile on FR 2878. The trailhead is on the right and a wide spot for parking is on the left. About 100 yards farther, a road leads into a parking lot on the left. If you did not notice the trailhead, pull over and park here.

Hiking Route

The initial challenge here is finding the trailhead. Two Forest Service signs stand near the junction of road and trail, but without regular maintenance, salmonberry bushes are happy to conceal them in exuberant greenery. The trail was well-built—or reconstructed—in the 1990s, so it is easy to follow even when trees and shrubs reach toward the middle.

The first section of the route heads southeastward and uphill. Just about the time it feels too steep, the path takes a turn to the left and flattens out for a short distance. Keep an eye out at the corner for a wooden bench on your right. This first one is off the trail about 6 feet. It offers views into a narrow gully beside the start of the trail. It is dry in high summer but may provide a gurgling brook and a focal point for bench-sitters in wet seasons.

The trail next wanders gently eastward for a short distance while you catch your breath, then ascends again when it turns more directly south. Rhododendrons appear among the tall evergreens from the start, with salal and bunchberry at the trail edge. As the route gains more elevation, occasional tiger lilies brighten the shady forest in early summer.

The second and third benches are right beside the trail, as if to make sure hikers know they are available after climbing a hill. There are few convenient rocks or logs, so the well-built benches are an appreciable contribution.

In less than a mile, the trail reaches the rim of the deep Slab Camp Creek Valley. A narrow line of trees filters views of the slightly higher Deer Ridge on the southern horizon, with Deer Park and Blue Mountain farther west. One of the nice benches is located a few feet above the trail here for hikers' viewing pleasure.

Follow the trail as it continues up and around the edge of the rim to the Ned Hill fire lookout. The little tower looks like a woodsman's weekend project, with now-dead trees and poles tied together to support a sketchy platform about 20 feet above the ground. It is enclosed with a split-rail fence silently suggesting hikers keep a safe distance. Big trees surround the ragged structure and small ones grow between its legs, adding challenges for photographers. Enough light is usually available to record the wide spaces between the logs of the platform and the lack of a ladder or stairs to assist ascent. Stay long enough to develop your own theories on how the tower was built here, then return to the longer views, which confirm the quality of the viewpoint.

3. BLUE MOUNTAIN LOOKOUT

RT Distance: 0.5 mile
High Point: 6007 feet
Elevation Gain: 170 feet
Season: Jun-Oct
No pass or permit is required.

History

The broad meadows below the 6000-foot peak of Blue Mountain were known by hunters as Deer Park from the late nineteenth century[1], and that remains an alternate name for the area. In 1928, the Forest Service built a small (10×10-foot) fire watch cabin on the mountain's highest point, overlooking the forests, meadows, and mountains in this section of the North Olympics. They replaced the little box with an attractive, gable-roofed house in 1931, which remained until 1970.[2]

The US Congress transferred the area from the Forest Service to the US Department of the Interior in 1933 as part of the Mount Olympus National Monument, a preliminary step to Congress establishing the Olympic National Park in 1938. A Civilian Conservation Corps (CCC) camp was located in Deer Park during the 1930s. Among other projects, CCC crews improved the road to the high ridge area.[3]

Blue Mountain Lookout cabin with Olympic Mountains in the background. (Olympic National Forest photograph, curated by Steve Ricketts.)

---

[1] Smitty Parratt, *Gods & Goblins; A Field Guide to Place Names of the Olympic National Park*, 2009, 35.
[2] Kresek, *1998*, 114.
[3] Gail H. Evans, *Olympic National Park Historic Resources Study*, Chapter 5. Putting the Unemployed to Work: Depression Years and Federal Relief Programs. The Civilian Conservation Corps / Camp Elwha (unpaged).

Their camp became part of the support buildings for the Deer Park Ski Area that occupied the meadows from 1936 to 1957.[4]

The Aircraft Warning Service (AWS) staffed the lookout cabin year-round during World War II. With views from the Strait of Juan de Fuca to the high Olympic Mountains, it offered a great vantage point for observing any planes approaching Puget Sound from the Pacific Ocean.

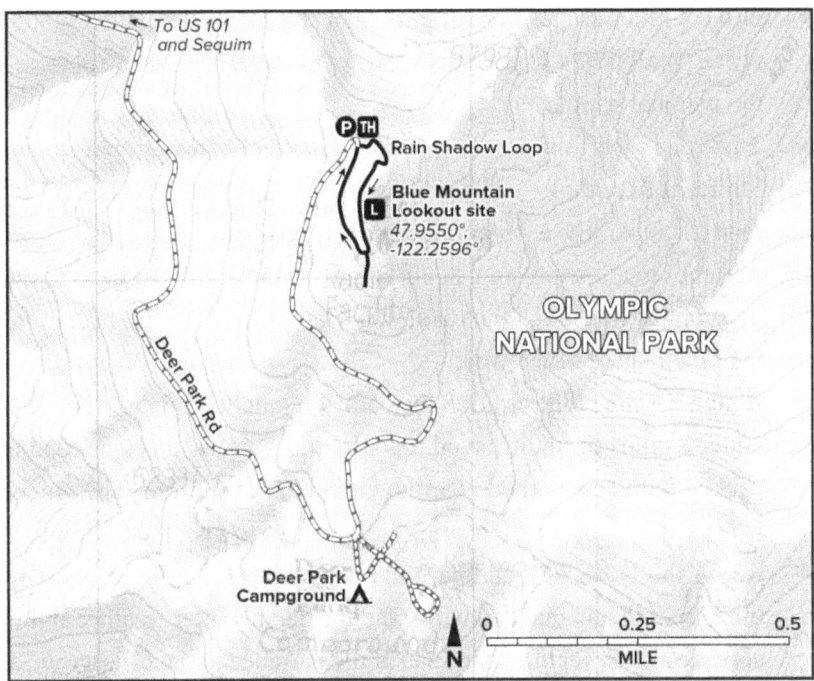

Hike Summary

This route offers a short hike on the very popular and very scenic Olympic National Park Rain Shadow Loop trail. Getting there requires driving 8 miles on a narrow, winding gravel road, often on the edge of a cliff scantily disguised by a slim line of young evergreen trees. Permits are not currently required for day visits; pets are not allowed on trails.

---

[4] Evans, Chapter 4. Wild and Quiet Places: Recreational Development. Popular Recreation/Skiing (unpaged).

Getting There

- From US Highway 101 between Port Angeles and Sequim, turn south on Deer Park Road at milepost 253. If coming from the east, exit from the right lane to Deer Park Loop, which passes under US Highway 101 before joining Deer Park Road on its way to the Olympic National Park.
- Drive 8 miles on paved road through a small commercial area, suburbia, small farms, and a narrow strip of state forest, before entering the national park.
- The road gets steeper and narrower after it leaves pavement. Stretches of potholes and washboard are not uncommon. The gravel road is generally a lane-and-a-half wide, with occasional wider stretches to allow passing. A cliff edge is concealed just beyond the trees on the outside of the road; don't let downhill traffic take more than their share of the way.
- A sign for the ranger station appears at a junction on the right, just under 8 miles from the paved road. In midsummer, that side road is packed with cars parked near the Grand Park trailhead. The ranger is usually out on patrol, leaving little reason to visit the building.
- Reach the Deer Park campground in another 0.1 mile. It is set in thick trees that manage to withstand the harsh winter weather at this elevation. Stay on the main road at the entrance to the campground, turning left and uphill toward Blue Mountain and the Rain Shadow Loop.
- Drive through high mountain meadows to reach the end of the road in 0.8 mile—a small parking lot with a grand view.

Hiking Route

The trailhead offers a ridgetop grove of dense spruce trees, surrounded by open meadows and rocky outcrops, which are more typical of the Blue Mountain peak.

The hiking trail to the Blue Mountain Lookout site is a 0.5-mile loop with a few short extensions to viewpoints and attractive large boulders that draw visitors like magnets. Arrow signs suggest a counterclockwise route is recommended. This route starts up a long, gradual hill with an open slope to the east and familiar views to the west. I have always preferred hiking the route in the other direction: winding through a grove of spruce trees and gaining views to the north, then emerging in fairly short order to the grand views of the Olympic Mountains, east and south.

The meadows slope away from Blue Mountain's high ridge trail at a 45-degree angle. In late summer, the grasses are tawny with occasional dots of color: blue harebell, white yarrow, and tall, green, native hellebore. Across a deep valley to the southeast stand dark green forested ridges. Enjoy the 6000-foot perspective looking south—here are the Olympic Mountains in all their glory—ridge after ridge of snow-edged peaks. Glaciers appear in the second or third row. Mount Olympus is not in sight, but this panorama is well worth the effort to get here.

Continue on the ridge to the small, rocky summit. It has three stony outcrops about 20 feet apart. Two of the rocky corners still support bronze Reference Mark discs, installed by the US Coast and Geodetic Survey in 1955. The National Geodetic Survey datasheet for this survey station indicates that the lookout cabin sat over the principal benchmark on the highest outcrop, the southeast corner of the triangle.[5] That marker is no longer found on the site.

The trail continues a little farther south before turning a corner to reveal the northward panorama of Port Angeles, Ediz Hook, trans-Pacific freighters, and the Strait of Juan de Fuca. The downward sloping trail—once a narrow ridge-top road—completes the loop with views of another steep ridge a short distance to the northwest. It too has tawny meadows set at 45-degree angles, and a dark green fringe of conifers set against the northern sky. Can you imagine life as a fire lookout in such a spectacular setting?

---

[5] US National Geodetic Survey, "Data Sheet PID SY1640 BLUE MTN LOOKOUT HOUSE 1955"; https://www.ngs.noaa.gov/cgi-bin/ds_mark.prl?PidBox=SY1640.

4. MOUNT PLEASANT LOOKOUT

RT Distance: 5 miles
High Point: 2636 feet
Elevation Gain: 1400 feet
Season: Mar-Nov
A Discover Pass is required.

History

Mount Pleasant offers wonderful views of all the forestlands between Port Angeles on the shores of the Strait of Juan de Fuca and the mountains of the Olympic National Park to the south. In 1936, US Forest Service Ranger Robert H. Mealey completed a lookout site evaluation report for Mount Pleasant. He recommended this site over another site close to the Port Angeles entrance to the Olympic National Park, approximately 1 mile to the west.[1] There is no record of the Olympic National Forest following up on his report.

A Washington State Division of Forestry biennial report mentions a road was partly built to the top of Mount Pleasant and the summit cleared in 1952; but the site badly needed a lookout tower.[2] The next year, the Division had a forty-foot tower with an open viewing platform constructed there.[3]

A Christmas Eve windstorm brought down the tower in 1963.[4] Ted Bradshaw, the summer lookout staff there from 1960 through 1966, reported in September 1966 "the old tower did a flip a couple winters ago and the new tower is just getting the newness worn off."[5] The Department of Natural Resources (DNR) rebuilt the tower in 1964, but abandoned it in 1968.[6] The *Port Angeles Evening News* reported a burglary there in January, its last year.[7] The intrusion could have been one factor supporting the decision to close. The growth of Port Angeles toward the tower and increased interest in monitoring wildfires from airplanes were likely contributors as well.

---

[1] Robert H. Mealey, [Lookout Site Evaluation Form] "Mount Pleasant 1936," Document 215-10.07, National Archives in Seattle.
[2] Washington Division of Forestry, *Forty-Seventh and Forty-Eighth Annual Reports for the Period Commencing October 16, 1950, and Ending November 10, 1952*, 43.
[3] Washington Division of Forestry, *Forty-Ninth and Fiftieth Annual Reports for the Period Commencing July 1, 1952, and Ending June 30, 1954*, 41.
[4] *Port Angeles Evening News*, December 28, 1963; January 14, 1964, quoted in https://washingtonlookouts.weebly.com/mt-pleasant.html.
[5] Ted Bradshaw, "Hi, Everybody," *Olympia District's Ten-Eight*, September 1966, [6].
[6] Kresek, *2015*, 23.
[7] *Port Angeles Evening News*, January 23, 1968, quoted in https://washingtonlookouts.weebly.com/mt-pleasant.html.

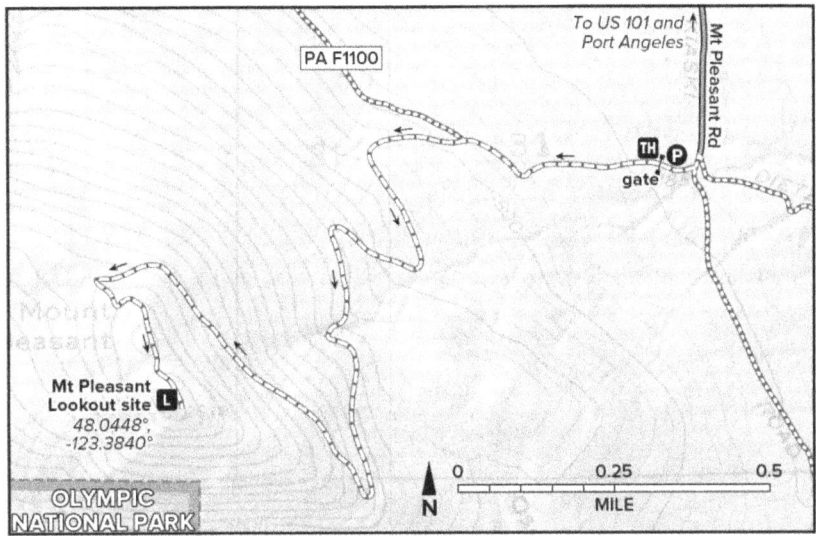

Hike Summary

This is a moderate road-hike through state forestland and open landscape dotted with tall trees. Large clearings harvested since 2015 offer great views of the Strait of Juan de Fuca and the coast from Ediz Hook to Dungeness Spit and even Port Townsend, Vancouver Island, and the Cascade Mountains.

Getting There

- From US Highway 101, turn south onto Mount Pleasant Road at a well-marked intersection on the east side of Port Angeles. It is about halfway between the city center and the big curve in the highway between Sequim and Port Angeles.
- Drive toward the Olympics through hillside view-homes and small farms.
- At 4 miles from US Highway 101, the road splits. Don't follow either branch; immediately turn right on a narrow forest road just

before the Y. An old green gate stands open at the mouth of the road. Drive about 100 yards and park outside the white DNR gate.

Hiking Route

The landscape around this trail changed substantially between two visits a decade apart. A shady forest lane has been replaced with a broad, open landscape adorned with scattered groves of trees. Solitude has given way to a path shared with dog walkers and neighborhood runners.

Mount Baker and Dungeness Spit from the Mount Pleasant hike route.

The route starts uphill steeply from the securely locked gate. Catch your breath at 0.25 mile: stop to admire a magnificent tree cluster on the left side of the road. A double-trunked big leaf maple wraps its branches around a tall thin evergreen, creating a large, arboreal illusion. While the main forest road continues westward, an attractive grassy road (PA F1100 on DNR maps) heads downhill at the bend. Remember, lookouts are always uphill; save that route for an extension you might explore later.

At 0.5 mile, the landscape opens to a great coastal panorama. Ediz Hook's narrow peninsula shapes a big harbor for the city at your feet. Large tankers and freighters pause their ocean crossings here for pilots to board before they enter Puget Sound proper. The hills on Vancouver Island rise across the strait. Soak in the scenery, then turn left at a horseshoe bend in the road and hike southeast as trees resume the edge of the route and fill the view.

Hilltop communication towers appear around the next major corner, at about 0.9 mile. They are due south and a reminder of the elevation yet to be gained. A clearcut stands between our route and the forest above, providing clear views to the east and downhill northeast, as well. Dungeness Spit reaches out to deep blue waters, along with rounded peninsulas as far as Port Townsend.

Tower service company arrow signs at curves in the road reinforce our navigational instincts to continue uphill. Hikers to the lookout site are going to the same place as the tower service people. With no alternate trail, we share the road.

At 1.4 miles, the road climbs a steep curve and continues toward the northwest. The elevation here is just under 2100 feet. At this height there are clear views from Ediz Hook to the Cascades, with ferry boats crossing to Victoria taking center stage on the sparkling blue strait.

After a long stretch northwestward, the road curves around the western end of the ridge at about 2350 feet. The route rises to a junction where a path crosses a grassy field and continues around the hill's perimeter. Signs to the towers direct us to follow the steep road on the left, once again into the trees. There are rhododendrons under the forest canopy, along with salal, sword ferns, and occasional birds sharing their enthusiasm for life in the trees. At this point, the destination has the hiker's focus. The road seems almost a tunnel, with thick forest on both sides. The summit loop is steep enough to require circling the entire tower site before arriving at the 2636-foot elevation.

There are few artifacts to be found and only concrete steps available for a lunch seat. At least one concrete block with a galvanized steel post and one eyebolt are sheltered under salal around the site. Sadly, there are no grand views on the summit. Despite proximity to the Olympic Mountains, the entire route is devoid of snowy peaks on the horizon. The top of Mount Pleasant is a great place to relax if you overheated on the ascent. Then, return to the fabulous views of the north Olympic Peninsula coastline and international waters—and maybe a hike extension on Forest Road PA F1100.

5. FOOTHILLS LOOKOUT

RT Distance: 1.2 miles
High Point: 2270 feet
Elevation Gain: 450 feet
Season: All Year
No pass or permit is required.

History

At the 2016 Forest Fire Lookout Association Western Conference, Ron Kemnow, an Oregonian who loves to share quotes from fire lookout documents on his web pages[1] told me a new fire lookout site had been found "right by the entrance to the Olympic National Park." Once we clarified he meant the Port Angeles entrance station, I was intrigued.

In the National Archives in Seattle, Eric Willhite found a series of June 1935 panoramic landscape images from the Osborne Photo Survey taken from this lookout site. On his website, http://willhiteweb.com, he shares the theory that a local forest ranger would climb the short trail to the firefinder base at the Foothills[2] viewpoint and scan the surrounding hills for "smokes," the term fire watchers use for the first sign of a wildfire. It's likely the storied ranger worked in the Ennis Ranger Station, which stood near the location of the current national park entrance station in the 1930s.

More recently, I found a 1936 evaluation of a lookout site called Panoramic Point, located less than 0.5 mile west of the Foothills site. The report's US Forest Service author didn't think more lookout locations were needed in this region: "We should not plan on too many points . . . much that can be seen from here may be covered from Mt. Pleasant."[3] We have no way to know if the lookout evaluator was unaware of the Foothills Lookout, or considered Panoramic Point virtually the same location. As the Foothills site still has a stand for an Osborne firefinder, it seems likely that it has long served as an informal national forest and park fire lookout site—before and after the state fire lookout tower on Mount Pleasant.[4] No record indicates a lookout building ever stood here.

---

[1] https://washingtonlookouts.weebly.com has a page for each fire lookout site in Washington state for which Kemnow has found information.
[2] Accessed August 23, 2016: http://willhiteweb.com/olympic_mountains/foothills_firefinder/port_angeles_397.htm.
[3] Robert H. Mealey, [Fire Lookout Site Evaluation] "Panoramic Point," 2, August 18, 1936; Document 19-15.09, National Archives in Seattle.
[4] See Chapter 4, "Mount Pleasant Lookout."

5. FOOTHILLS LOOKOUT

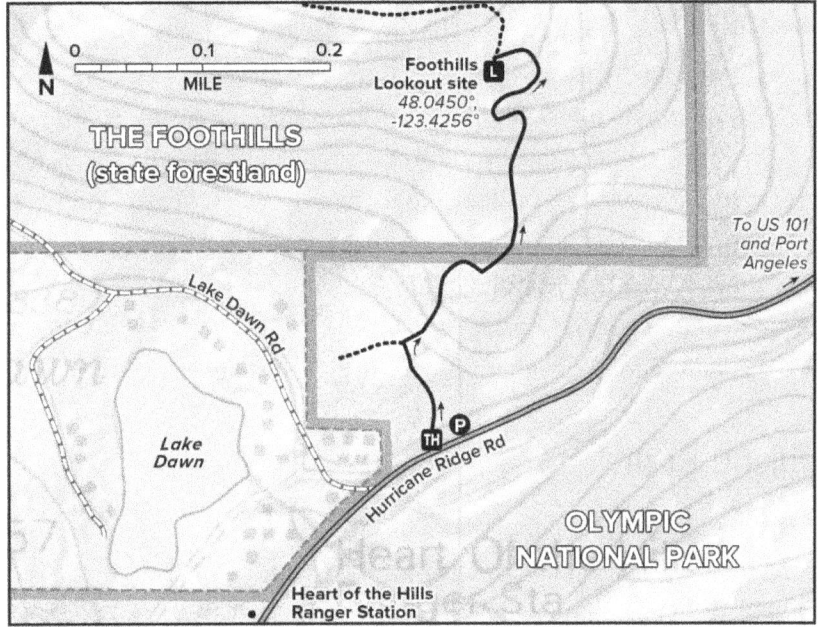

Hike Summary

This short adventure trail starts informally beside the Hurricane Ridge Road in Olympic National Park and winds a short distance uphill to a well-established but unofficial trail on state forestland a short distance north of Lake Dawn. At 0.6 mile, it reaches a natural viewpoint at the edge of the forest looking east toward Mount Pleasant and other forested peaks of the north Olympics.

Getting There

- Drive to the center of Port Angeles on US Highway 101.
- Follow the directions on the big brown sign at the intersection with Race Street that directs traffic up that street toward the Olympic National Park.
- In 1.5 miles, cross E. Park Avenue and drive past the main Olympic National Park Visitor Center and wilderness information office.

- Keep right at the Y to gain Hurricane Ridge Road; pass a viewpoint parking lot on the left.
- At 6.5 miles from US Highway 101, watch for paved parking on the right shoulder and a wide gravel shoulder on the left. This is just before a cross street called Little River Road on Washington Department of Natural Resources maps, and Lake Dawn Road on street signs. If you can see the Olympic National Park entrance gatehouse, you have passed the trailhead.
- Park close to the southern end of the paved shoulder.

Hiking Route

Start the hike beside the third large tree from the southern end of the paved parking. Climb a short bank to an apparent game trail, headed west. In 2020, it appeared that logs had been dropped on this path, but foot traffic had persisted. As you step over the second or third log in the first 0.1 mile, notice the tree's branches have been removed with a saw. Clearly, the trail has had some human improvements, although it is only as wide as a boot and closely bordered by large sword ferns, overhanging salal, and Oregon grape.

The author and the Osborne firefinder stand at the Foothills Lookout site. (Photo by Tolle VanLaanen, courtesy of the photographer.)

At 0.3 mile, this informal route meets a somewhat better established trail at a T. The left branch leads to the Little River or Dawn Lake Road. The right branch goes uphill, and thus the right direction. Although this track is easy to see ascending the hill ahead, it is still an unofficial path. It is about a foot wide and occasionally climbs straight up steep banks of 6 feet or more, where a well-built trail would switchback up the slope or include stone or log-supported steps.

At about 0.4 mile from the start, pass a side trail on the left. Continue on the path headed more directly toward the top of the ridge.

Just as you wonder how much farther it is to the top, the trail will open onto a stone outcropping at the edge of a cliff. A chest-high iron pipe with an 8-inch iron plate attached to its top stands in the middle of the rocky-floored open area. This is the base for an Osborne firefinder, used by lookout staff to sight forest fires.[5] The trail continues west toward the mountain-bike-oriented trails of the Washington Department of Natural Resources Foothills recreation area. The route leaves the ridge in another 0.25 mile, heading for lower ground.

---

[5] See the Glossary for information about the Osborne firefinder.

6. HURRICANE HILL LOOKOUT

RT Distance: 3.2 miles
High Point: 5757 feet
Elevation Gain: 650 feet
Season: Jun-Oct
A national park or another federal recreation pass is required.

History

As the name suggests, this 5757-foot summit gets severe weather, especially in winter. Prospector W.A. Hall gave the hill its name after he completed the long and steep ascent from the Elwha River on an extremely windy day in 1897.[1]

The Kresek lookout inventory published in 1985 dated this 13×13-foot fire lookout cabin from the 1930s,[2] which approximates the date "Hurricane Hill LO" first appeared on a published Olympic National Forest map, 1936.[3] The Forest Service also built a rough fire protection road to the ridge with a branch to the lookout in the 1930s.[4] The area became part of the Olympic National Park when it was established in 1938.

The site was occupied year-round during World War II, as Aircraft Warning Service (AWS) staff watched for enemy planes and the incendiary balloons that Japan released toward the western United States. A few of the balloons did land in Washington state, but only during wet seasons when they did no damage. Among the plane-watchers was Walt Crisler, a famous wildlife photographer for Walt Disney, who spent the winter of 1942-43 in the small Hurricane Hill lookout cabin with his wife, Lois.[5]

Hurricane Hill Lookout cabin, 1940s. (Herb Crisler photograph, courtesy of Olympic National Park.)

---

[1] Parratt, 62.
[2] Kresek. *Fire Lookouts of Oregon and Washington,1985*, 114 (hereafter cited as Kresek, 1985).
[3] US Forest Service Olympic National Forest, "Snow Peaks Recreation Area Guide," 1936.
[4] Robert L. Wood, *Wilderness Trails of the Olympic National Park*, 49.
[5] Parratt, 62.

In the 1950s, the park built a paved road through the mountains from the northeast. It passed through two tunnels before reaching the Hurricane Ridge Visitor Center. The lookout station's active life ended as the visitor traffic increased. The building was removed in 1960.

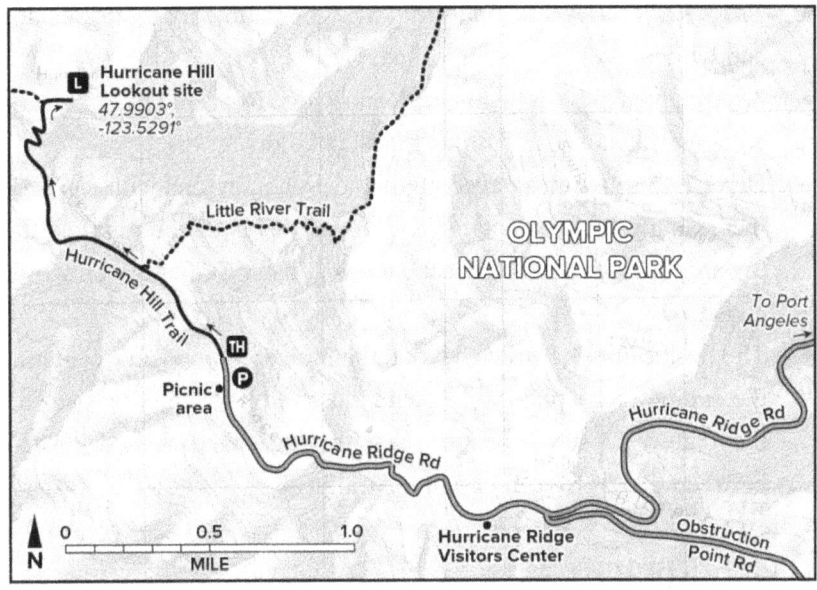

Hike Summary

This is a short hike from the end of the paved road on Hurricane Ridge. A broad asphalt path goes most of the way to the top, with spectacular views of the Olympic Mountains to the east, south, and west, all along the way. At the little summit, views of the international waters of the Strait of Juan de Fuca, Vancouver Island, and even Mount Baker join the panorama. The route has a short but spectacular flower season in midsummer.

Getting There

- Drive to the center of Port Angeles on US Highway 101.
- Follow the signs at the intersection with Race Street that direct traffic uphill to the Olympic National Park.
- Cross E. Park Avenue and drive past the main park visitor center and wilderness information office.
- Keep right at the Y to gain Hurricane Ridge Road and pass the park entrance gatehouse at 7 miles from US Highway 101.
- Drive 12.5 miles on a paved, two-lane mountain road with views of increasingly high mountains and deep valleys as the road climbs toward the ridge. The Hurricane Ridge Visitor Center is well worth a visit.
- The trailhead is 1.5 miles beyond the mountaintop visitor center at the end of a loop parking lot, with clustered parking spaces beside the roadway. A scenic picnic area with additional parking is located between the visitor center and the trailhead.

Hiking Route

The trail starts with views toward snowy peaks to the left (south) then opens on the right to a lovely, bowl-shaped valley. Flowers fill the valley's meadow at midsummer; the area appears a rich green or tawny pasture until snow flies in the autumn. A wide variety of wildflowers border the trail most of the hiking season. Avalanche lilies appear first, breaking through snow with their green spear leaves and cheery white flowers on sunny days. Summer brings brilliant mixtures of purple lupine, magenta paintbrush, and a wide variety of white flowers—bistort and Sitka valerian among them.

After passing a second valley on the right, and meadows descending steeply on the left, the trail climbs more seriously. Marmots pop out of their dens in the meadows to inspect passersby on the trail. If the sun is shining, one of the furry creatures is likely to stretch out on a nearby rock and enjoy the warmth.

Pass a trail junction in the middle of a meadow that leads a long way down to the Elwha Valley. The current steep pack route was a rough fire road in the 1930s that carried the construction materials for the Hurricane Ridge fire lookout cabin. After the park opened, it was the only road serving the ridge until the route from Port Angeles was completed in the 1950s.

The trail turns right at a viewpoint to the west, then follows the ridge east, gaining panoramic views of the snowy Olympic peaks to the south. In another 0.25 mile, come to a junction with a trail on the left, which climbs a short distance to a wooded ridge that is the high point—Hurricane Hill on Hurricane Ridge. On the south side of the ridge, among lumpy rocks that look as if a volcano could have thrown them there quite recently, are a few metal remains of the almost totally removed lookout cabin. There are two galvanized bars, a firefinder base and a benchmark: a bronze US Coast and Geodetic survey marker stamped: HURRICANE 1940. A more recent reminder of the site's history is a concrete bench etched HURRICANE HILL LOOKOUT, sitting right where the cabin stood many years ago.

Winter visitors to the park can also ski or snowshoe to the site from the Hurricane Ridge Visitors Center with a 3-mile trek, imagining the AWS staff who spent a few wartime winters here, safeguarding their fellow citizens below.

7. STRIPED PEAK LOOKOUT

RT Distance: 6.5 miles
High Point: 998 feet
Elevation Gain: 1500 feet
Season: All Year

No pass or permit is required for parking in this county recreation area.

History

In 1937, the federal Civilian Conservation Corps (CCC) built a forest fire lookout tower near Crescent Bay, Clallam County, for the Washington State Division of Forestry. Forestry's annual report also mentioned that roads and telephone lines were completed to each of the lookout stations built that year.[1]

View of the Olympic Mountains, southeast of the Striped Peak Lookout site.

In May 1938, US Forest Ranger R. M. Beeman evaluated the "new 50 ft. creosoted wooden tower with stairway and house." He said it provided "good early season coverage—supplements well our 3 lookouts (Kloshe Nanich, Hurricane Hill and Deer Park [later known as Blue Mountain]) for the regular season."[2]

By 1942, when this lookout was selected as an Aircraft Warning Service (AWS) station, everyone called it "Striped Peak." When the AWS program ended in 1944, the station was returned to Washington's Division of Forestry for forest fire monitoring.[3]

---

[1] Washington Division of Forestry, *Thirty-Third and Thirty-Fourth Annual Reports for the Period Commencing December 1, 1936, and Ending November 30, 1938*, 7-8.
[2] R. M. Beeman [Fire Lookout Site Evaluation], "Freshwater Bay Tower . . . State, May 11, 1938"; Document 7-6.2, National Archives at Seattle.
[3] Washington Division of Forestry, Memo to File: A.W.S. Posts Retained for Use by State under Cooperative Agreement with US Forest Service [handwritten document, dated "6/20/1945"] accessed in Department of Natural Resources Financial Records at Washington State Archives, Olympia.

State Forestry staffed the 53-foot lookout tower topped with a 7×7-foot observation cabin for another 22 years.[4] Considering the small size of the shelter at the top of the tower, it is fortunate State Forestry and the Department of Natural Resources also provided a cabin on the ground for housing the fire season staff.

David Barclay was probably the last person to staff Striped Peak Lookout, in 1966. He wrote in the DNR lookout staff newsletter, *Ten-Eight*, September 1966: "My tower is manned only on 4 and five days . . . This may be its last year in service."[5] The tower and ground cabin were removed in 1967 or 1968.[6]

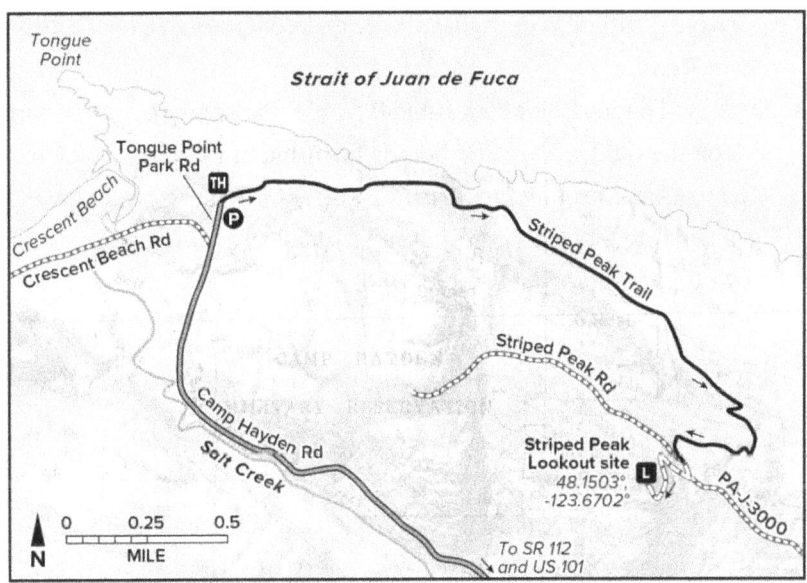

Hike Summary

The recommended route follows a joint Clallam County–Washington Department of Natural Resources trail that provides great views of many old-growth trees, the Strait of Juan de Fuca, and Vancouver Island. Continue in state forestland on little used roads to a high point offering expansive panoramic views. The Washington Department of

---

[4] Kresek, 1998, 115.
[5] David Barclay, "Dear Lookouts," *Olympia District's Ten-Eight*, September 1966, [11].
[6] US National Geodetic Survey, "Data Sheet PID TR2493 LOOKOUT"; www.ngs.noaa.gov /cgi-bin/ds_mark.prl?PidBox=TR2493.

Natural Resources provides maps of the trail and the area on their website: http://file.dnr.wa.gov/publications/eng_rms_n_oly_pen_lft.pdf.

Getting There

- Start from the junction of State Route 112 and US Highway 101, west of Port Angeles.
- Drive west 7.2 miles on State Route 112 and turn right onto Camp Hayden Road.
- Drive 3.5 miles, keep right at a Y, and continue on Tongue Point Park Road.
- Follow Tongue Point Park Road 0.5 mile. Park at the broad parking lot on the right with reader boards featuring maps of the Salt Creek Recreation Area and the Striped Peak Trail. Restrooms are available a short distance farther into the park, beside the ballfields and next to the waterfront campground.

Hiking Route

The trail starts on a closed forest road in the well-maintained Clallam County Salt Creek County Park, then seamlessly crosses into the state forestlands on a well-built footpath through a diverse and healthy forest. Tall evergreen trees host a mixed understory of ferns, salal, evergreen huckleberry, and leggy elderberry shrubs. The sounds and sight of saltwater are frequent and occasionally require a full stop to admire dramatic waves splashing on rocks far below, or kayaks maneuvering in narrow bays and coves. At 0.75 mile, a split-rail fence provides a reminder to take care while admiring the scenery—the view is spectacular, but the water is a long way down.

From this point, the trail goes slightly downhill as it passes over the stream that carved the cove from the cliffs above the shoreline. There are huge boulders in the stream, some topped with trees secured by roots wrapped around the rocky base. On the other side of the stream, a steep side-trail offers a route down to the cove and its beach. The cove is unique, but the trail is quite steep, and there are other opportunities to visit beaches in the area.

Now the main trail starts uphill in earnest. It circles the eastern end of the forested ridge atop Striped Peak, then delivers you to the viewpoint where the narrow footpath ends. Along the way, a couple of side trails lead uphill, and at least one ascends to the Striped Peak summit. While a little higher than the forest fire lookout site, the summit is fully forested and offers neither artifacts nor a view.

Just before the narrow footpath reaches a broad opening in the forest, another large reader board identifies this as a trailhead, too. The presence of this sign acknowledges the possibility of entering the trail system from the east, via state forest roads. That could be a preferable option on a busy summer weekend day when the recreation area is overflowing with visitors. The Department of Natural Resources map mentioned above provides directions for entering the area from the east. A state Discover Pass is required for parking on the state forest roads.

On the water side of the clearing, an opening in the forest reveals another vista. Although now farther from the water than at the split-rail fence, this higher elevation offers longer views—across the strait to Mount Baker and beyond. The ever-growing shrubbery here tends to reduce the width of the view, so this prospect is probably best in the winter and spring.

Now 2.4 miles from the Salt Creek Recreation Area trailhead, the trail offers few options. The last section of the route to the Striped Peak Lookout site is on state forest roads that twist, turn, and intersect before reaching the destination. Despite the frustration of knowing the lookout site stands on higher ground, follow the road down the hill. It twists to the left and Ts at a slightly wider forest road. This is labeled both PA-J-3000 and Striped Peak Road on the DNR map, but there has been no roadside sign at the junction in recent years.

Turn left at the junction, hike a couple hundred yards, and turn right on a side road with a Locked Gate Ahead sign. This road winds uphill and pauses at a closed gate, mid-slope. Is it located here to test the brakes of vehicles headed for the top? As a hiker, step around it undeterred, but wonder about its location just the same.

Approaching the top of the hill, notice a tall communications tower surrounded by trees and accompanied by a concrete block building that offers a constant hum. Workmen often putter around the facility at the highest part of the hilltop.

In a slightly lower clearing to the right, a shorter antenna stands near a square orange-and-white building inside a fence. This area offers satisfying artifacts and wonderful views not available around the taller communications tower. A permanent survey marker, or benchmark, is set in a 6-inch-tall concrete pedestal in the clearing. The metal plate is stamped "US Coast and Geodetic Survey; Lookout 1940." An iron I-beam, thick with rust, protrudes a couple of feet out of the ground nearby. It has a circular metal plate around its base. According to the 1974 National Geodetic Survey monitoring report, the survey station marker stood 28 feet north of the concrete pillars that supported the lookout tower. The cabin could well have stood in this sheltered position, a few feet downhill from the original tower.

On a clear day, this point offers the best views available on the entire route. Mount Baker holds pride of place in all its shiny, glacial majesty, with a picket of Cascade Mountains to its right and Canadian peaks to its left. More snow-covered peaks, the Olympics, stand across the valley to the south. Urban developments across the strait are easy to identify from this vantage point, and ship traffic on the marine waters is visible east, west, and center.

8. PYRAMID MOUNTAIN LOOKOUT

RT Distance: 7.5 miles
High Point: 3100 feet
Elevation Gain: 2400 feet
Season: Apr-Nov
No pass or permit is required.

History

In 1936, while President Roosevelt considered creation of an Olympic National Park, an Olympic National Forest ranger, Jim Bethel, was out evaluating forest fire lookout sites on the peninsula. He visited Pyramid Mountain that year, just north of Lake Crescent. At a 3140-foot elevation, Bethel located a good spot to build a cabin. He climbed to the top of a 30-foot tree, and decided a tower was not really needed for good views. His site evaluation may have been a factor when this location was chosen for a warplane-spotting station, six years later. He mentioned a 3-mile trail to the summit as an asset for a potential lookout station.[1] An established trail meant the area was well known to rangers and hikers in the popular Lake Crescent area.

Pyramid Peak Lookout 1954, photograph by Carsten Lien (University of Washington Libraries, Special Collections, UW41075)

Minnie Peterson, a famous woman horse packer in early Olympic National Park history, transported building supplies up to the Aircraft Warning Service (AWS) site, at 3100 feet, in the spring or summer of 1942.[2] Using US Army funds, Olympic National Park employees Joe and Rena Shurnick constructed a one-room, cedar-shake-covered cabin

---

[1] Jim Bethel, [Fire Lookout Site Evaluation] "Pyramid Mountain," August 27, 1936; Document 20-15.3, National Archives at Seattle.
[2] Gary L. Peterson and Glynda Peterson Schaad, *High Divide; Minnie Peterson's Olympic Mountain Adventures*, 2005, 102.

on the south slope of Pyramid Mountain that autumn.³ "Pyramid Peak Lookout,⁴ along with twelve others in today's national park, was called into service as an AWS observation post during the winter of 1942-43."⁵ At the end of the AWS program, spring 1944, the lookout station was retained by the national park and "remained in use as a fire detection lookout following World War II."⁶ Two Pyramid Mountain structures were entered in the National Register of Historic Buildings. "The lookout . . . measures 16 feet by 13 feet; just to the north of the lookout is an 8 foot by 7 foot woodshed."⁷ The lookout cabin is still standing.

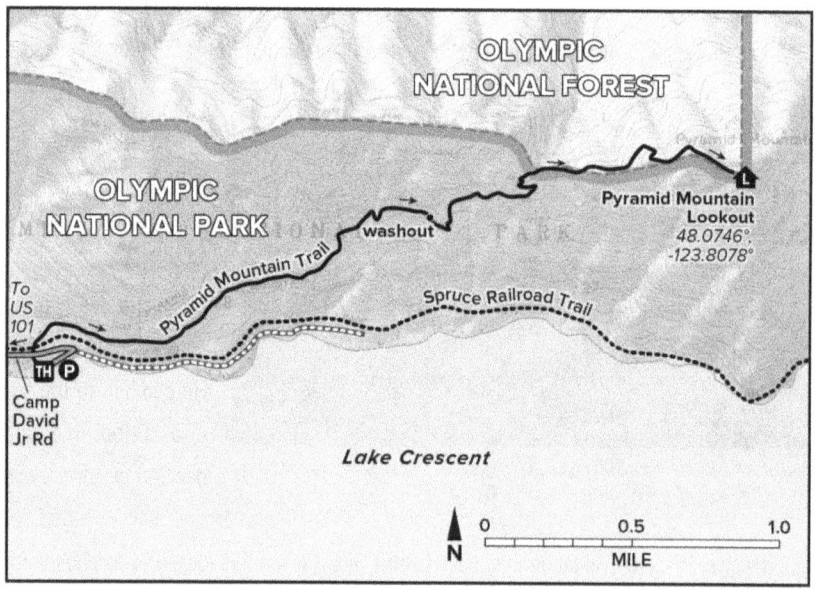

---

[3] US National Park Service, National Register of Historic Places, "Continuation Sheet, Section number 7 and 8, Pyramid Peak A.W.S. Lookout: Clallam County, WA," 1984, 1.
[4] Only the Aircraft Warning Service station was known as Pyramid Peak, the summit and fire lookout station are generally identified as Pyramid Mountain.
[5] US National Park Service, National Register of Historic Places, "Continuation Sheet, Section number 8 and 9, Pyramid Peak A.W.S. Lookout: Clallam County, WA," 1984, 2.
[6] US National Park Service, National Register of Historic Places, "Continuation Sheet, Section number 7 and 8, Pyramid Peak A.W.S. Lookout: Clallam County, WA," 1984, 1.
[7] US National Park Service, National Register of Historic Places, "Continuation Sheet, Section number 7 and 8, Pyramid Peak A.W.S. Lookout: Clallam County, WA," 1984, 1.

Hike Summary

The 3.75-mile route leads to one of the few standing lookouts on the Olympic Peninsula. Most of the trail is shady and pleasant. There is, however, an extremely narrow, high-exposure section of trail at 1.8 miles, which earns this hike an adventure rating. A winter landslide took out a section of the track in the early 2000s; the National Park Service has repaired and rerouted the footpath repeatedly to keep it passable. Do not assume this section of the trail is in good condition. It is not recommended for children or people with balance issues. Contact the Olympic National Park wilderness visitors' desk in Port Angeles, or phone them at 360-565-3100 for the latest conditions. No pets are allowed on the trail.

Getting There

- Drive US Highway 101 to the west end of Lake Crescent, milepost 221.
- Turn right (north) on Camp David Jr. Road, just past the Fairholm store. The paved road turns to gravel before reaching the large day use parking lot on the right, at 3.3 miles. Park here. It has a restroom, picnic tables, and views of the lake.

Hiking Route

Walk west through the parking lot and cross the road toward Pyramid Mountain Trailhead and the Spruce Railroad Trail. The paved railroad trail has been built in the twenty-first century for bicyclists and walkers. In the same period, the historical trail to the lookout cabin has had substantial redesign work. The path has been rerouted and 0.25 mile added to its historical distance.

The joint trailhead is 0.1 mile below the Spruce Railroad Trail at a 700-foot elevation. This section of the route is paved to provide easy access to the rail trail. After crossing the paved east-west trail, a feeling of crowds left behind is gained, with softer tread underfoot and a narrow forest path. The hike route rises slowly above the lake and the other trail, gaining 400 feet in the first mile. Enjoy the big-leafed madrones that thrive near the water, in among a mixed forest of firs, alders, and big leaf maples.

At 1.5 miles, cross June Creek, known as a spring water supply, but potentially dry later in the summer. The trail soon turns away from the lake, heading more northerly. In a short distance, another creek has caused some erosion crossing the trail; a notch in a big tree trunk offers a step to stable ground.

The forest thickens as the trail rises to 1650 feet, then descends to 1615 feet as it approaches and crosses the challenging washout site. The 0.1-mile wide opening in the forest has mostly sandy soil, so there are few plants to help with trail stability. The footpath was often less than a foot wide when visited in October 2018, about 5 months after Washington Trails Association volunteers worked on the route, removing downed trees and widening the footpath through the slide area.[8] The tree-free clearing provides great views of Lake Crescent, but safety must always take priority.

The dense forest on the other side of the clearing is particularly attractive as the trail curves around a spur and starts a series of switchbacks to gain elevation. The trail ascends 1000 feet in the next mile, traversing dense evergreen forest with salal and Oregon grape at its feet. At 3.0 miles, the trail reaches the ridge that is the boundary between the national park and Olympic National Forest to the north. Open spaces between trees offer views of the Strait of Juan de Fuca on a clear day. Lake Crescent sparkles blue to the south, with snowy Olympic Mountains beyond.

Hike another 0.9 mile to the lookout cabin for the best views of all. Some of the trees near the top show wind damage from harsh winters; salal sometimes seems the dominant foliage. A ridge rising 10 feet

---

[8] https://www.wta.org/go-hiking/trip-reports/trip_report.2018-06-03.1589074030, accessed May 18, 2021.

beside the trail blocks views to the south as you approach the top. From the summit's weather-worn cedar-shake cabin, landmarks can be seen almost all around. Lake Crescent gleams below, and Lake Sutherland to the southeast. Look northeast across the Strait of Juan de Fuca to glaciated Mount Baker and Glacier Peak, visible even in haze. Dungeness Spit and Ediz Hook stand out on the Olympic Peninsula shore, while large parts of the northern Olympic Mountains can be seen to the south, starting with Storm King on the other side of Lake Crescent. Only directly to the north do tall trees block the views.

The cabin itself is just a shell with no windows or doors to protect the interior. Guy wires hold it in place. Perhaps the next restoration project will include carpenters and glaziers to give the cabin a better chance at a long life. That would be a fitting memorial to the many men and women who watched for planes and forest fires throughout the Olympic Peninsula.

9. SOL DUC LOOKOUT

RT Distance: 9.5 miles
High Point: 4375 feet
Elevation Gain: 2200 feet
Season: Jun-Oct
A national park or another federal recreation pass is required.

History

Sol Duc is a name identified with a river, falls, hot springs, a campground, ranger station, and a lake on current and historical maps. No maps have been found with the name Sol Duc attached to a mountain peak or ridge near the Little Divide trail in the north Olympic National Park. Despite this, three sources agree that there was a fire lookout called Sol Duc established in 1919.[1] Kresek's inventory stated it was a camp, the Washington Forest Fire Association reported that they helped construct "a lookout house on Sol Duc Mountain," and Rooney's forest history includes the name and year in a list of early fire lookouts in the Olympic National Forest. Kresek's "Fire Lookouts of the Northwest" is the only source to provide a location, based on the best information available to him in the 1980s.

Kresek also reported the location was used as a lookout until the 1930s. That end date may well relate to the changing status of the area. When this lookout was established, it was within the Mount Olympus National Monument, managed by the National Forest Service, an agency of the Department of Agriculture. In 1933, Congress assigned the national monument to the Department of Interior, home of the National Park Service. In 1938, the monument became the Olympic National Park.[2]

Chris Morgenroth, a retired Olympic National Forest ranger, worked long and hard to have the national park established. He had also lobbied the monument's first Department of Interior supervisor to build a fire lookout on Bogachiel Peak, a thousand feet higher and just a few miles from the Sol Duc Lookout site. It was completed in 1934.[3] By then, a 15-year-old cabin at the Sol Duc site would have needed major repairs. The lookout cabin at Bogachiel Peak was recognized as a terrific location to observe a great deal of the north Olympic forests. There was no longer a need for this lower, obscure fire watch station.

---

[1] Kresek, 2015, 23; Rooney, 39; Washington Forest Fire Association, *12th Annual Report*, quoted in https://washingtonlookouts.weebly.com/solduc-mountain.html.
[2] https://www.nps.gov/parkhistory/online_books/olym/hrs/appa.htm.
[3] Chris Morgenroth, *Footprints in the Olympics; an Autobiography*, 1991, 186.

9. SOL DUC LOOKOUT · 53

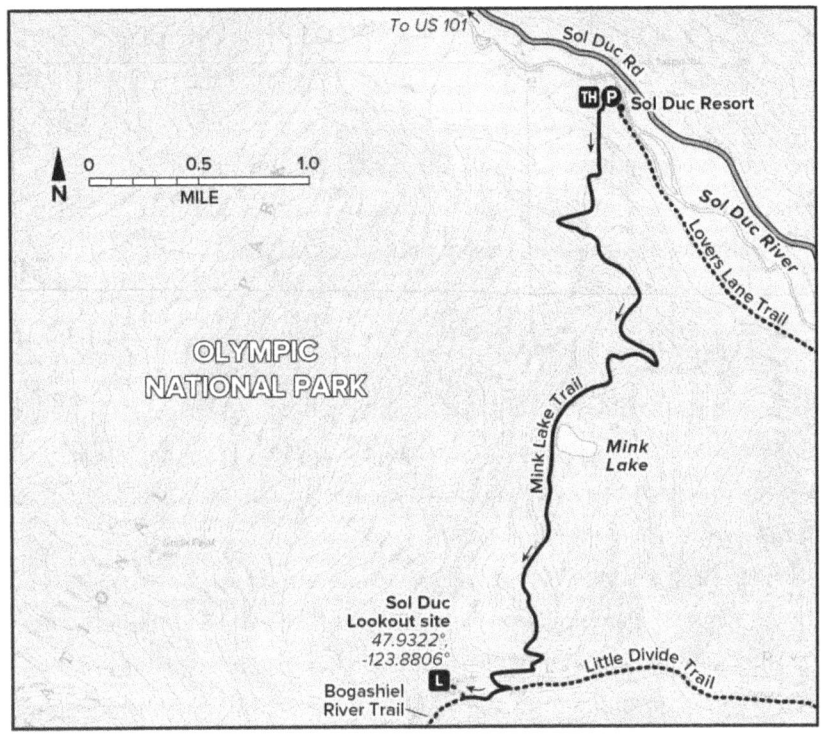

Hike Summary

This route starts at the Sol Duc Hot Springs Resort in the Olympic National Park and demonstrates the best and worst characteristics of national park trails: roots, rocks, and wildflowers in a shady forest. After 4 miles, it earns its adventure rating by leaving the park thoroughfare to follow a so-called social trail. Ascend a short distance to the top of a ridge that could easily have hosted a fire lookout camp—or cabin—in the 1920s and '30s.

Getting There

- Drive US Highway 101 between Lake Crescent and Sappho. Between mileposts 219 and 220, turn south on Sol Duc Road to enter the Olympic National Park. A federal pass or entry fee is required at the park entrance gatehouse.

- At 12.1 miles, turn right into the Sol Duc Resort. Drive to the parking lot row next to the forest. The trailhead is at the right end of the parking lot. The closest parking to the trailhead is by the picnic tables on open lawn opposite the last row of cabins.
- Walk to a gated road labeled Service Road Only. On its left is a trailhead sign for Mink Lake and Lover's Lane.

Hiking Route

This is a trail with several helpful signposts along the way, although none of them leads to the Sol Duc Lookout site. The route starts near the Sol Duc Hot Springs Resort, which may be considered a suggestion for after-hike relaxation.

The first signpost identifies its destinations as Mink Lake and Lover's Lane. The elevation here is 1650 feet. After a hundred yards, another sign sends Lover's Lane off to the left and notes that Mink Lake is 2.5 miles on the path to the right. The latter trail has an interesting border from the start. Vanilla leaf, huckleberry, starry Solomon's seal, and queen's cup flowers border the trail in late spring. Slender green deer ferns with black stems reach toward the tall conifers—hemlocks, fir, and cedar—overhead. After a short distance, twinflowers and star flowers replace the starry Solomon's seal. Vine maples drape gracefully among young hemlocks in the understory.

Mink Lake, beside the trail to the Sol Duc Lookout site.

The trail's only one-log bridge crosses a slim stream in the first 0.5 mile. Switchbacks start at 0.6 mile. New fern varieties and flowering plants distract from the ascent: sword ferns and bracken stand firm, while maidenhair stretch their graceful fingers toward the trail. Fairy bells, foam flower, roses, and red huckleberries join the blooming border plants in summer.

By 1 mile (2500-foot elevation), the narrow, shady woodland track is following a ridge on the right with the broad Sol Duc River Valley under open skies to the left. The river itself is about 0.5 mile away. The trail rises more gradually in the next 1.5 miles on its way to Mink Lake. Listen for the intermittent sounds of hidden streams. At 2.0 miles, pass Mink Falls on the left, a pretty cascade gleaming white as it descends a narrow canyon beside the trail. Two plants with heart-shaped leaves join the trailside display: violets and wild ginger.

At 2.25 miles, Mink Creek appears again, shortly before its namesake lake comes into view. Finally, a signpost identifies Mink Lake to the left and offers Bogachiel Peak for hikers who continue. The elevation is 3100 feet and the flowering shrubbery has changed: beargrass, green hellebore, marsh marigold, and late-season trilliums make their appearances as the trail offers more views of the water.

About 0.5 mile past the Mink Lake signpost, a ceramic insulator for telephone wire, hanging high on a conifer, adds mystery to the trail. Its host tree is too slim to have served a lookout camp early in the twentieth century. And, an insulator abandoned 80 years ago would have been overgrown with bark if it had stayed in place so long. A ranger station near Deer Lake seems a possible destination, but the details of its history are not known.

This section of trail also features plank bridges over bubbling brooks. Beside one of these structures sits a rocky pool overhung with ferns, wild roses, and broad-leafed branches. Then the footpath crosses a broad meadow, with low heather and huckleberries blooming in early summer and berry-covered in autumn. When the route starts uphill again, a sign reminds campers that no open fires are allowed: the elevation is above 3500 feet. The trail continues toward its major junction, climbing a narrow track to 4000-feet elevation and a T-intersection. The signpost there points left for Deer Lake and right to Bogachiel Trailhead (TH), meaning the trail west, down to the North Fork of the Bogachiel River. The trail toward Deer Lake is noted on park maps as the Little Divide Trail.

Turn right here and continue uphill. After less than 0.25 mile, the trail passes between two low slopes. A boot track heads to the right, off the trail and up through the trees on a gently rising ridge. Follow this to the high point on the ridge at 4375 feet.

At a couple of points, the trees grow too close together and you are forced onto the grassy slope on the south side of the ridge. There at your feet is a well-used trail. Follow it to the ridgetop. Gaining the narrow summit requires overcoming tree limbs that rarely encounter human touch. The trees on top are both dense and twisted by strong winter winds. No open space remains to support a tent camp or the cabin reported by the Washington Forest Fire Association. Small pines among the more usual Olympic conifers provide a surprise, but offer all that is really notable about the location. For clear views of Mount Olympus and all the forests in between, a retreat to a lower vantage point on the ridge is necessary.

About 0.1 mile from the park trail is a 20-foot-diameter clearing that looks like a strong candidate for the 1919 to 1930s fire lookout camp location. It offers great views of the surrounding forest landscape and space for a tent, radio, and campfire. It lacks the published elevation of the Sol Duc Lookout, but perhaps the tent was here and the viewpoint on the summit above.

Returning from the last scouting trip to this lookout site, we spotted a metal milepost sign, high on a tree beside the trail, thus confirming that hikers see entirely different vistas coming and going. The metal sign said "4," although my GPS said we were closer to 3.5 miles from the trailhead. Where a hiker finds one milepost sign beside a trail, sharp eyes can often spot more. Keep an eye out for other historical markers. Like the telephone wire insulator, an old milepost hints at a different history for this route than might be assumed from the blank page in the archival records.

10. BOGACHIEL PEAK LOOKOUT

RT Distance: 16.5 miles
High Point: 5474 feet
Elevation Gain: 3500 feet
Season: Jul-Oct
A national park or another federal recreation pass and a Wilderness Camping Permit are required.

History

The story of Bogachiel Peak and its fire lookout cabin is interwoven with the life of early north peninsula explorer and Olympic Forest ranger Chris Morgenroth. Morgenroth came to the United States as a young immigrant from Germany and arrived in Washington state in 1890. He homesteaded on the Bogachiel River when he was 19 and named Bogachiel Peak for the river two years after his arrival in the state.[1]

Newspaper articles published in Portland and Ogden, Utah, in the 1920s mentioned Bogachiel Peak as a lookout location.[2] It is likely rangers came here then to view the broad skyline for signs of fire without benefit of a shelter.

Bogachiel Lookout 1956, photograph by Carsten Lien (University of Washington Libraries, Special Collections, UW41077)

In 1933, the Olympus National Monument was transferred from the US Forest Service in the Department of Agriculture to the Department of Interior, with Mount Rainier National Park to oversee it.[3] Assistant Chief Ranger Preston Macy of Mount Rainier National Park came to the north Olympics in June 1934 to get acquainted with the landscape. He requested that

---

[1] Morgenroth, 40.
[2] Articles in the March 7, 1921, *Oregon Daily Journal* and the September 23, 1923, *The Ogden Standard Examiner*, quoted in https://washingtonlookouts.weebly.com/bogachiel-peak.html.
[3] The first Congressional bill to create an Olympic National Park was introduced in 1926. Several more were introduced in the 1930s before President Franklin D. Roosevelt signed the legislation in 1938.

retired ranger Chris Morgenroth be his guide for his exploration, which included several horseback trips. Morgenroth reported: "On September 13 and 14, Macy and I went up Bogachiel Peak and down the Hoh Valley . . . On this trip we finalized plans for building a Lookout house on top of Bogachiel Peak."[4]

Morgenroth's autobiography and Minnie Peterson's biography agree that she set up a work camp for the lookout cabin's construction a few days later and the work was completed in six weeks—by the end of October 1934.[5] This story is curiously contradicted by the Olympic National Park Final Construction Report. It says building materials were purchased by the Forest Service and delivered to Deer Lake Shelter, partway up the trail to the peak, in 1933. Campers broke in during cold weather and used the materials for firewood. The next year the National Park Service took over the construction project. In early September 1934, the peak was lowered 4.5 feet to level the site and a foundation was installed. New materials were brought up eleven miles from the trailhead. The building was worked on until October 8, when winter weather began. "When trails were again clear of snow on July 8, 1935, construction was resumed and the building completed on September 10, 1935."[6] Both versions provide much more detail than available on any other Olympic lookout building project and suggest a wide variety of interesting issues confronting mountaintop construction.

A piece of this lookout's later history also appears in Peterson's biography. In 1942, she brought in equipment for an aircraft warning station that needed to be staffed as much of the year as possible: "Air defense was not a seasonal activity so Minnie moved supplies to the peak as early as snowpack allowed. Kitchen, heat, and light were all powered by ninety-pound propane tanks that Minnie could just get on a horse."[7]

The lookout station had spectacular views of Mount Olympus, the Bailey Range, the Hoh and Bogachiel River Valleys, and the Seven Lakes Basin from its location on the top of the High Divide. It quickly became a popular work assignment, despite the 8-mile trail from the road. Minnie Peterson reported that a 1938 park ranger sought the job for that

---

[4] Morgenroth, 185-186.
[5] Morgenroth, 186; Peterson and Schaad, 84. As noted in the Chapter 8 Pyramid Mountain Lookout, Peterson was a famous woman horse packer in early Olympic National Park history.
[6] Olympic National Park Final Construction Report, May 1942, quoted in https://washingtonlookouts.weebly.com/bogachiel-peak.html.
[7] Peterson and Schaad, 102.

proximity. His girlfriend worked at the Hot Springs, and he didn't mind hiking back up to the lookout after a romantic evening visit.[8]

It is generally agreed that the lookout cabin was abandoned in the 1950s. None of the people who cared so much about it earlier were available to record its end.

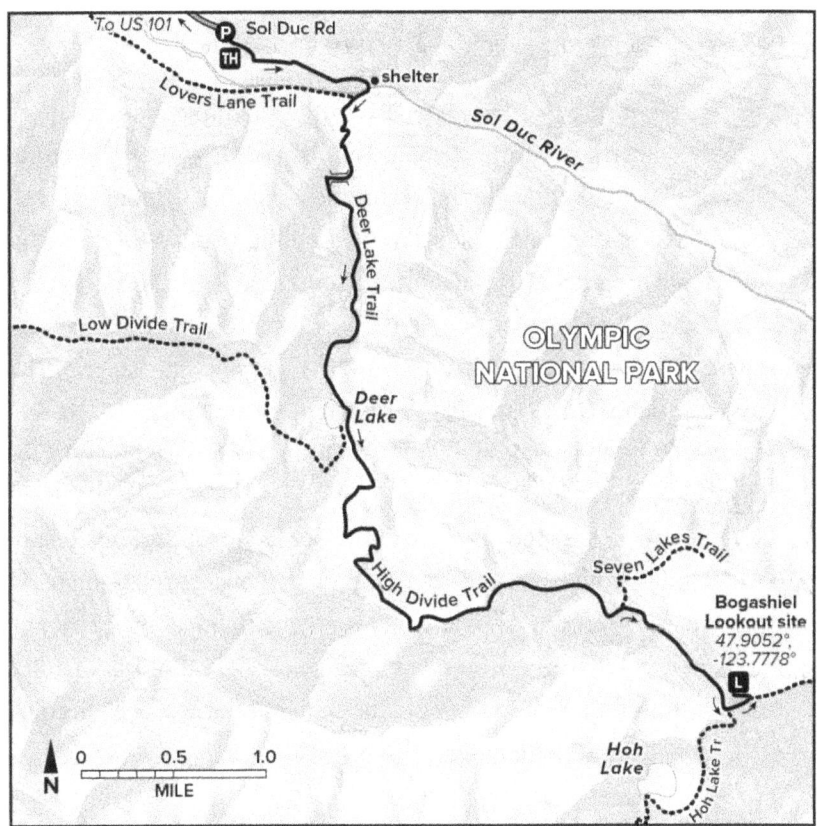

Hike Summary

This is a classic north Olympic National Park backpack trip. This hike description includes two nights at Deer Lake with a day hike to and from Bogachiel Peak. This allows a morning drive to the trailhead and hike completion in the morning of the third day. It provides time to enjoy the long views from the High Divide ridgetop, adequate consideration of

---

[8] Peterson and Schaad, 90-91.

the spectacular panorama of still glaciated peaks of Mount Olympus, and examination of the storied Seven Lakes Basin from the now bare fire lookout site. At 16.5-miles roundtrip and a 3500-foot elevation gain, a strong hiker could complete the trip in a long day.

Getting There

- Campsites in the Sol Duc area are in the Olympic National Park (ONP) wilderness permit system. Half of the campsites can be reserved via email at the beginning of the season. The other half can be booked up to one day ahead, at any of the ONP Wilderness Information Centers at Hoodsport, Lake Quinault, or Port Angeles. The fee is $8 per person per day.
- Drive US Highway 101 between Lake Crescent and Sappho. Between mileposts 219 and 220, turn south on the Sol Duc Road to enter the Olympic National Park. A national park pass or entry fee is required at the park gatehouse.
- At 12.1 miles, pass the entrance to the Sol Duc Hot Springs Resort.
- At 14 miles from US Highway 101, park in the large road-end parking lot. A restroom and picnic tables are available at the road end. This is a popular place on a summer weekend, with lots of folks taking the short walk to the Sol Duc Falls. Parking spaces become available every few minutes.

Hiking Route

This is the most popular trailhead on the Sol Duc Road, a forest entrance for resort visitors as well as through-hikers. There are 2 waterfalls to see in the first 2 miles, so especially heavy traffic should be expected in that distance. The pathway is broad and vacationers are generally welcoming. Most traffic ends at the falls—soon you will have the way to yourself.

The trail starts out at a 2000-foot elevation, in an old-growth forest with huge evergreens, ferns, and salal all around. Short bridges cross narrow creeks while the Sol Duc River gets louder as you approach it. Just before its broad bridge, a big, rustic log building—the Sol Duc Falls Shelter— appears on the left. It serves as a reminder that wet Olympic weather is often unpredictable, but usually cold and penetrating.

At 0.8 mile, cross the bridge high above the rocky river in its narrow gorge, with its triple falls obvious in moderate summer flows. This landmark receives so many visitors there are rows of benches along the western edge of the gorge. After the bridge, the trail turns right, then left, and continues west. In a short distance, the Lover's Lane Trail turns right, taking many visitors back to the Hot Springs Resort. A second trail sign says "Deer Lake—3." That's the route toward Bogachiel Peak.

About 1.5 miles from the trailhead, the rumble of Canyon Creek can be heard on the right. In a short distance, its turbulent flow appears below another broad bridge. In summer heat, hot hikers are often seen cooling their feet at the water's edge.

The trail gains 1550 feet in the 3.5 miles to Deer Lake, most of which seems to occur between the second bridge and the lake. Many early season wildflowers border the path at this moderate elevation: trilliums and Solomon's seal, May lilies, queen's cup, and tall devil's club. The tread is mostly rocky, designed by men with long strides like Chris Morgenroth, with tall stair steps and wide spaces between the stones in narrow waterways. Occasional side trails lead to campsites along the way.

Between Canyon Creek Campsites 1 and 2, the modern path follows a particularly old section of trail. A series of four thick trees on the left side of the trail have ceramic insulators attached to their trunks about 15 feet above the ground. The trees are about 50 feet apart; the insulators are mostly light-colored. It is certain that they guided telephone wires strung from the ranger station beside the Sol Duc Road to another station far above. No records remain to reveal whether they served the Bogachiel fire lookout cabin or other ranger stations in the backcountry. They were definitely part of the historical communication system and could have carried warnings of worrisome smoke deep in the mountains or wartime airplanes heard in the night.

Newer paths have more switchbacks than the straight lines provided by early trail-builders. The route now resumes its winding course up the hill while insulators would have continued on the original straight-line route. The trail parallels Canyon Creek all the way to Deer Lake. Its cascades can be heard twice above its bridge. The first time, a 30-foot drop is visible through the trees, landing in a broad pool that looks enticing, but too far below to visit. The creek's second rumble serves as notice that Deer Lake is nearby. The creek then becomes visible, rushing over and around angled rocks for 0.25 mile.

A bridge appears on the left, spanning the exuberant outlet from Deer Lake. A signpost with a map of the campsites around the lake appears just beyond the bridge. The main trail goes down the east side of the lake, with a ranger station just off the trail. Staffing levels are low, but the rangers are usually enthusiastic about the park, and happy to share their knowledge if you meet one. Site restoration signs appear at several points beside the lake—areas where the landscape needs time to recover from heavy foot-traffic.

On our 2018 scouting trip, we found a perfect campsite on the Deer Lake map. We were entertained by ducks in the evening, a doe and fawn on two occasions, and a young bear who came for a morning splash in the lake, then scurried uphill as we watched from the distance. Most tent sites are shaded by big conifers: hemlock, cedar, and fir trees. Thickets of huckleberries grow beside the trails. The abundance of ripe berries in late summer suggests bears don't rely on these shrubs for forage while hikers are around. In boggy areas, marsh marigold and tall green hellebore are common.

On day two, leave your tent, bear canister (required for safe food storage), and overnight gear in camp. Travel light to Bogachiel Peak. The net elevation gain in the 9-mile roundtrip hike to the summit from Deer Lake is less than 2000 feet, but elevation is gained and lost several times, making the total gain more than 2500 feet. From the trail junction at the southeast corner of Deer Lake, continue south. On the Deer Lake campsite map posted at the junction, this trail is labeled as the way to the High Divide and Seven Lakes Basin. Robert Wood and other writers of classic hiking guides call it the Bogachiel Trail. Many hikers on the trail identify "The Loop" or "Seven Lakes Basin" as their destination. Whatever it is called, this is clearly the main route in the area.

A short distance south on the trail is an unnamed lake with adjacent signs indicating campsites and restoration areas. The trail continues winding and rocky, but the landscape is changing, with more clearings and vistas opening to distant green hills and gray mountains. After a mile or so, pass a series of small lakes that have gained the name "The Potholes." The last one is set in trees on the edge of an open bowl of a valley. As the trail curves around the ridge, the tread broadens and roots give way to smoother surfaces. The improvement does not last all the way to Bogachiel Peak, so enjoy it when it appears.

When the route crosses over the ridge to the south, it looks down on the Bogachiel River Valley, 2000 feet below. The trail retains views into this watershed all the way to Bogachiel Peak. The steep slope is well-vegetated with low-growing plants that thrive in harsh winter conditions. Here, above the 4000-foot elevation, the flower show shifts to alpine blossoms. Several shades of paintbrushes, yellow monkeyflowers, rosy spirea, alpine fireweed, and beargrass catch the eye; lupine, harebells, and gentians represent the blues. The trail offers many panoramic views, punctuated by groves of trees on both sides of the trail. About 3.5 miles from Deer Lake, the route crosses several stretches of talus[9] that run far down the slope toward the river.

The next grove of trees shelters the side trail to Seven Lakes Basin. No lakes are visible from here, but a short, steep trail north leads up to a narrow ridge, suggesting the fabled valley lies just beyond.

Continue on the Bogachiel Trail another 0.5 mile to the next junction. Below, to the southeast is another deep valley, complete with a visible river. This is the Hoh River Valley. There are huge mountains

---

[9] Talus: mountain slopes of rocks and boulders.

beyond, with glaciers gleaming on steep slopes. Mount Olympus has three tall, broad peaks. The Bailey Range lies beyond to the east.

Signs at the junction indicate Hoh Lake is reached by continuing straight, while Heart Lake is on the trail to the left. The map shows Bogachiel Peak is above on the left, so it is apparent the Peak is reached via the route toward Heart Lake. In about 0.25 mile, a narrow trail to the left has a Bogachiel Peak sign. Informal social trails have been visible on the steep slopes leading to the top, but having a labeled trail is reassuring. The official trail is only a boot-width wide, but firm underfoot and it leads directly to the 30-foot-diameter summit.

In 2018, a family of goats dominated the summit clearing. Future visitors may find new greenery after the goat removals that started later the same year. The lookout site offers unobstructed views in almost all directions. Because of wildfire haze, they were not clear views in 2018, but Bogachiel Peak is obviously the place for spectacular panoramas of the Hoh and Bogachiel River Valleys, and into the Seven Lakes Basin. Even the Pacific Ocean can be glimpsed from here on a clear day.

Mountain goats on Bogachiel Peak, August 2018.

Artifacts are not a major feature of this fire lookout site. A few sparkles from shards of the cabin's window glass can be seen, and perhaps one of the last remaining nails. Please leave them here for others to discover. Enjoy the views and take home photos as reminders of your epic trek to Bogachiel Peak.

11. KLOSHE NANICH AND NORTH POINT LOOKOUTS

RT Distance: 9.2 miles
High Point: 3340 feet
Elevation Gain: 2730 feet
Season: Jun-Oct
The parking lot is in state forestland, so a Discover Pass is required.

History

In 1905, a forest fire swept through the Sol Duc River Valley from Lake Crescent to the village of Beaver, near Sappho. At the time, this area was part of the national Olympic Forest Reserve, established to provide a permanent supply of forest products for the country. By the mid-teens, the area had been replanted, and interest grew in building a fire watch post to oversee the young forest.[1] Fire lookouts were a new concept in western Washington, so it took a cooperative effort of the US Forest Service, Washington Forestry Division, and the private Washington Forest Fire Association to fund a small building in 1917.[2]

The original Kloshe Nanich Lookout cabin, 1919. (Photograph in Washington State Forester. *Fifteenth and sixteenth Annual Reports for the Years Ending November 30, 1919, and December 18, 1920.*)

The square white cabin with a small, second-story cupola stood on a rock ledge far above the Sol Duc River with great views over the trees at its feet, from the Pacific Ocean to Mount Olympus and the western half of Lake Crescent. The little building with its white cap was visible from the road running between the popular lake and the growing town of Forks, so it became a familiar landmark on that route for tourists and locals alike.

---

[1] An article in *The Oregon Daily Journal*, June 22, 1919, quoted in https://washingtonlookouts.weebly.com/kloshe-nanitch.html.
[2] Washington Forest Fire Association, *10th Annual report*, 1917, quoted in https://washingtonlookouts.weebly.com/kloshe-nanitch.html.

Some sources say the cabin was replaced in 1939 by the North Point Lookout, a few hundred feet higher in elevation, and about a mile farther up the winding mountain road. North Point is on the top of the ridge, and at that time had the advantage of views to the north, toward the Strait of Juan de Fuca, as well as the broad Sol Duc Valley to the south. A 14×14-foot cabin with a hip roof but no cupola was built on that site—and remains as a rare fire lookout building in the Olympic National Forest.

Despite North Point's broader views, records of the Aircraft Warning Service (AWS) show Kloshe Nanich was used as a year-round plane-spotting station during World War II, and was retained by the Forest Service at the end of the AWS program.[3]

When the town of Forks was threatened by a horrific wildfire in 1951, the North Point Lookout was mentioned as unfortunately unstaffed when it could have provided an important warning of the growing destruction.[4] A few years later, a north peninsula newspaper reported that this lookout was only being staffed on an emergency basis—during lightning storms and extremely dry weather.[5] The cabin was used as an intermittent fire watch station until about 1979, according to Forest Service staff.

The US Coast and Geodetic Survey placed a set of survey markers on and around the North Point Lookout house in 1954, with the location of the principal marker, the survey station, identified as "a cement monument 5 inches above the surface of the ground . . . on the south side of the lookout house."[6] From the geographic coordinates and the National Geodetic Survey description, it is clear the square, white building, now covered with vinyl clapboard siding and supporting solar panels and short-legged antennae, is the original lookout building constructed over seventy years ago.

The Kloshe Nanich Lookout building has not fared so well, but was too popular to disappear quietly. In 1996, a replica building was constructed on its site. Forest Service carpenters reported that there were only scattered nails and a rusty firefinder post (embedded in rock) remaining on the site when they started.[7] The pretty little building with the cupola erected in the '90s was popular with tourists who drove up the winding

---

[3] [US Forest Service] Region 6, "Report of Aircraft Warning Service Stations," May 1, 1944, Sheet II.
[4] Mavis Amundson, *The Great Forks Fire*, 12.
[5] *Port Angeles Evening News*, May 18, 1956, quoted in https://washingtonlookouts.weebly.com/north-point.html.
[6] US National Geodetic Survey, "Data Sheet PID TS0215 N POINT"; https://www.ngs.noaa.gov/cgi-bin/ds_mark.prl?PidBox=TS0215.
[7] "Forks pair recreates fire lookout," *Peninsula Daily News*, A1 + (undated clipping in Jefferson County Historical Museum Research Center files).

mountain road for its great views. I took a photo there myself on my first visit to these lookouts in 2003.

Less than a decade later, the Forest Service removed what remained of the replica building to keep visitors safe. Despite repeated repairs, the structure suffered from terminal dry rot, and the catwalk overhanging the cliff top was not reliable.[8] The building was removed in October 2012.[9] In 2014, Ranger Molly Erickson was successful in obtaining project funds to build a secure viewing platform on the site, now known as the Kloshe Nanich Viewpoint.[10] The structure was completed the next year, with the galvanized metal post and base for an Osborne firefinder still standing in the middle of its floor.

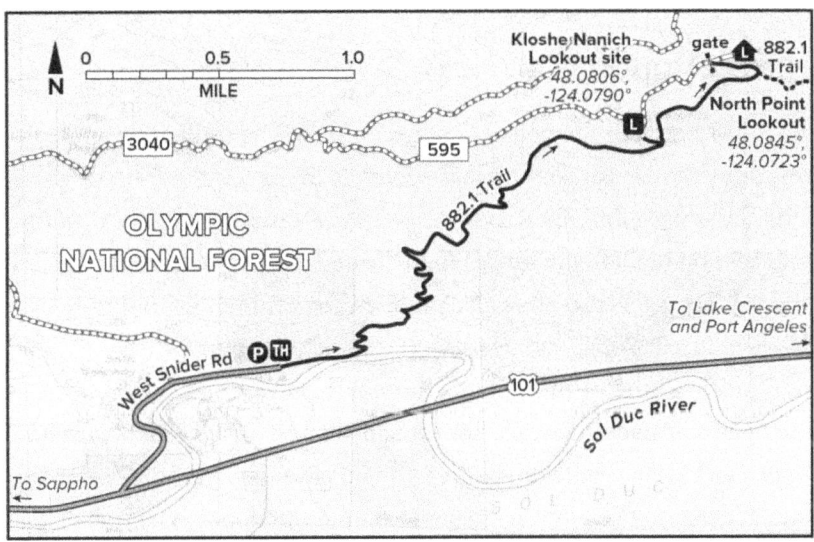

Hike Summary

Although mostly on south-facing slopes, the narrow path has lots of shade and eventual views of snow-capped mountains. It climbs pretty steadily, but the views from Kloshe Nanich and the opportunity to hike to a standing lookout building in the Olympic National Forest are worth the effort.

---

[8] Conversation with Ranger Molly Erickson, USFS, Olympic National Forest, Forks Office, 2012.
[9] https://www.fs.usda.gov/recarea/olympic/recarea/?recid=47711.
[10] The 2014/2015 project was supported by the Olympic National Forest Resource Advisory Committee while the author was serving on the committee.

Getting There

- Drive US Highway 101 between its junction with the State Route 113 and the Sol Duc Hot Springs Road. Between mileposts 211 and 212, turn north on West Snider Road, just west of a bridge crossing the Sol Duc River.
- Drive past classic Forest Service buildings at the historical Snider Creek Work Center. The road ends in 1 mile at a Kloshe Nanich Trailhead sign, in a small area of state forestland within the Olympic National Forest.

Hiking Route

A short section of fencing sits on each side of the trailhead, helping to disguise the old, paved road that serves as the short, flat trail entry, beside the broad Sol Duc River. At one-third mile, a brown and yellow signpost on the left announces the Kloshe Nanich Trail, and the ascent begins. Ranger Erickson is also credited for getting this trail to Kloshe Nanich, North Point, and even Muller Mountain, built in 1994.[11]

The first mile of trail climbs through hemlock and fir forest dense enough to provide shade for hikers and support an attractive variety of plants and shrubs beneath the trees: twinflower, sword ferns, salal, and huckleberries. The whir of tires and deep mutters of diesel trucks start to fade as the trail passes a ravine with a murmuring creek.

At 1.25 miles, the forest thins, and green ridges of the Olympic forest on the south side of the Sol Duc Valley come into view. Cross a stream—or streambed, depending on the season—at about 1.5 miles.

The trail soon turns a corner, heading north. Tall vine maples—more than 20 feet in height—stand out under 50- to 100-foot conifers; their colorful translucent leaves glow brightly when they catch the sunlight. The whorled leaves of the pipsissewa catch attention beside the trail here, particularly in spring when the creamy umbrella blossoms hide

---

[11] Craig Romano, *Day Hiking Olympic Peninsula*, Seattle, Mountaineer Books, 2007, 278.

11. KLOSHE NANICH AND NORTH POINT LOOKOUTS · 69

their shy faces. The trail next curves toward the east, coming to viewpoints revealing higher and higher peaks to the south and east, before reversing direction with each switchback, reaching for the rock-rimmed ridge above.

Cross two more small streams as you continue to switchback toward Kloshe Nanich. The underside of the viewpoint platform appears above before you reach the multidirectional signpost that asserts the Snider Road is 3.5 miles downhill and the Kloshe Nanich Lookout is 0.5 mile above. Follow the short spur trail to the lookout site and its wonderful viewpoint.

On the way up the hill, notice the square storage building that serves as the foundation for the broad wooden platform that welcomes visitors to this historic vantage point. There are reader boards, a picnic table, and outhouses near the platform to serve visitors, but unfortunately, no information is presented. Perhaps displays will eventually tell the area's human and natural history.

Enjoy the views from the 20×20-foot platform. Savor your lunch on one of the small benches, if a seat is available. Notice the metal post and broad cap rising from the floor; it once held the circular firefinder map and its viewfinder.

Rather than continue your hike to the North Point Lookout on the nearby road, consider the signpost at the junction below. It includes an arrow pointing north: "Lookout *Loop* 1.5." There is no trail higher on the ridge to complete a loop connecting the two lookouts, only a road that features an American Tower Company *No Trespassing* sign beside a gated road leading to communication towers and the North Point Lookout cabin.[12] To avoid approaching the lookout building from the forbidding gated road, return to the Kloshe Nanich Trail, and continue hiking through the forest toward the high point on the ridge where the communication facilities are clustered.

---

[12] I was assured by a US Forest Ranger in 2016 that exclusive use of the land is not in the Forest Service contract. It is possible the sign has been removed, although removal is not a likely priority.

It is 1 mile from the signpost below Kloshe Nanich to the North Point Lookout cabin. Partway to North Point is a two-direction signpost, pointing right to *Muller Mt. 5 miles*, and left to *Lookout .5 mile*. Follow the almost level trail to the left. It emerges on a road between the gate and the communication towers, support buildings, and North Point Lookout cabin. Ascend the road a few hundred feet toward the well-signed buildings—there are lots of warnings and "who to contact in case of emergency." At the high point of the road end, carved out of the forest, is a little white building on top of a small knoll. The easy way to reach the top of the rise is a short trail that goes behind the building.

North Point Lookout cabin with vinyl siding and antennae, 2017.

From below, the building looks classic: white clapboard siding and a gray pyramid roof. The details reveal the steps taken to protect the structure from Olympic winter weather. This is not a fresh coat of paint, but vinyl siding on three exterior walls. The building doesn't have big wooden shutters covering classic fire lookout windows; all the windows have been covered with the horizontal siding to protect whatever is stored inside. Only one sheltered side of the building lacks vinyl. It has a padlocked wooden door and no windows.

The historical National Geodetic Survey markers sit near the northeast corner of the square cabin. They confirm this as the location of the historical lookout building. There no longer is a view from North Point. If you look carefully, you can spot the Kloshe Nanich viewing platform on its rocky point through the trees, while descending the curving trail toward the famous landmark.

12. ELLIS LOOKOUT

RT Distance: 7.2 miles
High Point: 2338 feet
Elevation Gain: 1450 feet
Season: Apr-Oct
No pass or permit is required.

History

Only bits and pieces of the Ellis fire lookout history have been uncovered. The two fire lookout inventories published in the 1980s agree that a small cabin was built at 2338 feet on a hill about two miles south of Ellis Mountain in 1952.[1] In his listing, Ray Kresek mentioned the cabin was "atop the middle ridge."[2] The elevation, combined with Kresek's description of the location, places the historical observation station on a knoll now occupied by several tall cell and repeater towers.

Ellis Lookout, 1960. (Boyd Church photograph, courtesy of the Fire Lookout Museum.)

One additional document unfortunately contributes confusion rather than clarity. An Annual Report of the State Forestry Division (which became the Department of Natural Resources in the mid-1950s) includes the information that the 1952 construction project at Ellis Lookout was a replacement 14×14-foot ground house.[3] No record of an earlier lookout building here has yet been found. Whatever its history, sources agree that the cabin was removed in 1970.

---

[1] Kresek, *2015*, 22; Spring and Fish, 197.
[2] Kresek, *2015*, 22.
[3] Washington Division of Forestry, *Forty-Seventh and Forty-Eighth Annual Reports for the Period Commencing October 16, 1950, and Ending November 10, 1952*, 42.

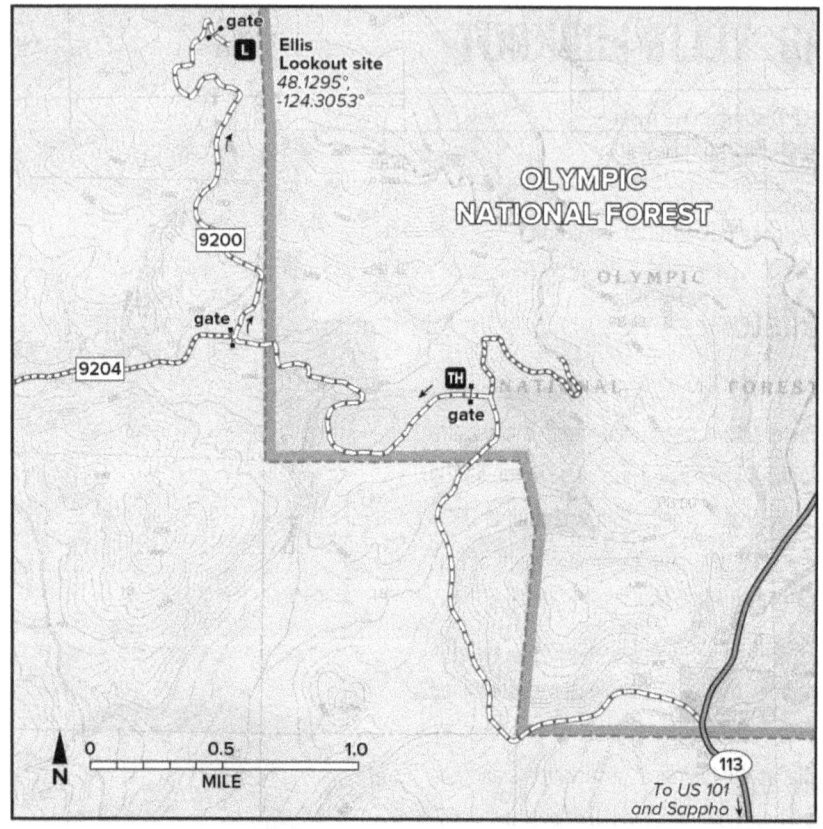

Hike Summary

Drive through private and federal forestland to state forest. Start the hike near a Department of Natural Resources (DNR) gate, crossing a private tree farm before reentering state forestland. The gate at the foot of the final hill warns of High Radio Frequency ahead. The hilltop is where the Ellis fire lookout site is found among today's tall communication towers. For orientation purposes, it is useful to remember the Ellis Lookout was not located on Ellis Mountain, a couple of miles to the north.

Getting There

- At Sappho, turn north on State Route 113 from US Highway 101.
- At milepost 2, promptly turn left. This turn is easy to miss, as the road into the forest is not visible until you reach the milepost. Some directions follow the route to the Beaver Falls Quarry, but the only sign identifying the quarry is not visible before the turn.
- Drive west, passing through private land and a short section of unsigned Olympic National Forest. When you reach a sign on the left encouraging fire prevention (about 0.8 mile from State Route 113), you have entered state forestland.
- The road turns north and in about 1.4 miles turns west again and comes to a yellow DNR gate. If the gate is open and you want to drive farther, check with the regional DNR office in Forks (360-374-2800) to learn if the gate will remain open. The road near the gate is too narrow for parking. When hiking from here, stop at the last bend in the road before the gate, and park on the wide shoulder there.

Hiking Route

The 7.2 miles identified as the length of this hike assumes the yellow DNR gate is closed. An open state forest gate could be tempting, but should not be relied on without checking with the DNR office. This section of the route travels 1.6 miles through state forestlands, with fairly dense mixed forest on both sides of the road. The course starts gently downhill to the west, then curves south around a minor hill before continuing northwestward, alternately gaining and losing elevation as it goes. Beginning at 880 feet, the elevation increases 100 feet by the next intersection, but it feels like substantially more.

Turn right at an intersection of state and private forest roads. Beside the junction, on the east side of the north-south road and north of the junction on the east-west road, are signs identifying these gravel tracks as Rayonier Timber Company roads 9200 and 9204. The Department of Natural Resources has a different numbering system, which appears on their road maps, but not here.

The road hiked to this point continues west, through a blue Rayonier Timber Company gate. The route to Ellis Lookout turns right, following Forest Road 9200. At the junction, a white painted 4×4-inch post with red vertical letters and an arrow points to the right: **ELLIS—›**. The route gains elevation steadily from here, winding up the hill and gaining 1300 feet in the next 2 miles.

A quarter mile after the gate, a narrow creek burbles under the road and disappears downhill. Enjoy thick forest on the right-hand hillside and intermittent views across the Hoko River Valley to the left. A variety of wildflowers grow on the road edge, each in its season. Spring brings violets, salmonberry, oxalis, and may lilies, followed by rambling raspberries, foxgloves, and pearly everlasting through the summer.

Above 1800 feet elevation, views into the valley include parts of the 2-mile long Lake Pleasant, several miles to the south. Near that viewpoint, about a mile and a third from the blue gate, cross from private timber land into state forest again. Unless there are timber sale or contract signs on the trees, the border is likely invisible. A tributary of the Hoko River parallels the outside of the road at its higher elevations. It remains unseen but occasionally murmurs down the slope.

The road ends in a wide opening with a tall, forested hill opposite a gated gravel track, which leads the last 0.25 mile up to communication towers and buildings. The closed white gate on the final road bears a sign warning *High Level Radio Frequency Fields* ahead.

I have visited this site twice, in 2012 and 2017. I have not yet found convincing remains of the buildings constructed here in 1952 or earlier. In 2012, my companions and I found a Department of Natural Resources survey marker dated 1984 near the towers. In 2017, my husband and I found a DNR survey disc dated 1974, on a 4-inch-tall metal post at the foot of the wooded hill opposite the closed white gate.

After finding the 1974 survey marker, we climbed to the top of that forested hill, in case it might be the "middle ridge" Ray Kresek reported as the historical cabin's location. We found no open ground or building remnants to support an idea that hilltop had been the fire lookout site.

We also kept an eye out for a US Coast and Geodetic Survey marker stamped "Ellis, 1913, 1954." The agency's 1954 site visit activities included replacing an original azimuth marker here with this one: "33 feet north of the lookout house, 15 feet west-northwest of an anemometer, 15 feet southeast of the road, 6 feet west of an aerial pole, and 9 feet northwest of a weather box. The mark projects 4 inches."[4] Finding this bronze disc could establish the location of the Ellis Lookout site definitively.

On both trips to the area, we hiked to the crest of the hill where communication towers are located, admired views of the sparkling blue Strait of Juan de Fuca to the north, and searched for artifacts of a fire lookout cabin. On one visit, we found a large chunk of concrete with a metal bar protruding. If this were a hilltop with no other structures in sight, I would be satisfied we had found the lookout station's historical location. With several communication facilities now on site, the source of the concrete remnant cannot be easily assumed.

In 2017, we also followed the spur road beyond the highest gate on the hilltop. It led to a relatively short metal antenna tower and a wooden telephone pole-type tower with its own small metal antenna among the modern repeater stations and cell phone towers. Could these have been accessories to a fire lookout station removed in 1970? When you visit the area, make your own interpretations and select your own site for the long gone lookout cabin. If you find some convincing evidence, be sure to share the information.[5]

---

[4] US National Geodetic Survey, "Data Sheet PID TS0219 ELLIS RESET"; https://www.ngs.noaa.gov/cgi-bin/ds_mark.prl?PidBox=TS0219.

[5] Send a comment to my website, www.LeslieRomer.com, or post on the *Fire Lookouts of Washington* Facebook page.

OLYMPIC PENINSULA EAST

Hikes accessible from US Highway 101
from its junction with State Route 20 at Discovery Bay
to Potlatch State Park on southern Hood Canal.

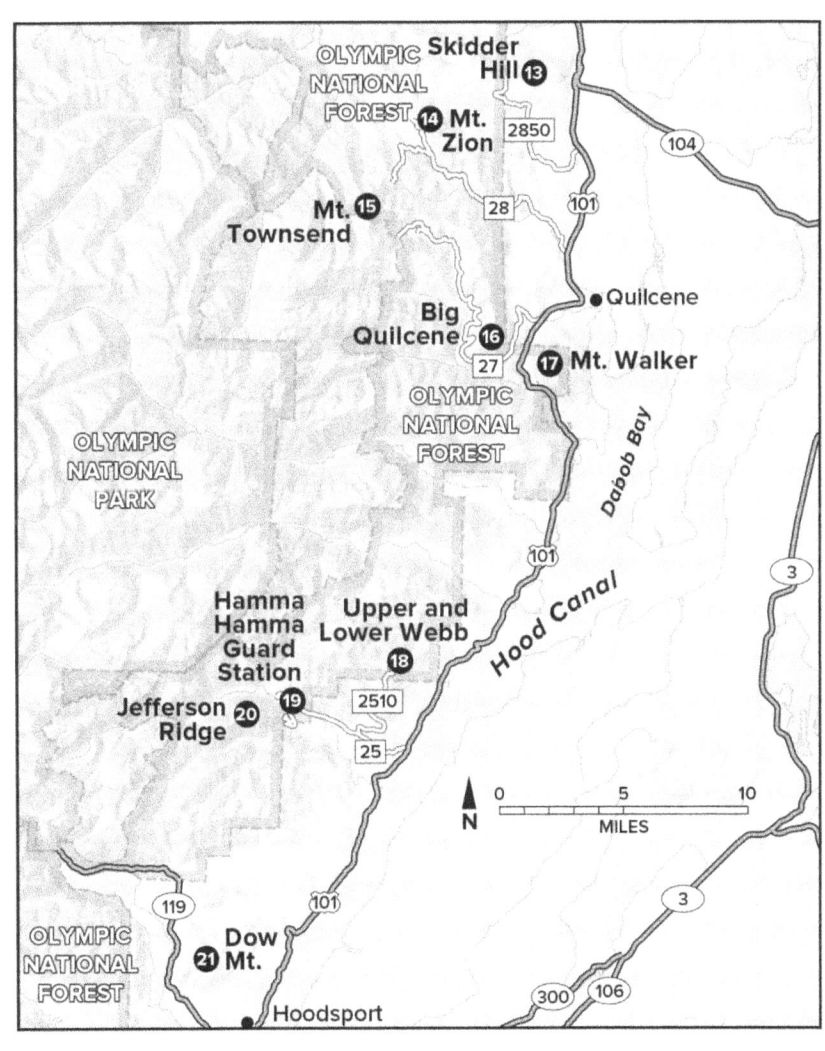

13. SKIDDER HILL LOOKOUT

RT Distance: 10.5 miles
High Point: 2125 feet
Elevation Gain: 1500 feet
Season: All Year
No pass or permit is required.

History

Two hills, Big and Little Skidder Hills, appear on maps, but the lookout station was always known by the shorter name. In 1957, the Washington Department of Natural Resources built a forty-foot wooden fire lookout tower near the top of Big Skidder Hill with a 14×14-foot live-in cabin on top. It replaced the Shine Lookout, which had stood 1.5 miles from Hood Canal, 12.5 miles to the southeast, since 1942. The Shine tower was removed the same year.[1]

In July 1966, Olga Hughett, editor of the state fire lookout staff newsletter, proudly announced her granddaughter, Karen Roening, was serving her second year as fire lookout staff at Skidder Hill.[2] Olga served many years as the Blyn fire lookout staff, retiring from lookout duty in 1965. The Skidder Hill tower stood guard on state forestland south of Discovery Bay until 1971, when it was removed.

Skidder Hill Lookout, 1960. (Photograph courtesy of Doug Houck.)

---

[1] Olga Hughett, "Eleven Lookouts Watch for Fires in Jefferson County," *Port Townsend Leader*, August 2, 1962, 7.
[2] [Olga Hughett, "Staff Updates"], *Olympia District's Ten-Eight*, July 1966, [1].

13. SKIDDER HILL LOOKOUT · 79

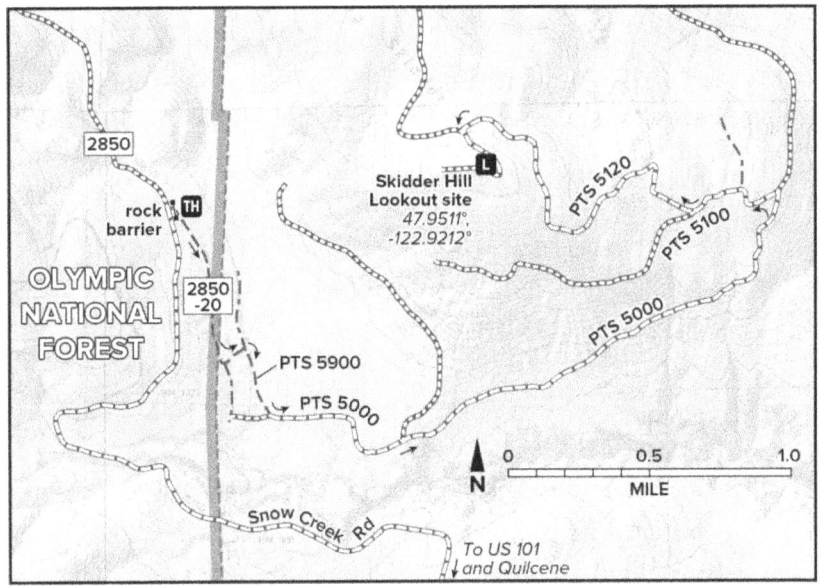

Hike Summary

This hiking route starts with the adventure of a decommissioned national forest road and a series of low berms and ditches on its way to gravel roads in state forestlands. The upper slopes of Big Skidder Hill provide broad views of Hood Canal, the Olympic Mountains, Discovery Bay, the Strait of Juan de Fuca, and many distant peaks.

In 2020, Pope Resources sold their timber lands in the region to Rayonier Inc., eliminating an alternate hiking route from the north on private forest roads.

Getting There

- Drive US Highway 101 between Quilcene and its intersection with State Route 104.
- Between mileposts 289 and 290, turn west on Snow Creek Road.
- Drive 1.0 mile and follow a sharp right turn in the road. At 1.4 miles from the highway, the pavement ends.
- At 3 miles, stay to the right at a Y.

- At 5.9 miles, the county road ends. A variety of signs indicate the change from local to national forest jurisdiction. Sometimes a brown sign stands here, identifying the route as Forest Road (FR) 2850.
- At 6.6 miles, go right.
- At 6.8 miles, stay right at a Y. The left branch is signed FR 2852.
- At 7.7 miles, park near knee-high rocks blocking the decommissioned side road (2850-20) on the right.

Hiking Route

FR 2850 and the land surrounding it are within the eastern border of the Olympic National Forest. This hike begins on a closed national forest road (labeled 2850-20 when it appears on maps) that is occasionally used by dirt bikes or other all-terrain vehicles to access the maintained forest roads on the adjacent state forestlands. The first 100 yards follow rough tracks pressed into a small clearing in the forest, replanted to disguise the former road. The tracks lead to an old roadway now carpeted with moss and grass, heading south-southeast through thick, healthy forest. Just when you think this abandoned road is a really nice hiking route, a 3-foot thick alder tree lies across the path. Foot and wheeled traffic have left a rough trail around the root ball at the west end of the obstruction. The branches are weathering away, so climbing over the trunk in the middle of the track is becoming less arduous with time.

At 0.7 mile from the trailhead, this road is closed with a large berm on the edge of a clearcut running east and south. Another short track—with smaller berms—snakes the short distance east to a narrow parallel road within the clearcut area. Follow this track, turn right on that narrow road, and continue to the southern edge of the young tree plantation.

There are several ditches and berms interrupting the first 0.25 mile of this gravel route. A couple of the ditches contain water in wet seasons, but are usually easy to cross. As the road approaches the southern border of the tree farm, it curves left (eastward), toward tall trees and a road junction.

The junction at 1.6 miles was marked with both red-and-white and brown vinyl road signs when scouted, probably indicating a transition in design. The main road here is PTS 5000, while the road just exited is signed PTS 5900. In 2020, roadside flagging indicated a future timber harvest is planned for the forest south and west of this junction.

Turn left on PTS 5000. The next major junction comes at 2.2 miles, in the midst of a shady hemlock and alder forest. Continue to follow PTS 5000 to the northeast, while PTS 5700 heads around a corner toward the northwest. At this point, the elevation is 900 feet, somewhat lower than the starting point. The track through the forest rises steadily from here, gaining a 1000-foot elevation in about 2.5 miles on its way to the Big Skidder Hill ridge.

After climbing for 0.5 mile, the route gains views of Hood Canal in the southeast, Little Skidder Hill and Mount Walker directly south, and higher, sometimes snowy peaks to the southwest. One of the highest on the front range is 6200-foot Mount Townsend,[3] a very popular flower and fire lookout hike in summer. In March, its eastern slope has vertical stripes of snow, while tufted coltsfoot, bright yellow swamp lanterns,[4] and furry, gray pussy willows grace the roadside at this lower elevation.

A little farther north, highway sounds and the sight of miniature cars on the very straight roadway far below disrupt the peace. The view of placid Lake Crocker is disconcerting. How can it be so tranquil, so close to all that noisy traffic?

The track turns a corner toward the northwest, and Discovery Bay and the broad Strait of Juan de Fuca appear at the northern edge of the Olympic Peninsula. On clear days, Mount Baker and its white-capped neighbors appear to the north-northeast. The views disappear as the route gains tall trees on both sides. At 3.25 miles, turn left on PTS 5100 where rhododendrons make their first appearances under the tall trees.

---

[3] See Chapter 15, "Mount Townsend Lookout."
[4] You may know this familiar spring beauty as skunk cabbage.

There are more road junctions on the ridge than lower on the route. After another 0.2 mile, turn left again to stay on PTS 5100. The next right turn onto a narrower track, PTS 5120, is intuitive as it curves uphill while the wider road slopes down.

Mount Baker over north Puget Sound from the Skidder Hill hike route.

Finally, our route meets an old road from the west at a T. Turn left to continue on PTS 5120. Go one-third mile and look to the hillside on your right as you turn a corner in that direction. An eyebolt on a foot-high, anodized metal post signals your arrival at the Skidder Hill Lookout site. Careful hunting under the hemlocks will reveal all four concrete footing blocks fairly close together. Apparently these supports are all that remain of the proud tower that watched over the broad forests in this corner of the peninsula from 1957 until 1971.

14. MOUNT ZION LOOKOUT

RT Distance: 3.5 miles
High Point: 4278 feet
Elevation Gain: 1350 feet
Season: Late Apr–Nov
A National Forest Pass or another federal lands pass is required.

History

The US Forest Service built the first fire lookout structure on this high peak in the northeast Olympics in 1929.[1] This photograph shows a square mountaintop cabin with a big shutter hanging open above each wall's broad windows. Snow surrounded the building in that long-ago winter image, but Mount Zion is in the rain shadow of the taller peaks to the west. Rains are light and spring comes early to this almost 4300-foot site.

Rollin Shaw was the lookout at Mount Zion for many years, taking his wife and three or four sons to the high cabin with him.

Mount Zion Lookout in snow, February 1943. (US Forest Service photograph found in National Archives, Seattle. Courtesy of Ron Kemnow.)

The family also kept a herd of goats up on the hill,[2] which is hard to imagine with today's dense forest. Images from the historical Osborne panoramic photo series,[3] as well as stories about the Shaws' animals, however, indicate the forest around the peak was completely logged in the 1930s.

---

[1] Spring and Fish, 198.
[2] Rooney, 51.
[3] Osborne panoramic photos taken at Mount Zion lookout in 1935 are posted at https://willhiteweb.com/washington_climbing/olympic_mountains/mount_zion_trail/hiking_047.htm.

The Aircraft Warning Service (AWS) added an 8×16-foot cabin to the fire lookout station when they enlisted it as a year-round observation station in 1942.[4] When the wartime program ended in 1944, the facilities were assigned to the Olympic National Forest (ONF). The national forest employed summer lookout staff here until 1962, at least.[5] The building was removed in 1975.

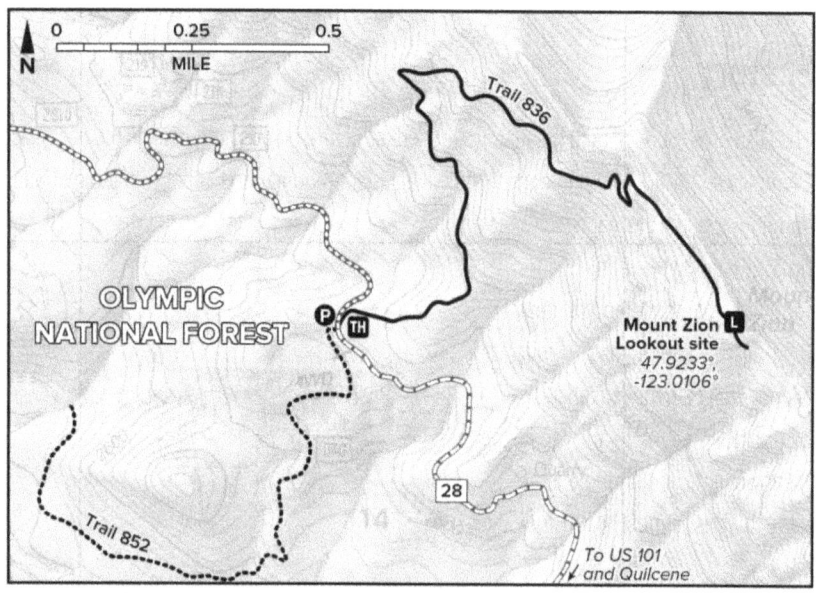

Hike Summary

The basic hike to the site of the Mount Zion lookout is short and steep through fairly thick forest. There are many wildflowers in May through early July and occasional views of the northern Olympic Mountains. The hike can be extended on side trails accessed at the summit and across the parking lot, which is shared with the low-elevation Shady Hollow Trail.

---

[4] [US Forest Service] Region 6, "Report of Aircraft Warning Service Stations," May 1, 1944, Sheet III.
[5] Olga Hughett, "Eleven Lookouts Watch for Fires in Jefferson County," *Port Townsend Leader*, Aug 2, 1962, 7.

Getting There

- Turn west from US Highway 101 on Lords Lake Loop Road between mileposts 292 and 293, a couple of miles north of Quilcene.
- At 3.4 miles, the road turns left at the fence surrounding the Lords Lake reservoir. At a junction shortly after the lake, bear right uphill, passing Road PT03800 on the left.
- Enter the Olympic National Forest at 4.1 miles on Forest Road (FR) 28.
- At 7.7 miles, come to a big intersection with FR 27 and FR 080. Bear right and continue on FR 28 (some signs read 2800).
- At 9 miles, reach the famous, but unfortunately unsigned, Bon Jon Pass; bear right on FR 28. Sometimes, a broken vinyl road sign is visible on the left, just beyond the junction, which can help identify the intersection.
- Drive 2 more miles to a well-planned parking lot and outhouse. Hikers who arrive in the a.m. can usually find space for their car at this very popular trailhead.

Hiking Route

The Mount Zion trail is famous for its wonderful display of native pink rhododendron blossoms each spring. When it occurs, of course, is dependent on that year's weather pattern. Having a 1300-foot elevation range does help extend the bloom season for rhodies, as well as the many other flowers that find a welcome on the partially shaded trail.

The path starts fairly steeply, including a series of shallow, wood-fronted steps in the first 0.3 mile. Leggy rhodies with pink blossoms line the trail in late spring, as well as tiny pink roses with yellow centers, blossoms of vanilla leaf and salal, and a profusion of firs and hemlock.

Some parts of the trail have a canopy of tall rhododendron shrubs meeting overhead. Most of the understory offers a wide variety of other flowers, too, although they appear in small patches, under trees and around rocks, rather than as a broad border. The early summer display offers a wide variety: white flowers beside the ascending trail include star flower, bunchberry, strawberry, thimbleberry, queen's cup, and Sitka valerian. There are also blue lupines, orange paintbrush, pink pipsissewa and penstemon, and multicolor columbine.

At 0.9 mile, an opening in the trees offers views of the snowy peaks of the Gray Wolf Ridge to the west, as well as dark green ridges across the valley to the south. The elevation is about 3700 feet. At 1.3 miles, a side trail to the left leads to a rocky outcrop with panoramic views. This is a good diversion on the way up or down and a great way to see more of the landscape.

Just when sky becomes visible through the trees at the top of the ridge (1.9 miles from the trailhead) a tall, rectangular shadow appears on the right, and a narrow trail leads through the forest to a historical outhouse. Why historical? The door is difficult to open and there is no seat inside. Since it is not operational, its next best function is as a historical object.

After returning to the main trail, continue uphill a short distance around the edge of a large boulder and turn left onto the big viewing rock. On late spring and summer weekends you can expect to join an extended picnic party of families with children of all ages and groups of young to mid-aged adult hikers on Mount Zion's summit. At the far end of the rocks are a few small sitting boulders and a little shade. One of the boulders features an undated US Army Corps of Engineers bronze disc survey reference mark with an arrow pointing east. The arrow is intended to identify the direction of the principal benchmark, or survey station, from the reference mark.

According to federal records, a US Coast and Geodetic Survey marker was installed at Mount Zion Lookout House in 1955.[6] Only a Corps of Engineers disc has been found near the lookout site recently. The old outhouse offers the sole physical reminder of the lookout station that stood on top of this peak.

---

[6] US National Geodetic Survey, "Data Sheet PID SY1604 MT ZION LOOKOUT HOUSE"; https://www.ngs.noaa.gov/cgi-bin/ds_mark.prl?PidBox=SY1604.

A trail off the southeast corner of the summit leads gently downhill in 0.5 mile to another broad rock outcrop, with broader views to the south and west than Mount Zion's summit, and more space for the extended picnic party. Another option for extending your hike is to visit the Shady Hollow Trail with its trailhead directly across the parking lot. It leads gently downhill to a pretty stream-crossing in 1.5 miles. The 500-foot elevation gain returning from the creek is a small price to pay at the end of a great day in the woods.

If your after-hike route takes you south on US Highway 101 through Quilcene, consider stopping at the little grocery store on the north side of the town center for one of their truly generous ice cream cones.

15. MOUNT TOWNSEND LOOKOUT

RT Distance:
6.1 miles (N)
9.0 miles (upper S)
10.6 miles (lower S)

High Point:
6212 feet
6280 feet
6280 feet

Elevation Gain:
2200 feet
2900 feet
3500 feet

Season: Jun-Oct
No pass or permit is required.

History

The US Forest Service built a fire lookout cabin on the north summit of Mount Townsend in 1933. It was slightly downhill and about 0.5 mile north of the mountain's highest point, 6280 feet.[1]

Longtime forest ranger Robert Bulchis worked summers for the Olympic National Forest while studying Forestry at the University of Washington. In 1935, two Civilian Conservation Corps (CCC) men helped him pack his gear for the summer up the ten-mile-or-more trail from the Lower Quilcene River, using two burros. "Nearby, slightly below the level of the lookout, was an open lean-to which was the home of my burros. The only other structure was an open air outhouse nearby where one might sit and meditate as he enjoyed the grandeur of the panorama he faced."[2]

Mount Townsend Lookout. (Olympic National Forest photograph, curated by Steve Ricketts.)

Mount Townsend was one of the fire lookouts evaluated by US Forest Service staff in 1936 and 1938. James Bethel reported "L.o. [sic] house is at present on ground. tower [sic] not feasible or practical . . . This point is a little too high for an efficient L.o. but since

---

[1] Kresek, *2015,* 24.
[2] Robert Bulchis, [*Oral History*], April 1997, accessed October 31, 2018 at http://justinmuseum.com/oralbio/bulchisbio.html.

it covers some country which is impossible to get from any other pt. it must be accepted."[3] The cabin was abandoned by 1955[4] and destroyed in 1962.[5]

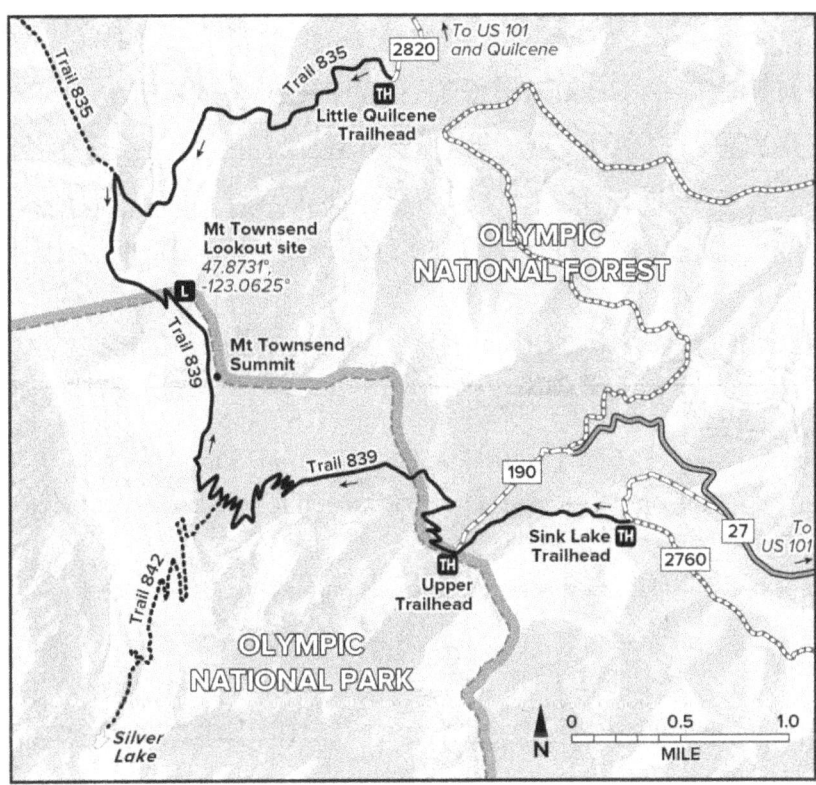

Hike Summary

At a 6212-foot elevation, this is one of the highest lookout sites in the Olympic Mountains and the easiest hike to a high elevation Olympic fire lookout site. There are three trailheads for hiking Mount Townsend. The routes vary primarily in length and elevation gain. The route from the north is shorter and has less elevation gain. The trail from the south has two trailheads about a mile apart. All routes offer spectacular flower

---

[3] James Bethel, [Fire Lookout Site Evaluation] "Mt. Townsend," July 11, 1936; Document 26-11, National Archives in Seattle.
[4] US National Geodetic Survey, "Datasheet PID SY1606 Townsend"; https://www.ngs.noaa.gov/cgi-bin/ds_mark.prl?PidBox=SY1606.
[5] Kresek, *2015*, 24.

displays if there are blossoms anywhere in the Olympics. Be aware that this is an extremely popular hike and finding a parking space at any of the three trailheads may be a challenge on a summer weekend.

Getting to the Southern Trail from Quilcene (coming from the east or north)

- Follow US Highway 101 1.5 miles south from Quilcene to Penny Creek Road at a big bend in the two-lane highway and turn right.

Getting to the Southern Trail from Shelton (coming from the south)

- Follow US Highway 101 for 50.5 miles from Shelton.
- After passing Fish Hatchery Road, watch for the highway to take a 90-degree turn to the right.
- In the middle of this curve, turn left onto Penny Creek Road.

Getting there from the junction of US Highway 101 and Penny Creek Road to the Southern Trail

- Drive 1.4 miles on Penny Creek Road to Big Quilcene River Road (gravel). Bear left on the road whose signs soon indicate a change to Forest Road (FR) 27 (paved).
- Drive 12.5 miles to a junction with FR 2760. **For the lower trailhead and longest hiking route**, take this side road 0.7 mile to the Sink Lake Trailhead of Trail #839.
- **For the upper trailhead**, continue on FR 27 for another mile to FR 2700-190.
- Turn left and continue another 0.75 mile to the upper trailhead of Trail #839.

Getting to the Northern Trailhead

- Two miles north of Quilcene, turn west from US Highway 101 on well-marked Lords Lake Loop Road.
- Drive 3.3 miles. At the lake, stay left.
- This road soon becomes FR 28. Drive 6 miles to its junction with FR 2820. Go over Bon Jon Pass along the way; it is a name that appears on maps, but has no sign.
- Follow FR 2820 for 4 miles to park for Trail #835 Little Quilcene Trail.

The Southern Hiking Route

The trail starts with a moderate ascent through shady forest full of rhododendron bushes of all sizes. In late May and June, these are adorned with large blossoms that begin deep pink and fade to pale shades as their season passes. The trail stays within sound—and occasional sight—of the vigorous Townsend Creek for the first mile. Only glimpses of the surrounding mountains are offered in this section of the hike, so enjoy the rhodies and other shade-loving spring flowers.

The fir and hemlock forest starts to open in the second mile, with more flowers on the trailside slopes. At 2 miles, a broad rock ledge appears on the left side of the trail, offering a snack or lunch spot with grand views southeastward across the valley to the Welch Peaks, a small waterfall, and out to Puget Sound. The ledge is divided by a small stream—bare rock for sitting on one side and an impressive floral display protected by the running water on the other: chocolate lilies, columbines, and strawberries on a typical late spring visit. Brighter summer sun brings out lupine, tiger lilies, paintbrush, bunchberry, and strawberry blossoms.

The switchbacks that follow are slightly less steep than the first section of trail. Mixed bouquets of wildflowers grace broad hillsides in summer: vivid red and orange paintbrush, periwinkle harebells, deep purple lupine, yellow arnica, and tall cow parsnip with lacy white blossoms. Snow-capped mountains appear above the islands and water of Puget Sound: Mount Rainier and it neighbors, Mounts Adams and St. Helens to the south, Glacier Peak and eventually Mount Baker to the northeast.

Approaching the ridge, trail signs offer arrows to Windy Camp and Windy Lake. The trail levels briefly here, but is braided as it wanders through the camp area. Fallen trees also cause a little confusion, so focus on your route and watch for the trail leading uphill.

In another 0.5 mile, the trail heading for the peak passes a major junction with the route to Silver Lake. The lake is a worthy destination, but at the price of a noticeable loss and gain of elevation. Only the truly hardy combine the lake and summit destinations in one hike.

Views open in all directions as you reach the ridge of Mount Townsend. It is hard to choose between the mountains in all directions and the alpine flowers at your feet. The variety of flowers changes in the higher elevation. Blooms above 6000 feet are sturdy survivors of wind and frost, and often miniature versions of their cousins farther down on the mountain.

The trail bypasses both the mountain summit at 6280 feet and the fire lookout site 0.5 mile farther at 6212 feet. The peak is reached by a side trail to the right, leading to the obvious highest point. If you would like a landmark, a bronze US Geological Survey benchmark disc stamped "Mt Townsend" is attached to a rock close to the summit.

Continuing on the main trail, the historical forest fire lookout site is up another side trail, about 0.5 mile farther north. The artifacts include guy wires still sticking from the ground and window glass sparkling among the grass at these coordinates: 47.8731°, -123.0625°.

On a clear day, there are spectacular views into the central Olympic peaks, as well as across Puget Sound to high-rise towers in Seattle. Ground-hugging plants take advantage of the bright sunshine available on the open landscape of Townsend Ridge. Phlox, cinquefoil, and buckwheat carpet areas of the broad summit. Unusual flowers, like purple avens, Piper's bellflowers, and mountain death camas also make their home here. Many butterflies find their way here in midsummer, feeding on the nectar of the diverse plant life.

With trailheads both north and south of the Mount Townsend ridge, a through-hike is an attractive possibility. Plan ahead with friends and exchange car keys on top for an opportunity to see the whole mountain and all its features.

Hiking Route from the North

While all of Mount Townsend's trailheads will be busy on summer weekends, Trail #835, Little Quilcene Trail, has the advantage on weekdays of fewer hikers on the trail and cars at the trailhead. By the time you reach the fire lookout site, you will probably have seen all the same flowers found on the southern route.

Trail #835 starts uphill in rolling countryside, gaining 800-foot elevation in 0.9 mile. At that point, a well-used side trail takes off to the left. Continue on the main footpath to its junction with the Tubal Cain Trail at 2.0 miles from the trailhead. The Tubal Cain route heads north and downhill as Trail #835; the elevation at the junction is 5280 feet. Turn left and uphill toward Mount Townsend. The trail signs here lack trail numbers. On maps, the Mount Townsend trail is #839.

Hike slightly less than a mile, gaining almost 1000 feet, for views into the Central Olympic Mountains and their valleys, and glimpses of the Strait of Juan de Fuca and Vancouver Island to the north. Many unusual flowers appear along the way during the summer. Pass a sign for the Buckhorn Wilderness entrance a short distance before a well-established but unsigned trail takes off on the left. Follow this old trail as it winds up toward the Mount Townsend Ridge and its northern peak. When you reach the cable sticking out of the ground on your left (coordinates: 47.8731°, -123.0625°), you have reached the Mount Townsend fire lookout site. On a crystal clear day, you can see glaciated peaks in the Cascades from Mount Baker to Mount St. Helens, and perhaps beyond.

16. BIG QUILCENE LOOKOUT

RT Distance: 5.0 miles
High Point: 3235 feet
Elevation Gain: 1000 feet
Season: Jun-Oct
No pass or permit is required.

History

The scant records of the Olympic National Forest fire lookout on Big Quilcene Ridge indicate a cabin was built on this viewpoint in 1930.[1] In 1962, Olga Hughett, the Blyn fire lookout, reported in the *Port Townsend Leader*, "The Forest Service is planning a new lookout where a good road comes out on the top of the Big Quilcene Ridge. This summer it will be manned on real fire-weather days under an emergency set up . . . a man, firefinder and trailer."[2]

Clues to the fate of the 1930s cabin or details of plans to rebuild in 1962 have not been found. Pieces of old concrete, suggesting a building foundation, remain on the site.

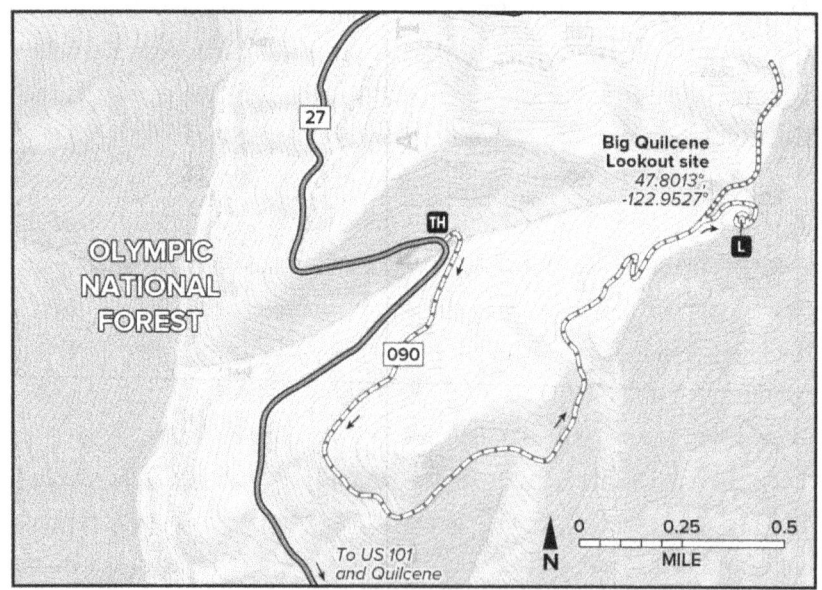

---

[1] Rooney, 39.
[2] Olga Hughett, "Eleven Lookouts Watch for Fires in Jefferson County," *Port Townsend Leader*, August 2, 1962, 8.

Hike Summary

Hike a gently climbing forest road on the woodsy Quilcene Ridge. About halfway up the hill there are great views across the Quilcene River Valley to high peaks beyond. The once bare ridgetop is now surrounded by trees.

Getting There

- Drive US Highway 101 1.5 miles south from Quilcene. At the big bend in the two-lane highway, turn west on Penny Creek Road.
- Drive 1.5 miles on Penny Creek Road (paved) to the Big Quilcene River Road (gravel). Bear left on the road, which becomes Olympic National Forest Road (FR) 27 (paved) in 1.9 miles.
- At 7.0 miles from US Highway 101, arrive at a junction with FR 090, the route to the Big Quilcene Lookout site. A vertical vinyl road sign labeled 090 should be visible on the right side of the minor road.
- An FR 27 sign with arrows pointing in both directions (←27→) usually stands across the main road from 090.
- As the hike route to the Big Quilcene Lookout site is a 3-digit forest road that gets little maintenance, parking at the junction and hiking the minor road is a good idea.[3]

Hiking Route

This old forest road begins wide enough for walking beside a friend, but narrows as it continues. There is a good mix of tree and shrubbery species along the way, with hemlock, fir, and ocean spray dominating near the start. Foxgloves and pearly everlasting border the track where the sun reaches them. At 1.0 mile, the route reaches its southernmost

---

[3] The National Forest road numbering system identifies the traffic anticipated on each road with the number of digits in the road number. An FR with three digits is not maintained for sedans. It is likely to be narrow, rough, and potentially returning to nature.

point, traces a wide curve, and heads northeast. There are big views across the Quilcene River Valley here. Buck Mountain and its forested neighbors are directly south, while taller, rockier Mount Warrior stands among other 7000-foot peaks harboring snow patches to the southwest. This is the best viewpoint on the hike; be sure to check it out in both directions.

The road becomes narrower after the curve, with grass growing in the median and young alders reaching for sunlight from both shoulders. An occasional rhododendron peeks between the tall trees at this elevation, suggesting a visit here in May or June could be a visual treat. The elevation gain is moderate all the way; just enough to keep you warm on a cloudy day.

After a little more than 2.0 miles, the road splits. Follow the branch to the right, heading uphill. The old road coils around the top of the peak, coming to a large opening in the forest at 2.5 miles. A fire ring sits near the center of the cleared high point. Trees have filled in the perimeter, blocking the views that served firewatchers on Quilcene Ridge. Strawberry vines and kinnikinnick grow at the foot of leggy rhododendrons near the summit. Even with the panorama obscured, it is a popular spot for picnics and beer bashes—a possible explanation for the lack of remnants of the lookout cabin that once stood here.

View into the Olympic mountain range from the route to Big Quilcene Lookout site.

17. MOUNT WALKER LOOKOUTS

RT Distance: 5.0 miles
High Point: 2802 feet
Elevation Gain: 2000 feet
Season: All Year
No pass or permit is required.

History

Mount Walker is a tree-covered peak above Quilcene Bay and Hood Canal, a few miles south of Quilcene. The high Olympic Mountains to the west catch most of the rain from Pacific weather systems, making this corner of the Olympic Peninsula much drier than the rest, and giving this area its rain shadow reputation. The dry weather patterns combined with early logging practices to cause sizeable forest fires on and around Mount Walker in the first hundred years the area was settled.

Aerial view of the Mount Walker Lookout cabin, 1957. (US Forest Service photograph by Leland J. Prater.)

A fire that started in post-logging slash near Port Ludlow burned for five years in the 1860s and stripped Mount Walker and Quilcene Ridge, twenty-five miles from the first flame. Major fires on nearby 4400-foot Green Mountain burned 9600 acres of timber in 1925 and 1500 acres in 1938.[1]

This fire history and Mount Walker's height above Hood Canal undoubtedly contributed to its selection as a fire lookout building site. The lookout cabin on the high point at the north end of the Mount Walker ridge was built by the US Forest Service in 1931.[2] A few years later, a Civilian Conservation Corps (CCC) camp was established near Quilcene, on the lowlands north of Mount Walker. Crews from the camp completed construction of

---

[1] Jefferson County Historical Society, *Fire!*, Port Townsend, n.d., [based on a 1997 exhibit].
[2] Kresek, *2015*, 24.

a road up to the ridge in 1936[3], helping make the lookout cabin a popular stop for tourists visiting Hood Canal.

Another high spot near the south end of the ridge was used as a fire patrol viewpoint without a structure. The location also served as a US Army Corp of Engineers survey station, and is still marked with a bronze disk dated 1955.[4]

Most years, the lookout's principal responsibility was the Olympic National Forest land to the west, between Mount Walker and the rocky, often snow-capped Olympic mountain peaks. Robert Bulchis, a forestry student who worked as Walker's lookout in 1936 and '37, remembered the cabin facing north, with the tall trees removed from all but its south side.[5] This perspective also worked for plane-watchers stationed here during World War II. The year-round job of Aircraft Warning Service staff was to watch for enemy flights headed inland toward Puget Sound. The cabin was returned to the Forest Service after the war, and fire management operations resumed.

Despite the spot's popularity with hikers and tourists, the lookout building was removed in 1967. With modern logging and fire management technology, fewer wildfires were occurring in the area and airplane flyovers were preferred to locally stationed fire-watchers.

Hike Summary

The steep Mount Walker trail is a popular conditioning hike on weekends. Add another mile hiking the woodsy road to and from the ridge's south end. Enjoy great views at both ends and hunting for artifacts of the lookout cabin on the north end and for the fire patrol station near the middle. Visit in late spring for a great rhododendron show all along the trail.

---

[3] Rooney, 47.
[4] US National Geodetic Survey. "Data Sheet PID SY5574 MT WALKER"; https://www.ngs.noaa.gov/cgi-bin/ds_mark.prl?PidBox=SY5574.
[5] Robert Bulchis, [Oral History].

17. MOUNT WALKER LOOKOUTS

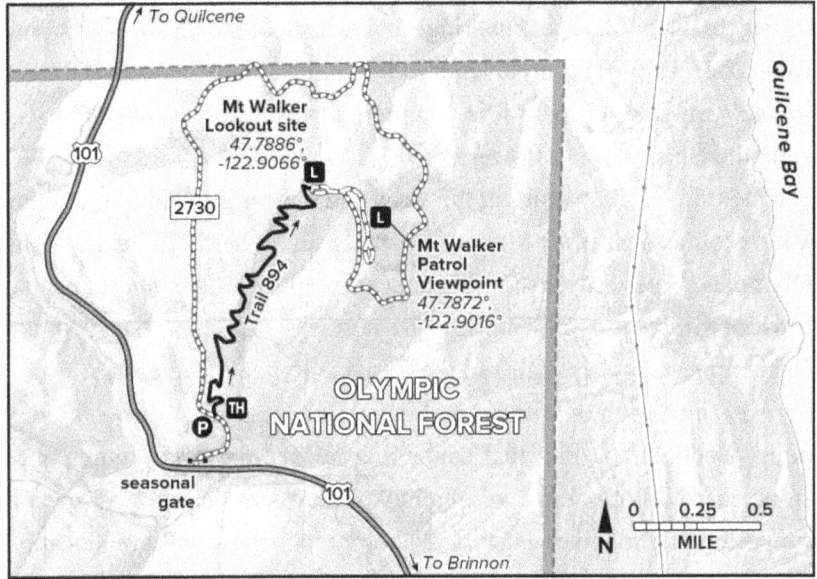

Getting There

- Drive US Highway 101 between Quilcene and Brinnon.
- Between mileposts 295 and 305 the highway climbs toward Mount Walker from both directions.
- When approaching mileposts 300 or 301, watch carefully for a sign on the west side of the road pointing east to the Mount Walker Viewpoint Road. Turn quickly onto that road. The speed limit on US Highway 101 is 55 mph and the area is forested, so the intersection is easy to miss.
- Drive 0.25 mile to trailhead parking on the left if the gate is open. In late fall and winter, park outside the gate and walk the short distance to the trailhead on the right.

Hiking Route

The forested trail to the top of Mount Walker is easy to follow. There are no junctions with the road or other paths along the two-mile route to the ridge. The trail starts steeply and the angle eases only briefly on its way to the north end of the ridge and the site of the historical lookout cabin. Beautiful pink rhododendron blossoms appear beneath the trees in late spring, along with less common calypso orchids, candy stripe, and other shade-loving flowers.

The trail officially ends at the clearing on the north end of the ridge. Views to the west offer Mount Constance and other high peaks of the Olympics. Forested coastal hills appear in all directions and the small town of Quilcene is downhill to the northeast. On clear days, Mount Baker appears to the north and the Cascade Range to the east.

An 8-inch eyebolt sticks out of the ground near the north-end viewpoint bench, suggesting that something tall requiring guy wires once stood nearby. With no record of a lookout tower at this site, I suspect it supported a radio tower. Historical photographs show the cabin location at or near the site of the picnic table that stands about halfway between the bench and the hilltop parking lot. The low concrete berm around the table may have surrounded the cabin or a carport used by fire lookout commuters.

To achieve a 5-mile hike, follow the road to the other end of Mount Walker's ridge and enjoy the perspectives to the south and southeast. Views southeast reach down to Dabob Bay, Toandos Peninsula, Hood Canal, and the Kitsap Peninsula. Clear skies offer views of Mount Rainier and Seattle.

Historical records say the south fire lookout viewpoint was at 2759-foot elevation.[6] A short trail off the road—about halfway between the north and south ends of the ridge—leads to a small clearing with a bronze Corps of Engineers survey marker at coordinates 47.7872°, -122.9016°. The elevation at the benchmark is 2757 feet, according to USGS topographic maps, providing a satisfying artifact for a site which served thirty-some years as a fire watch point, despite never having a building.

---

[6] Spring and Fish, 198.

18. WEBB MOUNTAIN LOOKOUTS

Lower Webb:
RT Distance: 4.6 miles
High Point: 1880 feet
Elevation Gain: 615 feet
Season: All Year

Upper Webb:
RT Distance: 4.3 miles
High Point: 2775 feet
Elevation Gain: 825 feet
Season: All Year

No pass or permit is required.

History

These two neighboring fire lookout stations have a confusing and intertwined history. Lookout inventories published in the 1980s used similar photographs of the same unique three-story "California windmill"-style building,[1] with one book identifying it as a state forestry station at approximately 1900-foot elevation built in 1934,[2] and the other identifying it as a US Forest Service lookout at 2775-foot elevation, built in 1930.[3] Both were built by the US Forest Service. The lookout building at the higher elevation, on the top of Webb Mountain, was built between 1936 and 1942. Photographs of these buildings appear on pages 105 and 107.

The dates for construction of the higher Webb Mountain Lookout are indicated by a US Forest Service evaluation of the lower Webb Lookout written in 1936, and a statement in Harold Chriswell's *Memoirs*. Robert Mealey's 1936 report identified the lookout location on Fulton Creek Road—downhill and about 0.5 mile east of the Webb Mountain summit. The evaluation didn't mince words: "This L.O. is in a very poor place. The funds expended are from a F.S. standpoint an absolute waste except that it covers dangerous lands which are adjacent to F.S. lands. I recommend that this lookout be abandoned and reestablished farther back on the same ridge."[4]

---

[1] The California windmill-style building featured first and second floor walls that tapered in under a catwalk, a straight-walled third floor with windows, and an overhanging roof. (See photograph on page 107.)
[2] Kresek, *1998*, 113, 115. By the 1980s, the location of the lower Webb lookout was on state forest land. The construction date is supported by the photograph on page 105 and its documentation.
[3] Spring and Fish, 92, 198.
[4] Robert H. Mealey, [Fire Lookout Site Evaluation] "Webb LO," July 1, 1936; Document 26-17, National Archives, Seattle.

Harold (Chris) Chriswell was the US Forest Service District Ranger in the Hoodsport Ranger District, 1942 to 1944. The Upper Webb Mountain Lookout was one of five fire lookout stations in the district selected for the WWII Aircraft Warning Service (AWS). Preparation for AWS work "included . . . closing in the lower part of the short lookout towers on Webb L.O." and 2 others.[5] This remodel changed the cabin on posts to the "California windmill" look that made it famous.

Chriswell described the AWS staff: "The people who manned these AWS Posts were older couples who took on the 24-hour watch job as a patriotic effort to serve their country in time of war . . . The work was difficult because most of the time it was very boring . . . and they must never miss the flight of any aircraft through their area, day or night."[6]

Harold White and Marion White were among the couples who served as AWS plane watchers at Webb Mountain Lookout.[7] In August 1961, the Department of Natural Resources lookout staff newsletter remembered the seventeen years of service by Harold White, who retired in 1959: "His was the pleasant, far-reaching voice on Webb Mt. for seventeen years [meaning he had started in 1942] . . . For us he watched over Hood's Canal and vicinity, for the US Forest Service he looked far into the Olympics and smoothly operated both radios."[8]

In 1962, the newsletter reported that the lookout building at the top of Webb Mountain was transferred from the Olympic National Forest to the state Department of Natural Resources, and was no longer a shared operation.[9] The building was taken down in 1967.

---

[5] Harold Chriswell, *Memoirs*, 53. Chriswell's Memoirs are quoted in several chapters with the permission of his daughter, Bonnie Chriswell Johnson.
[6] Chriswell, 54.
[7] Photo of Harold and Marion White on the steps of the three-story Webb lookout, from National Archives, Seattle AWS files accessed at https://willhiteweb.com/olympic_mountains/webb_mountain/lookout_map_211.htm.
[8] [Olga Hughett], "TEN-SEVEN. Remember Harold and Marion White," *Olympia District's Ten-Eight,* August 1961, [3].
[9] [In a note written by editor Olga Hughett, at the end of] Jay Bates, "From SH-14, Webb Lookout," *Olympia District's Ten-Eight,* July 1962, [2].

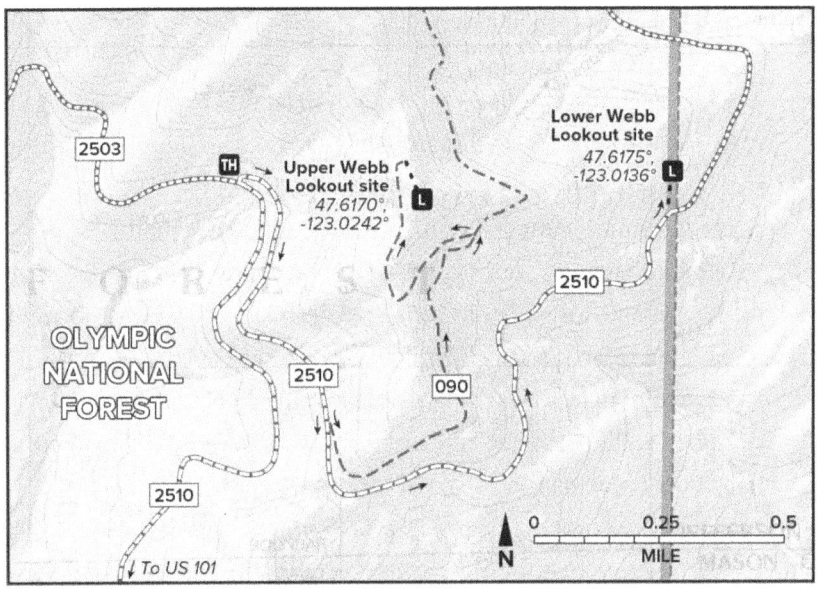

Hike Summary

Although located close together and including adventurous components, these two hikes have different characters, and have been described separately for that reason. Both lookouts were known as "Webb Mountain Fire Lookout" when they were active. I have used the names Upper and Lower Webb Mountain here, adopting the labels used by the Willhite and Kemnow websites. The Upper site and its route are located in the national forest, on roads that have been decommissioned and abandoned to regrowth.

The Lower Webb Lookout site is located in state forest. Most of the hike route is on national and state forest roads, passing through pretty forest landscape. The last 0.1 mile is on an informal uphill trail to the lookout site. The rewards for the short hill climb are fabulous views of Hood Canal, wooded Kitsap Peninsula, and cities and mountains beyond.

Getting There

- Leave US Highway 101 at the Hamma Hamma Recreational Area road sign just north of milepost 318, between Eldon and Triton Cove. This puts you on Forest Road (FR) 25.
- Drive 2.4 miles; turn right on FR 2510. The road number appears on a small sign on your right. A sign on the left side of the road warns "Road Closed ___ miles ahead." This blank appears to leave forest managers' options open in case of future need.
- Pass several side roads; at 3.1 miles from US Highway 101, stay right. At 4.7 miles, keep right; at 5.9 miles, keep left. The alternative route has a gate.
- Pass a borrow pit[10] at 6.2 miles. At 6.3 miles, keep left.
- At 6.9 miles, watch for a water bar and dip, followed by road deterioration. The Olympic National Forest portion of FR 2510 starts here. National forests have little money for road maintenance outside of highly popular recreation areas, while the state is able to finance roadbuilding with part of its timber harvest revenues.
- Park at FR 2510's junction with FR 2503, 8.0 miles from US Highway 101. In 2020, the next 0.6 mile of FR 2510 had deep ruts and a potential washout before coming to a wide space at its junction with side road 090, the turnoff for the Upper Webb Lookout route.

---

[10] A *borrow pit* is a construction term for a hole, pit, or excavation created for the purpose of removing gravel, clay, or sand, usually for a nearby project, such as a forest road.

Hiking Route to the Lower Webb Mountain Lookout Site

The first 2.2 miles of this route are straightforward. Stay on road 2510 as it curves around Webb Mountain, gradually losing a few hundred feet of elevation as it descends to 1730 feet. This is classic Olympic Peninsula forest with lots of native rhododendrons, ocean spray, and huckleberry bushes. After 2 miles, emerge from the healthy forest with its mossy rock walls and birdsong into a landscape that is recovering from its traumatic haircut in 2010. If you have an aversion to clearcuts, remind yourself of the importance of public school funding.

At the edge of the open landscape, the road curves to the right, uncut forest stands on the ridge to the left, and a somewhat steep hill rises directly ahead. Several small groves of trees stand about 100 feet from the solid forest at the high point of the hill. One cluster includes three different species: a hemlock, an alder, and a Douglas fir. Find an informal trail close to the edge of the forest and follow it toward the high point. Along the way, you will notice several yellow signs on the edge of the standing forest: "Property Boundary National Forest behind this sign."

Lower Webb Mountain Lookout under construction by CCC crew in 1934. (US Forest Service photograph by Lee P. Brown, courtesy of Olympic National Park.)

Approaching the hemlock-alder-Douglas fir grove, notice a pair of trees at the national forest boundary circled with multicolor ribbons. At the foot of one is an unusual benchmark. It is a Bureau of Land

Management survey marker for a 1973 cadastral survey. A cadastral survey is conducted to resolve a boundary issue. Some topographic maps show two north-south section lines through this area. It is likely that this BLM survey established the property line now observed between the state and national forests.

Under the three landmark trees are large sawn-off posts, several set in the ground and standing upright, others horizontal and bolted together. These are artifacts uncovered by the 2010 logging, and considerately left for visitors to appreciate. Then, consider the views not available in the forest. The northern half of Hood Canal opens broadly before you. Directly across the water are the verdant hills of the Green Mountain State Forest in Kitsap County. (There are forest fire lookout sites to visit there, too. And one of those modern communication towers is probably providing the signal for your cell phone.)

Please take only photographs and leave the clues of historical activities here for others to discover and enjoy.

Hiking Route to the Upper Webb Mountain Lookout Site

The route to Upper Webb Mountain Lookout heads uphill from FR 2510 about 0.6 mile south-southeast of 2510's junction with 2503. It was labeled FR 2524 on older maps when it was drivable, and 090 since it has been downgraded. Whether you want to visit the higher lookout site on the same trip as Lower Webb Mountain depends on your taste in hiking. Upper Webb is a route for bushwhackers and people with a very good sense of direction or reliable navigational tools.

The hike starts out as a little-used road with a mossy median. Glimpses of Hood Canal can be seen through the trees as elevation is gained. At about 0.8 mile from FR 2510, the route reaches a junction with a narrow path on the left. An unlabeled vinyl road signpost stands on that side of the road, often hiding in the shrubbery. A surprisingly large colony of ginger plants grows in the ditch at its foot, for those on the watch for its exotic spring blooms. About 20 feet into the trail are two rotting, square gate posts, and a few feet farther into the trees is a 6-foot signpost with a blank wooden signboard. This used to be known as Road 091, but it has the remains of a berm at its entrance, indicating the route has been decommissioned and nature is welcome to remove all signs of humans here.

Webb Mountain Lookout House, October 1944. (Official US Forest Service photograph #432611 by Blodgett, courtesy of Olympic National Forest.)

Soon it is clear that nature is winning. Alder and other brush are reclaiming the roadway. Enthusiasts occasionally clear the trail, but hikers here usually need to use their observation skills to follow the old roadway through and around fresh growth and downed trees. The course first goes 0.2-mile southwest and then zigzags a little more than 0.25-mile northwest. A ridge going north becomes more obvious on the right as you proceed. Stay on the faint trail to the end of the ridge, where the route follows the terrain and turns the corner. In a few feet, the way becomes easier to follow. Continue on this old road base until it ends, and a narrow trail appears headed up a 6-foot bank, on your right.

Follow it to the highpoint on Webb Mountain, where you may find a geocache[11] box against a stump.

Continue south on the ridgetop, gaining little elevation. In about 0.1 mile, notice a reverse track headed downhill to the north. At the foot of that short trail is a remarkably sturdy old outhouse.

Return to the ridgetop and continue south to the summit of Webb Mountain. A grassy clearing here hosts two US National Geodetic Survey (NGS) bronze markers. The NGS datasheets for this series of survey markers provide measurements for discovering where the unique California windmill-style fire lookout tower stood until 1967. The main benchmark, or survey station, stamped "WEBB MTN 1955," is located at these coordinates: 47.6170°, -123.0242°. A 3-foot-tall, rusty, green metal stake that stands a few feet from the survey marker guides the eye to its location. The survey marker was "ten feet east northeast of the northeast corner of the lookout house," according to the station description recorded in 1955. An additional bronze reference mark is located in vegetation about 20 feet southwest of the survey station. It is also close to a low stone retaining wall first mentioned in the survey marker records in 1973, after the lookout house had been torn down.[12]

Try to imagine a three-story building shaped like a Dutch windmill (the second story tapering to narrower than the first or third) in this location, with the surrounding trees removed. During fire season the lookout staffer drove to his or her assignment, parked a car in the ground level garage, and climbed stairs to the viewing room and catwalk. Webb Lookout had spectacular views of Hood Canal and the Olympics, as long as it stood.

---

[11] In the first decade of this century, many fire lookout sites were used as locations for geocaches. This is one that still remains at a lookout site in this region.
[12] US National Geodetic Survey, "Data Sheet PID SY1624 WEBB MTN"; https://www.ngs.noaa.gov/cgi-bin/ds_mark.prl?PidBox=SY1624.

19. HAMMA HAMMA GUARD STATION LOOKOUT

RT Distance: 2.0 miles
High Point: 655 feet
Elevation Gain: 235 feet
Season: All Year
No pass or permit is required.

History

The Hamma Hamma Guard Station is not only one of a small number of standing fire lookout stations in Washington's coastal region, it is the only fire lookout on the Olympic Peninsula available for rent. The Forest Service is proud of the guard station's heritage as a building constructed by the Civilian Conservation Corps (CCC) in the 1930s, but they apparently lost track of the building's design, if not use, as a fire lookout station. Eric Willhite discovered the unique fire lookout features incorporated into the building's design among documents at the National Archives at Seattle, in 2019.[1]

His findings include a Work Sheet (Form R6-E19) identifying the structure as "Guard and L.O. Cabin with Gar[age] & Stor[age]." A May 1936 letter to the Olympic National Forest Assistant Forest Ranger in the Portland headquarters had proposed the building, with an unusual feature to improve visibility. It said a large bay window was necessary to eliminate a blind spot in the forest guard's view. He described the design as providing a wide room on the south side

The Hamma Hamma Guard Station as it has looked since the 1930s.

---

[1] http://www.willhiteweb.com/washington_fire_lookouts/hamma_hamma_guard_station/fire_278.htm.

of the building and windows giving improved views up and down the valley, as well as the territory across the valley.[2]

It is generally accepted that the building was constructed, not just remodeled, in 1936, despite one historical photograph of the completed building labeled "1933." Olympic National Forest staff, as well as website descriptions of the historic site, agree that the building was constructed in 1936 by the CCC.[3] More than one person told me they thought the photo labeled 1933 must have been misdated when it was filed decades after the image had been recorded.

The Civilian Conservation Corps is not mentioned in any of the documents posted on the Willhite website in 2020, but the unusual craftsmanship demonstrated at the site is characteristic of CCC work. Of particular note are the rockwork included in the registration station and the fences around the building, as well as the chevron woodwork design on the garage door and window shutters. Their "skill and craftsmanship" earned recognition for the building on the Washington Heritage Register in 1984,[4] and a nomination for the National Register of Historic Places.[5]

Hike Summary

This is a distinctly family-friendly hiking route, year-round. Follow the short, scenic Living Legacy Trail from the Hamma Hamma Campground to view this historical building. Along the path, read interpretive signs to learn some of the history of the Civilian Conservation Corps and their work in this area. Stay on the trail when close to the guard station to respect the privacy of renters.

---

[2] A portion of the letter, photocopied at National Archives at Seattle, appears on http://www.willhiteweb.com/washington_fire_lookouts/hamma_hamma_guard_station/fire_278.htm.
[3] Conversations with current and retired Olympic National Forest staff, and statements in the description of the Hamma Hamma Cabin as a recreation site: https://www.recreation.gov/camping/campgrounds/233740, accessed 12/11/2019.
[4] Washington Department of Historic Preservation database entry, Resource ID:675663; https://wisaard.dahp.wa.gov/Search/1162/Detail/5335.
[5] https://www.recreation.gov/camping/campgrounds/233740, accessed 12/11/2019.

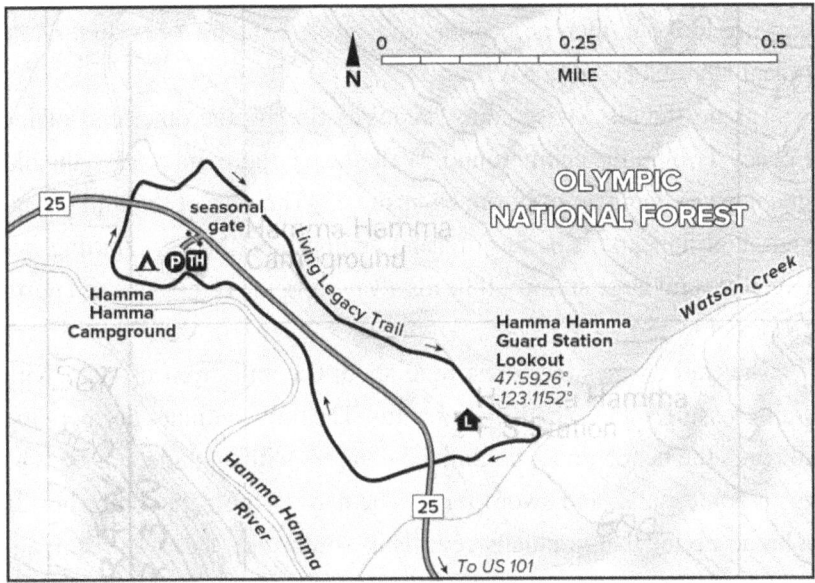

Getting There

- Between Eldon and Triton Cove, leave US Highway 101 at the Hamma Hamma Recreational Area road sign, just north of milepost 318. This puts you on Forest Road (FR) 25, well known in the East Olympics as the route to Lena Lake and other popular trails.
- Drive 6 miles to the Hamma Hamma Campground on the left.
- During the summer, drive through the campground to the big reader board near the river to park. During months the campground is closed, park outside the gate and start your hike there.

Hiking Route

On the bulletin board in the campground is a map of the Living Legacy Trail, as well as information about camping there. It recommends starting the trail beside the Hamma Hamma River and hiking the loop in a counterclockwise direction. I prefer starting uphill and hiking the route clockwise, rewarding the climb with views of the historic guard station and fire lookout, then descending to complete the hike beside the turbulent Hamma Hamma River.

Taking the clockwise course requires finding the other end of the Legacy Trail in the campground. Walk the campground road to the old green water pump across from campsite #5. The start of the trail has no sign, and appears to be an informal campground byway, starting between several large stumps. It heads away from the campsites, and north to cross FR 25.

The trail crosses the forest road about 0.1 mile from its start, with trail-crossing signs to confirm its status. The trail continues north, rising to reach the bench under tall, mixed conifers with an understory of Oregon grape, salal, and sword ferns. The narrow footpath climbs beside a broad ravine that gradually reveals its source as a narrow stream, audible only in winter.

At its high point, the trail turns southeast and follows the low ridge toward the cabin. The ridge retains a surprising number of wet spots supporting cedar and alder, as well as trickles of water crossing under the narrow trail. The area's logging history is suggested in the variety of stumps that stand near the trail.

A few broad stumps feature horizontal slots cut near their tops. The cuts were made to make room for springboards loggers stood on while using long, two-man saws to cut the trunk at waist height. Some stumps hosted seeds that became tall trees with their support, while others took many years to mature to nurse-stump status, hosting only saplings and little shrubs 80 years after their harvest. Still others have rotted enough to offer homes between their roots for small forest animals.

The trail approaches the guard station and fire lookout cabin from the back. The best views of the cabin are gained at the trail's junction with the cabin's access road. Take a look at the information about the Civilian Conservation Corps' stone construction of the registration station and fence posts on the interpretive board there. If the cabin is unoccupied (no vehicles and no lights), walk the road past the registration station and take a peek at the five large windows forming a broad bay window on the south side of the building. They may well inspire you to rent the cabin to examine the expansive view from the inside.

Return to the interpretive sign and take a look at the tall spar pole that stands beside the building. Was its only purpose to support the radio antenna on top? It appears to have climbing spikes up the side. Numerous other fire lookout cabins had climbing posts nearby to help expand viewing range. If watching for fires were part of my job, I think I would climb the pole if it helped my work.

When satisfied, resume the trail, which soon turns south to follow the rock-strewn Watson Creek, tumbling downhill toward the Hamma Hamma River. The path crosses the road again, about halfway to the river's edge. As you approach the river, a side trail leads out to a viewpoint high above the flowing water. A couple of benches provide spots for picnic lunches or watching for ducks that enjoy surfing the white-tipped river. Colorful harlequin ducks nest here in spring, while American dippers hunt tasty treats from the rocks in midsummer. In spring and summer, wildflowers and berries grace the lower trail, too.

The Hamma Hamma River beside the Living Legacy Trail.

From bright pink salmonberry blossoms and pendent, white Indian plum flowers will come summer berries, while leggy wild rose bushes and broad rhododendrons offer their cheery blossoms for appreciative hikers in their season.

Short, and easy to visit before or after another destination in the Hamma Hamma Recreation Area, this trail offers enjoyable hiking in all seasons. Observe the river in its various moods. Experience the trail with flowers in bloom or a dusting of snow. If you are traveling through the Hood Canal region, it is a fine place to take a break with nature.

20. JEFFERSON RIDGE LOOKOUT

RT Distance: 6.6 miles
High Point: 3850 feet
Elevation Gain: 2750 feet
Season: Jun-Nov
No pass or permit is required.

History

Olympic National Forest (ONF) fire guards started climbing up to Jefferson Ridge for views deep into the Hamma Hamma River drainage sometime in the 1930s. An icon representing an emergency fire lookout station appeared on the 1937 Hoodsport District Fireman's Map, discovered in the National Archives, Seattle, in 2019.

The first lookout building on the ridge was a tower raised in 1961, probably the last lookout station newly built in the Olympics. It was also the only fire lookout station built in the northwest with materials delivered to the site by helicopter.[1] A clever forest ranger apparently recognized he had the materials to build a fire tower during the same period a helicopter was assigned as firefighting support to the Hoodsport Ranger Station.[2] A photo caption on page 1 of the June 8, 1961, *Shelton-Mason County Journal* states the lift occurred a week earlier. A Port Angeles newspaper repeated the story in April 1962,[3] causing some confusion among twenty-first century lookout historians. With the materials

Jefferson Ridge Lookout tower 1961. (US Forest Service photograph, curated by Steve Ricketts.)

---

[1] "Airlift in the Olympics" [photo caption], *Shelton-Mason County Journal*, 1, June 8, 1961. The clipping is in the collection of Stan Graham, retired US forest ranger.
[2] Part of the history posted at http://willhiteweb.com/olympic_mountains/ jefferson_ridge _point/lookout_trail_212.htm, accessed October 2018.
[3] The *Port Angeles Evening News* article was quoted in https://washingtonlookouts.weebly .com/jefferson-ridge.html.

delivered at the beginning of summer 1961, it is likely the construction was completed that year.

Most sources agree that a 41-foot tower with a 15×15-foot flat-roofed cabin was built on the narrow Jefferson Ridge. Its service lasted only six years. It was damaged by fire in 1967 and never used again. A 1976 newspaper article reported that a US Army unit "disassembled and cleaned a partially burned lookout at Jefferson Ridge" that year.[4]

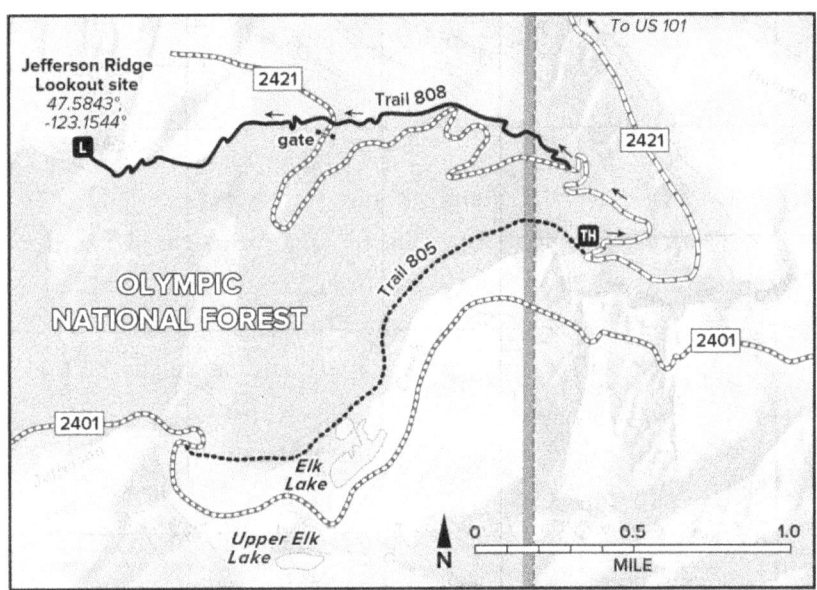

Hike Summary

This is a beautiful and challenging forest hike despite fire damage. It begins on a steep forest road in the midst of a landscape cleared by the combination of an August 2018 wildfire[5] and state forest salvage logging in 2020. When scouted to 3000-foot elevation in October 2020, the national forestland appeared generally healthy, with occasional charred

---

[4] The newspaper clipping is reproduced at http://willhiteweb.com/olympic_mountains/jefferson_ridge_point/lookout_trail_212.htm.
[5] The Maple fire, as the 3300-acre burn was known, was caused by three loggers poaching big leaf maple trees for sale to hardwood mills for musical instrument manufacture. They tried to use fire to remove a bees' nest from a maple tree they wanted to cut, but lost control. By September 2020, court proceedings had been completed for only one of them. He pled guilty and was sentenced to 20 months in prison.

tree trunks, fallen trees, recovering shrubbery, and flowering plants surrounding the trails. The Olympic National Forest will rely on volunteer crews for trail maintenance, and did not know in late 2020 when the upper trails would be restored,[6] earning the route an "adventure hike" designation. Check with the Hoodsport Visitors Center (360-877-2021) or the ONF Quilcene Ranger District Office (360-765-2200) for current information. Avoid visits to the Jefferson Ridge Trail in times of high winds, as dead limbs will continue to fall for several hiking seasons.

Getting There

- Between Eldon and Triton Cove, turn west from US Highway 101 at the Hamma Hamma Recreational Area road sign, just north of milepost 318. This is Forest Road (FR) 25.
- Drive 6.8 miles to the junction with FR 2480 on the left.
- Turn left and drive over the bridge crossing the usually busy and frothy Hamma Hamma River.
- At a short 0.2 mile from FR 25, turn right and uphill on steep FR 2421. Deep water bars were installed in early 2021, requiring high clearance and recommending 4-wheel or all-wheel drive vehicles.
- Drive 1.6 miles on FR 2421 to the loop parking area close to the Elk Lake trailhead.

Hiking Route

Begin with 0.8-mile on a fairly steep and narrow forest road. Since the forest fire and salvage harvest, dense forest has been replaced here with open land dotted with occasional spindly groves of trees. Enjoy the views of forested landscapes in all directions beyond the immediate clearcut. New panoramic views are available in this area—down into the Jefferson Creek Valley and Elk Lake, and east to Hood Canal and

---

[6] Telephone conversation with Olympic National Forest public affairs staff, November 2020.

beyond. The forested slopes on the south side of the valley offer a dark green vista on a sunny day.

Prior to the fire, a small sign, "Jeff. Ridge Tr.," announced a narrow path that traversed the state forestland bordering the Olympic National Forest. In April 2021, a new 4×4-inch signpost stood beside the new steep, rocky trail. From the new trailhead, the wooded summit of Jefferson Ridge and the often snow-covered rocky peaks beyond are visible to the southwest. The roughed-out track here connects with an established but fire-damaged ridge trail at the national forest boundary.

Despite a few charred and downed trees, the ONF trail still winds up the ridge through open, shady woodland. That area was harvested in the 1990s, but has the feel of an old-growth forest. Shade-loving plants like Indian pipes and coralroot grow here, along with pipsissewa and rattlesnake plantain. Partway through this trail segment, rhododendrons appear in the understory, adding brilliant pink to the forest palette each June. As you emerge from the forest at a horseshoe bend in the road, pass a small "Jefferson Ridge Trail" sign.

Walk around the curve in the gravel track to a slightly different Jefferson Ridge Trail #808 sign. This is where the hike described on the Olympic National Forest website begins. There are two more segments to the route, separated by another narrow road crossing. Occasional giant trees appear along the upper trail, with intermittent views of Hood Canal and beyond. Clouds often get stuck on Jefferson Ridge, but everything from Glacier Peak and the Seattle skyscrapers to Mounts Adams and St. Helens adorn the eastern skyline on clear days.

Beargrass joins rhododendrons at this higher elevation. The tall white plumes often disappear by mid-August, suggesting elk or deer munch as they meander these trails. The views to the east are longer as the elevation increases. Puget Sound waters appear as silver strips beyond Hood Canal and the peninsulas in the Sound, with lowlands and Cascades beyond.

At 1.9 miles and 2800-foot elevation, cross the road again. It is still FR 2421, but it has a gate just out of sight to the south. The trail crosses the gravel track, then continues with a very narrow footpath diagonally ascending a 20-foot-tall road cut. Narrow logs serve as a trail border trying to keep the soil from sliding down the steep hill.

Once on the upper ridge, trees are thinner and berries gain more sunshine beside the trail. Huckleberries—blue *and* red—salal, and tiny raspberries bloom in late spring and berry in late summer. The footpath becomes rockier with steep stretches of slippery gravel in between. It switchbacks from one side of the ridge to the other, offering alternate glimpses of the Hamma Hamma River and Jefferson Creek Valleys, below.

View of Jefferson Ridge 2021, above fire-damaged and salvage-logged slopes.

This section of trail also includes, unfortunately, a false summit. Up, up, up, it rises; a treeless rock suggests it is the summit, but the trail continues past, and into a grove of trees. Beyond the trees, the trail continues down to a saddle between high points on the ridge. The last knob is a short climb. A foot-high rock wall announces human effort has modified the landscape. A rusty metal plate bolted to the ground confirms arrival at the Jefferson Ridge Lookout site.

There are also spacious rocks here, and a good space for lunch. The trail continues another 20 feet. Before the fire in 2018, impressive remnants of the 1960s tower remained at the very end of the trail: 8×8-inch creosoted timbers, steel rods, metal beams with bolts attached, and melted glass. I hope all of these artifacts have survived the modern flames to offer reminders of the tower and the people that once watched for fires in this part of the Olympic forests.

21. DOW MOUNTAIN LOOKOUT

RT Distance: 7.0 miles
High Point: 2514 feet
Elevation Gain: 1700 feet
Season: All Year
No pass or permit is required.

History

Dow Mountain and the creek that rushes down its slope were both named for John D. Dow, who homesteaded here beside Lake Cushman in the 1890s. He staked a claim on the first copper mine at the north end of the lake in 1888 and spent some years early in the twentieth century working as an engineer for the Olympic National Forest.[1]

Dow Mountain Lookout, undated photograph by Stan Stiegel, courtesy of the Forest History Society, Durham, NC.

Dow Mountain, above the southeastern shores of the lake, has its summit, north, and eastern slopes in state forest, while the southwestern slopes and main access road are in Lake Cushman Management property. The earliest record of a fire lookout on the peak was "Dow Mt. LO" on a 1930 Olympic National Forest map found in the National Archives in Seattle.

In 1936 and 1938, Olympic National Forest rangers visited and wrote reviews of the state's lookout site on Dow Mountain, considering its potential to provide better "coverage of the S. side of Washington & Elinor, but not give a very good view up the Canal—to the

---

[1] Janice Krenmayr, *Footloose Around Puget Sound*, 218; Olympic National Park. *Historic Reserve Study*, 2009, chapter 3, 16 accessed at https://www.nps.gov/parkhistory/online_books/olym/hrs/chap3.htm.

N.E."[2] They liked that there was "a R.R. grade to within 200 yds. of top." Federal forest rangers Robert H. Mealey and R. M. Beeman described the established state lookout station as a "temporary 20 ft. tower. Ground telephone line. Nearest water 20 minutes down grade to east." They recommended a 40- or 60-foot tower near an 80-foot spar tree,[3] with the cost of staffing shared: "If this point agreed as primary caliber, we should build tower and select man, perhaps asking half his salary from Association or State."[4]

Apparently nothing came of these Olympic National Forest evaluations. The Washington Forest Fire Association funded construction of the first fire lookout cabin on Dow Mountain in 1942.[5] The Association was an organization of private timber companies focused on preventing and fighting forest fires, 1908 through the 1950s. They worked cooperatively with the State Division of Forestry, providing resources for projects that met their priorities when state funds were not available.

In 1963, the Department of Natural Resources replaced the 12×24-foot cabin with a 40-foot tower with a live-in cabin on top. The tower stood here in 1967, but a 1972 report on the site by the National Geodetic Survey reported the tower torn down and the mountaintop leveled for use as a helipad.[6]

Hike Summary

This woodsy hike has two distinct sections, starting on a gravel road with occasional polite vehicular traffic and the noisy Dow Creek on your right, and then a mossy old road on the upper mountain where only bird songs and breezes offer company. There's enough elevation gain to keep you puffing, but plenty of shade to prevent overheating most of the year. The Lake Cushman Management Corporation manages most of Dow Mountain. Some of the acreage is considered watershed and they could refuse access to hikers but are generally hospitable. You may

---

[2] Robert H. Mealey, [Fire Lookout Site Evaluation]: "Dow Mountain," July 9 [no year]; attached to Document 6-5.3, National Archives in Seattle.
[3] A spar tree is a topped tree used as the main support for block and tackle and cables for moving cut logs in a harvesting operation.
[4] RMB [R. M. Beeman], [Fire Lookout Site Evaluation]: "Dow Mtn," Sept. 26, 1938, Document 6-5.3, National Archives in Seattle.
[5] Spring and Fish, 199.
[6] US National Geodetic Survey, "Data Sheet PID SY1711 DOW RESET"; https://www.ngs.noaa.gov/cgi-bin/ds_mark.prl?PidBox=SY1711.

want to phone for permission to park in their lot and hike the Dow Mountain Road: 888-777-6443.

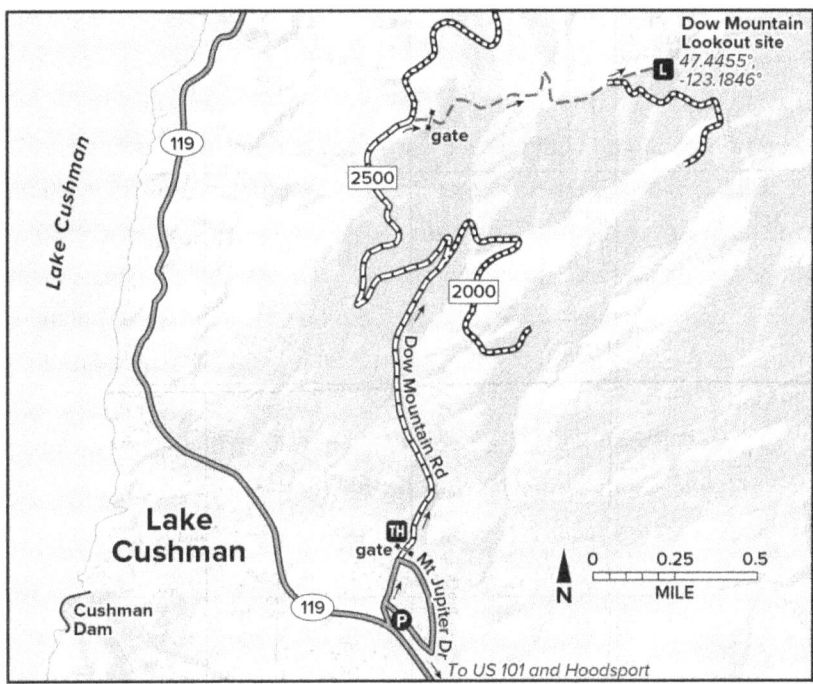

Getting There

- From US Highway 101 in the center of Hoodsport, turn west on State Route 119 toward Lake Cushman.
- Pass Lake Cushman Realty.
- At 3.7 miles from US Highway 101, turn right into the Lake Cushman Management Corporation parking lot and park. The offices are generally not open before 10 a.m. Cut through the trees at the back of the lot and walk left on Mount Jupiter Road to its junction with Dow Mountain Road. Turn right and continue about three blocks to the gate on Dow Mountain Road. There are signs on these residential roads forbidding parking. The signs on the gate say access is restricted to Lake Cushman Corporation vehicles. All others are trespassing and risk being locked behind the gate.

Hiking Route

Dow Mountain was a popular hike in the 1970s, but the public wore out its welcome before the end of the twentieth century. This is a nice hike, easily accessible on paved roads for all of South Puget Sound. Hikers need to treat the retirement homes and weekend retreats along the lower section of the route with respect if we hope to retain the current access.

The forest environment comes into focus even before hikers reach the gate and start up the hill. Homes in the threshold neighborhood are surrounded with evergreens: cedars, fir, and hemlocks, some garlanded with long strands of lichen. *Usnea longissima*, one of my favorite botanical names in the Olympic forests, welcomes us to the Dow Mountain plant show.

Above the gate, houses are farther apart, hidden down private lanes, and only occasionally displace the healthy mixed forest that climbs the slope. A short distance up the road, a cluster of moss-topped water tanks sits in an open area to the left. An occasional side lane proclaims its private nature as it disappears narrowly into the forest. Tall trees—especially cedars and big leaf maples—shelter the road on both sides with sword ferns, Oregon grape, salal, moss, and a changing array of other small plants at their feet. Dow Creek mutters its power on the right, but is rarely seen.

At 1.0 mile, a narrow road heads off on the right, signed as Watersong Drive. Sometimes a glimpse of the boisterous creek can be seen here. In another 0.25 mile, the route reaches a promising junction. Signposts identify the road on the right as 2000 and the left branch as 2500. Some years, another sign on 2000 identifies a construction company eager to build homes farther up that route. This seems a sure indication that 2500 is the route for hikers.

Road 2500 serves as a transition between the first and second sections of the hike. It climbs at a steep angle for a few hundred yards, reaches a level area with a grassy old logging landing on the right, then continues uphill to the left. This track carries less traffic and is quieter and softer. The bank, cut here for roadbuilding, is well covered with moss, Oregon grape, and the shiny leaves of the little twinflower vine. The route continues curving to the southwest (away from the summit) for 0.5 mile, then turns a corner and begins the upper route in earnest.

At 1.75 miles, you have reached the gateway to an untrammeled path. A narrow grassy road appears on the right, with a red gate just visible at the next corner. Beyond the red gate is a forest road where a few branches may fall, but the tread is soft, wild rhododendrons are common, and birds sing happily in the trees. Even deer appear in the lane on quiet days.

Continue up this old track, passing a downhill road on the left in another mile. On Dow Mountain ridge, the path gains, loses, and regains the last few hundred feet of elevation repeatedly during the last 0.75 mile. Water views occasionally appear between the trees. The water on the west side of the ridge is Lake Cushman; Hood Canal is on the east.

The old road emerges from the forest with a clear view of south Hood Canal and a broad forested landscape in the distance on the right. Rectangular storage sheds and free-standing solar collector panels are slightly downhill in the foreground, with a newer road going downhill to the southeast. Old boundary markers on the other side of the hiking track are labeled Tacoma Power, the leaseholder of the federal land around Lake Cushman. Signs on the trees say the upper hiking route is protected as a wildlife refuge under an agreement with the Washington Department of Natural Resources.

Continue up the ridge on the old road. In 0.25 mile, reach a clearing with a variety of orange survey markers around its perimeter. A 3-foot tall vinyl wand at the edge of the trees on the right is labeled "Witness Post. Do not disturb any nearby Survey Marker." At its feet was a 2-foot hole the last time I visited, suggesting that the bronze survey marker disc, set in a large block of concrete that stood here earlier this century, has been dug up and removed. Fortunately, the artifacts of the last fire lookout tower here cannot be moved so easily. In the trees about 20 feet southwest of the Witness Post lie two large pyramidal concrete footing blocks. Down the hill another 20 feet are the other two heavy blocks that anchored the tower built by DNR in the early 1960s.

Enjoy your lunch, take some photos, and watch for wildflowers on your return trip. Twinflowers, star flowers, and a host of other blossoms appear along this route in spring. Pink, native rhodies appear in late spring, along with pipsissewa and other native beauties you aren't likely to find at home.

OLYMPIC PENINSULA WEST

Hikes accessible from US Highway 101
west of its junction with State Route 113 at Sappho
to its junction with the Donkey Creek Road.

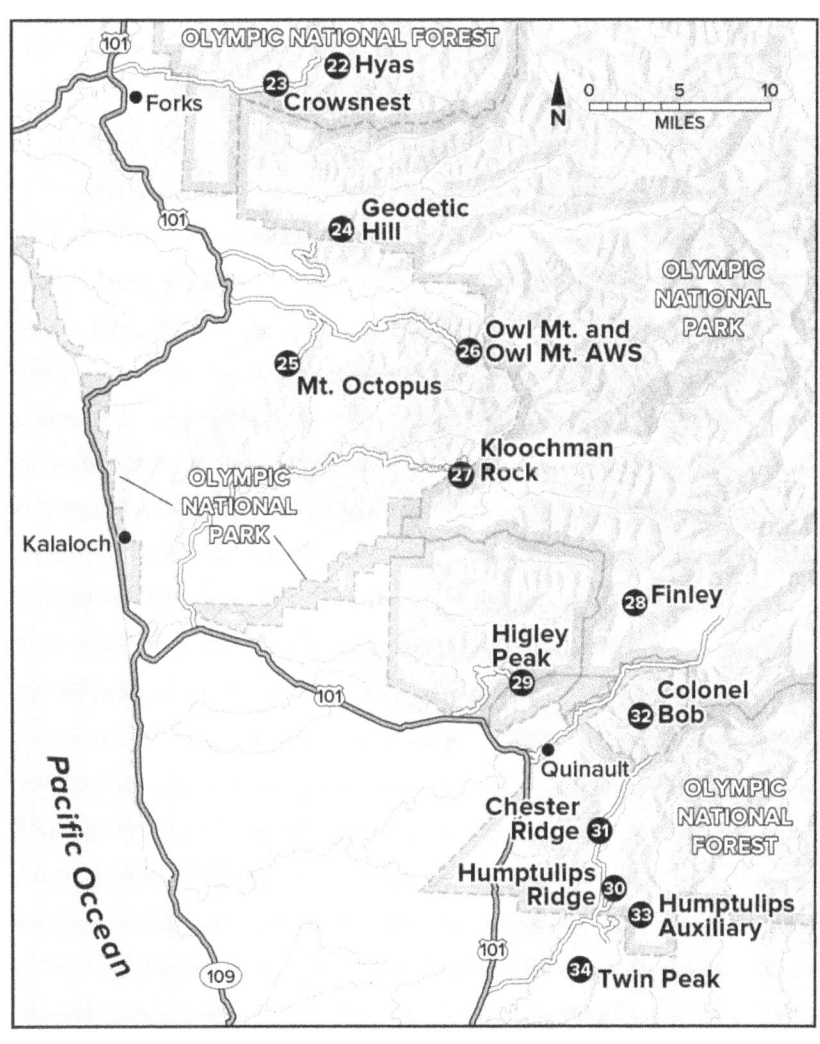

22. HYAS LOOKOUT

RT Distance:2.6 miles
High Point: 3077 feet
Elevation Gain: 750 feet
Season: Apr-Oct
No pass or permit is required.

History

Hyas Lookout tower, 1971. (Courtesy of Molly Erickson.)

In 1943, the Aircraft Warning Service (AWS) built a cabin on this short ridge for wartime plane-watchers. The 12×16-foot structure was built from "native materials"—presumably logs, boards, and cedar shakes produced on site. The station was transferred to the Olympic National Forest in 1944, when the AWS program ended.[1]

J. R. (Jack) Rooney included a 1953 photo of himself on duty at the Hyas fire lookout in his book on Olympic National Forest history.[2] It appeared an odd-shaped building, with a small, two-story section on one end of a rectangular structure. A pole ladder provided access to the second story and similar poles served as porch and stair railings.

In 1956, the Forest Service replaced that building with a 40-foot tower with a cabin on top.[3] It was removed in 1971, but the hilltop continued to be used as an Emergency Lookout (ELO) site into the 1990s.[4] Until trees grew to block the view, Hyas lived up to its Chinook jargon name meaning "great," for the wide perspective it gave on forests in all directions.

---

[1] [US Forest Service] Region 6, "Report of Aircraft Warning Service Stations," May 1, 1944, Sheet #III.
[2] Rooney, 41.
[3] Kresek, *2015*, 23.
[4] Ranger Molly Erickson, Olympic National Forest, Forks office, Personal conversation, 2012.

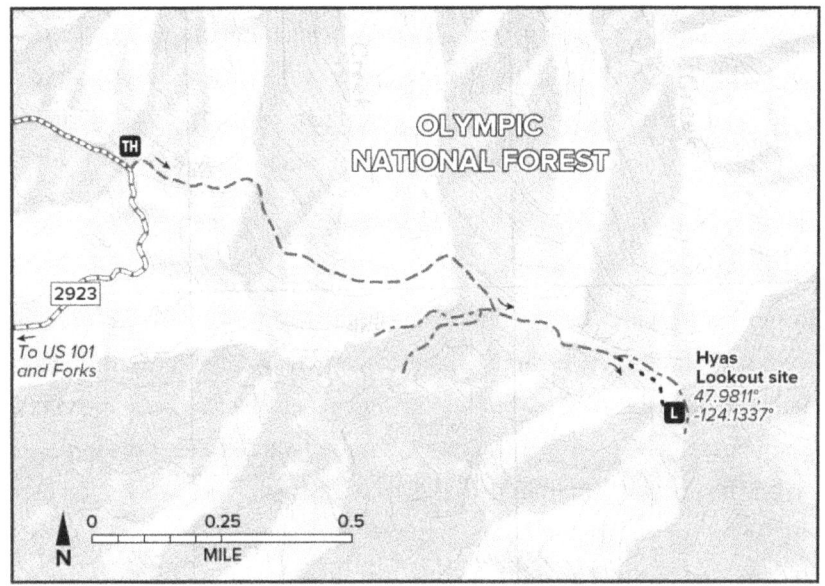

Hike Summary

This whole hike is an adventure. Start with a bushwhack on a short, abandoned road that nature is working to reclaim. At the foot of the Hyas Lookout knoll, the old path continues to a great viewpoint but bypasses the lookout site. Rather than follow the route around the end of the ridge, find and follow the old boot track up the final rise through open forest to a fine array of permanent artifacts.

Getting There

- From US Highway 101 just north of Forks, turn east on the Sitkum-Sol Duc Road, which appears on forest maps as Forest Road (FR) 29. Enjoy driving this broad road with the Sitkum River on the right and a canopy of trees frequently meeting overhead, filtering the daylight.
- Drive 8.8 miles and turn left on FR 2923, marked by a small sign near the right shoulder of the narrower, gravel road. This is a steeper route, with occasional sharp curves and potholes.

- Drive about 6.5 miles from FR 29 to an abandoned spur road on the right. The road junction is now just a wide spot on the right, at a curve in the road, so here are the coordinates: 47.9877°, -124.1564°.
- Pull off Road 2923 at the mouth of the side road and park.

Hiking Route

In the 1960s and '70s, driving to the Hyas fire lookout was a popular weekend outing.[5] After the lookout tower was removed, road maintenance eventually stopped, but hunters have continued to come this way. They occasionally drive in a couple hundred yards to set up camp, but no one had recently maintained or driven the track when we visited here in 2017.

The first part of the route, a little less than 0.9 mile, follows a bench overlooking the creek valleys to the north. There are downed trees, vigorous saplings, and young shrubs with thorns to challenge your progress. Any path between the high—often rocky—wall on the right and the steep bank edge on the left will do. Carrying clippers or a machete is also legitimate preparation for this adventure trail. An oxalis carpet sometimes covers the tread, while elderberry and salmonberry frequently reach for sunlight between the tall conifer and deciduous trees.

This trail section ends where the path splits in two. A broad roadbed continues to the right toward the southwest, while our path continues more narrowly to the southeast. This trail seems clear at first, but again, young trees appear, competing for growing space in the old track. In less than 0.25 mile, a footpath appears to the right between columns of trees on the edge of a narrow saddle of land between broader ridges. Follow the path on the right on fairly level ground until the slim ridge broadens and a 100-foot hill rises in front of you.

---

[5] E.M. Sterling, *Trips and Trails, 1: Family Camps, Short Hikes and View Roads in the North Cascades and Olympics*, 187.

Ascend the hill on the boot path that winds between widely spaced hemlocks and spruce to the high point. Find four angle beams set in concrete and a concrete doorstep that probably sat at the foot of the stairs leading up the 40-foot tower. Oxalis, low-growing May lilies, elderberry, and salmonberry shrubs thrive under the tall evergreen trees that block all the views now. The delicate flowers attest that little foot traffic finds this location.

To gain an idea of the views that lookout staff had here, return to the lower trail and follow it around the lookout hill. The track ends in a clearing—most likely a former logging landing—with great views of the ocean and all the forestlands between.

23. CROWSNEST LOOKOUT

RT Distance: 1.25 miles
High Point: 2020 feet
Elevation Gain: 180 feet
Season: Apr-Oct
No pass or permit is required.

History

As a fire lookout station, a crow's nest is usually a platform built high in a sturdy tree that offers panoramic views of the surrounding forest. While crow's nest lookouts have been common in other parts of the western United States, very few were used in western Washington.

A ranger at the Olympic National Forest Forks District Office told me about this lookout site in 2012, when I asked about other obscure fire lookouts in the area. She consulted a retired ranger who had been the district's fire manager in the 1970s and '80s, then gave me a copy of a section of the district's fire management map from that period. It showed the Crowsnest Lookout site and a helipad on a ridge southwest of the Hyas Lookout. Both Crowsnest and Hyas were labeled as Emergency Lookouts (ELO) on that map.[1]

The US Coast and Geodetic Survey installed a set of bronze survey discs between the Hyas fire lookout building and Crowsnest Lookout in 1954. "The azimuth mark, a standard disk set in a 12 in by 12 in concrete post, and stamped HYAS 1954, is about 0.35 mile east, by road, from the road fork which leads to the Crowsnest Lookout."[2] This establishes a longer history for the Crowsnest Lookout, suggesting it was more regularly occupied in the 1950s than the "emergency" label that appeared on later maps implies.

Hike Summary

Before or after visiting the Hyas fire lookout site, stop off for a short trek up this interesting ridge. Jeeps occasionally travel the track until they meet a thick tree blocking the way. Near the destination, a slim path navigates steep slopes between a helipad site on one hillock and a

---

[1] Conversation with Ranger Molly Erickson, Olympic National Forest, Forks office. July 2012.
[2] US National Geodetic Survey, "Data Sheet PID 0671 Hyas"; https://www.ngs.noaa.gov/cgi-bin/ds_mark.prl?PidBox=SD0671.

lookout tree on the next—all overlooking broad, forested valleys. Although this route has been easy to follow whenever I have hiked it, it is not maintained, so it must be considered an adventure hike.

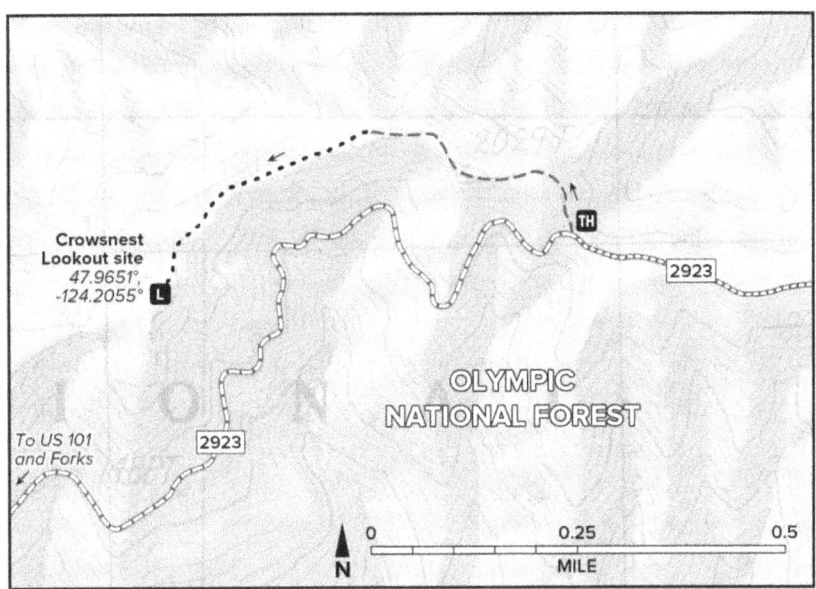

Getting There

- From US Highway 101 just north of Forks, turn east on the Sitkum-Solduc Road, Forest Road (FR) 29 on forest maps. Enjoy the drive on this broad gravel road with the Sitkum River on the right and a canopy of trees frequently meeting overhead and filtering the daylight.
- Drive 8.8 miles and turn left on FR 2923, marked by a small sign near the right shoulder of the narrower gravel road. This is a steeper route, with occasional sharp curves and potholes.
- Drive 2.9 miles from FR 29 to an abandoned spur road on the left. In 2020, Eric Willhite mentioned a recent timber thinning in this area, so the appearance may have changed since I visited the site in 2017.[3] The junction is on the left side of the road at these coordinates: 47.9661°, -124.1950°.

---

[3] http://willhiteweb.com/fire_lookouts/crows_nest/lookout_007.htm.

Hiking Route

At the northern edge of the grassy parking area, two tracks take off into the forest. Follow the one on the left, uphill and southwesterly. When I scouted the route, there were signs of recent jeep traffic on the old route. The roadbed was covered with moss and grass, but no tall vegetation blocked the course for the first 0.2 mile.

Then (and probably now) a tall, broad tree trunk blocked the way. Use the narrow trail on the left edge of the ridge to get around the tall barrier. The old roadbed resumes beyond the tree, but only a narrow route continues. The way is carpeted with oxalis trefoils, accented by occasional starry Solomon's seal and heart-shaped wild ginger leaves. At 0.35 mile, arrive at a large, open area that served as a helipad when there was a fire lookout station nearby. We don't know if helicopters actually landed here, but each ELO on the historical Forks District fire management map had a helipad location marked, and this clearing appears a likely spot.

At the southern edge of the clearing, another broad tree trunk blocks the path on the continuing ridge. Bypass it on the left edge, revealing a short level trail leading to a steep descent to a saddle between two knolls. There are hillside cuts on either side of the steep narrow path, suggesting a strong blade of some kind was used to create the smooth narrow track that quickly loses 20 feet as it slopes down to the level saddle.

There are views between trees along most of the route, looking out over miles and miles of forest on both sides. The Hyas Creek Valley to the west appears deeper and broader than the Rainbow Creek Valley on the southeast.

The second knoll lacks a broad open area in its center, but has widely spaced mature conifers scattered across its diameter. None of these offer the signs of a classic crow's nest tree, such as wooden cross-bars or metal spikes up its trunk for climbing, or a wooden platform high in the crown. One 100-foot tall fir had all of its lower limbs removed, a broad blaze close to the ground, and appeared to have been topped. This could have been a climbing tree, or the damage to its limbs may only have been coincidental. Until more historical information is found, this is the best candidate for the elusive Crowsnest Lookout station, recorded in both US Coast and Geodetic survey marker datasheets and the Olympic National Forest fire management maps.

24. GEODETIC HILL LOOKOUT

RT Distance: 6 miles or more
High Point: 3018 feet
Elevation Gain: 1000 feet
Season: Apr-Nov
No pass or permit is required.

History

Long before there was a fire lookout station on Spruce Mountain between the Hoh and Bogachiel rivers, the US Coast and Geodetic Survey installed markers here to help with navigation and land measurement. The broad summit gained the name Geodetic Hill because of those devices, sometime after the survey monuments were installed in 1913.[1]

Geodetic Hill Lookout, 1954. Carsten Lien photograph. (University of Washington Libraries, Special Collections, UW41076)

The Olympic National Forest considered the site for a lookout in 1934, and again, early in 1938. By '38, a trail to the site was planned from the Bogachiel Guard Station, north of the mountain. R. M. Beeman wrote in the later evaluation that he thought

---

[1] US National Geodetic Survey. "Data Sheet PID SD0670 SPRUCE"; https://www.ngs.noaa.gov/cgi-bin/ds_mark.prl?PidBox=SD0670.

"engineers, occupying the summit for triangulation [surveying] might have built a ladder up one of the 100 foot, 4-foot diameter trees, and built a platform in the top."[2]

This area between the Bogachiel and Hoh Rivers was included in the Olympic National Park when it was established in 1938. The treetop observation point was probably the basis for "Spruce" being listed in January 1942 as a fire lookout tower to be used as a World War II Aircraft Warning Service (AWS) station.[3] Park records say a shake cabin was built in 1942 for year-round use on Geodetic Hill, as part of the park's contribution to the AWS effort.[4]

A National Geodetic Survey (NGS) report described the cabin in 1954 as "20 feet long by 12 feet wide, with a steep gable roof about 15 feet in height."[5]

Until the 1970s, the site was reached by a 12-mile trail coming south from the Bogachiel River Valley. The NGS driving directions for monitoring visits in the 1960s and '70s approach from the south, which is closer to the route used today. In 1974, the Rayonier Timber Company reported the destruction of the fire lookout building in their monitoring report to the National Geodetic Survey: "The station, reference marks no. 1 and no. 2, and the azimuth mark . . . were firmly set and in good condition. The Geodetic Hill cabin was completely burned by the park service around 1972."[6]

Hike Summary

Despite the lookout site's location in the Olympic National Park, between the Bogachiel and Hoh River Valleys, drive state forest roads from the Hoh Valley to the hike starting point. Walk little-traveled state forest roads to a junction with the Spruce Mountain ridge; then, embark

---

[2] Feb 9, 1938 annotation on a memorandum written to Ranger Floe by W. D. Bryan, Forest Ranger, July 20, 1934. National Archives in Seattle. Document 7-6.3.
[3] January 12, 1942 memorandum: "Forest Service Lookout Stations to be Occupied" posted on http://willhiteweb.com/washington_fire_lookouts/aircraft_warning_service/forest_service_stations/aws_273.htm.
[4] Gail E. H. Evans and T. Allan Comp, "Aircraft Warning System [sic] History of Olympic National Park" from Historic Resource Study 1983 Olympic National Park, accessed at http://www.windsox.us/VISITOR/HISTORY_BUILDINGS/AIRCRAFT_WARNING_SYSTEM.html
[5] US National Geodetic Survey, "Data Sheet PID SD0669 GEODETIC HILL CABIN 1954"; https://www.ngs.noaa.gov/cgi-bin/ds_mark.prl?PidBox=SD0669.
[6] US National Geodetic Survey, "Data Sheet PID SD0670 SPRUCE"; https://www.ngs.noaa.gov/cgi-bin/ds_mark.prl?PidBox=SD0670.

on a short adventure hike on game trails to reach the 0.25-mile-wide ridgetop and the easily identified fire lookout site.

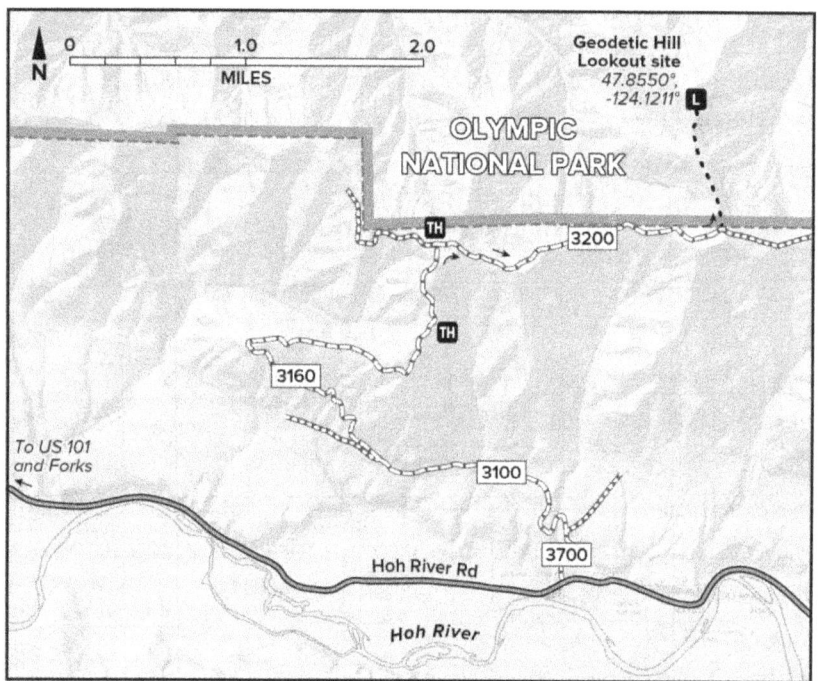

Getting There

- Drive US Highway 101 to the Hoh River Road, 0.6 mile north of milepost 178, south of Forks and the Bogachiel River. Turn east onto the Hoh River Road. **Please Note**: Some older directions to the site recommend State Forest Road H3200, which suffered an impassable washout a few miles east of US Highway 101. The Hoh River Road is the only feasible driving route at the time of publication.
- Drive 6.7 miles through forestlands with occasional campgrounds, farms, and vacation services.
- Turn left on Forest Road H3700. After a short 0.3 mile, turn left on H3100. It curves around narrow valleys and crosses pretty cascades streaming down green hillsides.

- At 1.8 miles from the Hoh River Road, at a junction with lesser tracks headed downhill and straight ahead, turn right and uphill on H3160.
- H3160, sometimes called the Goat Trail by Department of Natural Resources staff in Forks, is a steep but usually well-maintained forest road. In April 2018, the gravel track appeared recently graded with shallow water bars cut into its surface to drain rainwater from the crown of the road. The bars slow traffic but undoubtedly extend the drivable life of the roadway.
- Drive 5 miles on H3160 to reach H3200 on the east-west Willoughby Ridge. It is a narrow road with frequent wide shoulders for parking if the driving becomes tedious. Whether you park at the junction of H3160 and H3200, or somewhere along H3160's hill climb, you are in state forest.

Hiking Route

Park beside the hill-climbing Goat Trail (H3160) for the opportunity to view landscapes not visible from either the Willoughby or Spruce Mountain ridges. Mount Olympus and others of the Olympic Range's highest peaks can be seen between widely spaced trees wherever this road follows the eastern edge of its ridge. When the road dips to the west, enjoy views into the narrow valley of Willoughby Creek and the forested ridges beyond it.

After turning right at the junction of the two state forest roads, you are hiking on the 11-mile Willoughby Ridge. Hike 2 miles on this narrow road, enjoying intermittent views to the north and healthy forestland all around.

Openings in the hemlock and fir forest on the north side offer views into the narrow valley of Hades Creek. The shiny, dark-green needles of waist-high true fir saplings gleam beside the gravel track. No doubt generations of future seedlings will replace these as years pass. After a while, the much broader Bogachiel River Valley comes into view. Tall trees hide the river itself, but the contours of the broad valley are easy to spot.

After 2.0 miles on the Willoughby Ridge, watch for landmarks of the Spruce Mountain Ridge and the place to turn north toward the Geodetic Hill site. The spur ridge is a quarter-mile wide, and the forest is thick. A very broad stump with a broken top about 4 feet tall serves as a landmark for leaving the forest road. A piece of red survey tape was left as a marker in one of the stump's crevices in 2018. When standing beside the stump, a rectangular yellow National Park Service (NPS) boundary sign can be seen on a tree about 100 feet into the forest.

Between two visits to the site—a decade apart—the forest between the road and the Olympic National Park boundary received a commercial pre-thinning. Most of the thin trees were cut close to the ground and dropped on the same spot. The young forest was dense here, so the felled trees formed a loose mat, 2- to 3-feet above the ground, which may still be difficult to traverse. The trees in the national park are older and naturally spaced farther apart, so this particular challenge ends as you enter the national preserve.

No formal trail approaches Geodetic Hill on this route. Directions to the survey markers in the 1974 report to the National Geodetic Survey offer good instructions: "Turn north on the spur ridge, keeping on top of the ridge, and go north 0.9 mile to the station in a clearing."[7] There are clear signs of elk and deer on the ridge. Their grazing patterns create hike-able trails by midsummer; at other times of the year, just stay close to the ridge crest as you travel northward. With open forest and the land sloping downhill to both east and west of the ridge, finding your path should be straightforward.

The route holds only one significant surprise. Just when the lookout site seems near, the ridge appears to end. The route disappears downhill, and another hill appears ahead. At closer look, the not *too* steep decline is only 50 feet, and the corresponding rise is not as steep as it first appears.

---

[7] US National Geodetic Survey, "Data Sheet PID SD0670 SPRUCE"; https://www.ngs.noaa.gov/cgi-bin/ds_mark.prl?PidBox=SD0670

As you approach the final knoll on the ridge, notice the openness of the forest floor. The understory plants—ferns, Oregon grape, and salal—are spaced farther apart here. A scattering of shattered window glass sparkles in one area. Rusty pieces of an old woodstove appear under low plants in another. A piece of old lumber with bolts attached, twisted wire and a guy wire controller, and several other remnants of an old building confirm this as the location of a long-ago fire and plane watch station.

These same artifacts appear in snapshots an older friend took while hiking here in 2000. Please leave what you find where it is, so another explorer can enjoy their own discoveries many years in the future.

The author near the site of the Geodetic Hill Lookout. (Cindy Ziobron photograph, courtesy of the photographer.)

25. MOUNT OCTOPUS LOOKOUT

RT Distance: 5.0 miles
High Point: 2444 feet
Elevation Gain: 800 feet
Season: May-Oct
A Discover Pass is required.

History

Chris Morgenroth and Cornelius Huelsdonk, pioneer settlers in the Bogachiel and Hoh River Valleys, accepted the challenge to scout a trail between the Hoh and Queets Rivers in the west Olympics in late December 1892. When they reached the top of a ridge between Nolan Creek and Snahapish Creek, Morgenroth noticed short ridges running in every direction from their high points. They named the promontory Mount Octopus for its many arms.[1] Morgenroth became well known in the early twentieth century as one of the first forest rangers in the new Olympic National Forest and then an active supporter of the proposal for an Olympic National Park. His friend, Cornelius, was brother to John Huelsdonk, who became famous as the Ironman of the Hoh.[2]

Mount Octopus Lookout tower, 1960s. (Linda Pickering photograph, courtesy of the photographer.)

In 1914, the US Coast and Geodetic Survey identified this mountain as easily recognized from the sea for its sharp peak, and established a survey station, or benchmark, on its high point. They were not aware of the name given to the peak by the earlier explorers, and labeled it Bull Hill.[3]

---

[1] Morgenroth, 42-43.
[2] Daryl C. McClary, "Huelsdonk, John (1866-1946) and Dora (1863-1947)" accessed at https://www.historylink.org/File/7480.
[3] US National Geodetic Survey, "Data Sheet PID SD0675 Bull Hill"; https://www.ngs.noaa.gov/cgi-bin/ds_mark.prl?PidBox= SD0675.

The Washington Department of Natural Resources (DNR) started developing a road to the already identified Mount Octopus Lookout site in 1954.[4] In 1957, they completed construction of a 40-foot wooden tower with a 14×14-foot cabin on top.[5]

Among the people who staffed this fire watch station were three sisters, Beth, Barbara, and Kathy Barlow. Kathy told their tale in the July 1966 DNR fire lookout staff newsletter, describing her first year on Mount Octopus. Her older sisters had spent two and three summers there, respectively. She thought 1966 was a great year for seeing wildlife from the tower, having seen many deer, many elk tracks, and a few elk. One feature she didn't like was the coyote chorus: "It was rather a hair-raising thing to hear at 3 A.M."[6]

DNR abandoned the building in 1974.[7]

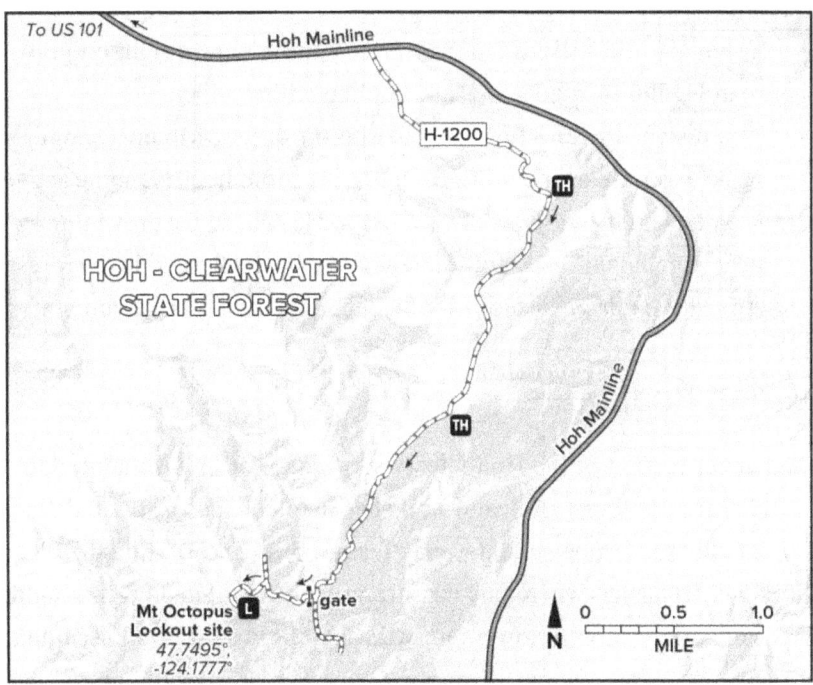

---

[4] Washington Forestry Division, *Biennial Report [for 1954]*, quoted in http://washingtonlookouts.weebly.com/mount-octopus.html.
[5] Spring and Fish, 23.
[6] Kathy Barlow, "Hi from Mt. Octopus," *Olympia District's Ten-Eight*, September 1966, [5].
[7] Kresek, *2015*, 23.

Hike Summary

This is a forest road hike with moderate elevation gain in a state forest. The beauty here depends on the retention of mature forest and the variety of trees and wildflowers sustained in it. On clear days, you may see Mount Olympus from the north side of the peak.

Getting There

- Drive US Highway 101 between Kalaloch and the Hoh Oxbow. Turn east at milepost 176 on the Hoh Mainline Road toward the Clearwater Corrections Center.
- Drive 4.4 miles. Between mileposts 4 and 4½, turn right on gravel road H1200. A road sign stands on the left shoulder.
- The distance to the fire lookout site on one of Mount Octopus's peaks is a little over 5 miles from this junction. In 2017, some active logging had recently occurred close to H1200, so we drove through the clearcut landscape and parked on the first stub road in the forest. Adjust your drive distance for the length or type of hike you prefer.

Hiking Route

The uncut section of the Hoh-Clearwater State Forest has matured to a healthy diverse forest. A beautiful mix of hemlock, cedar, fir, and alder borders the road. One shoulder may feature thick moss while the other hosts verdant salal, where one has strong shade and the other, sunlight. A wide variety of wildflowers grow beside the road as well. Trillium, violets, and oxalis bloom in spring; foxgloves, fireweed, daisies, and even northern gentian appear here later in the summer. Park on a side road along the way, or near the gate on the road described below.

At 4.1 miles from the junction with the Hoh Mainline Road, turn right on a road with a gate, starting or continuing the hike. In 2017, there was a broken wooden sign on the left shoulder of the gated road with the digits *"100"* remaining, as well as two little yellow signs with red arrows pointing to the gate. The gate has the numbers 26-11-19 painted on it, matching the "legal description" of the peak's location: Township 26 N, Range 11 W, Section 19.

A few hundred feet beyond the gate, the road splits. Take the left branch, heading uphill. I have a photograph of Mount Olympus taken from this road in 2006. Having only visited Mount Octopus in inclement weather more recently, I cannot promise a similar view for your visit, but do keep an eye out; it was a pretty grand sight.

The vegetation becomes lush as the road curves up around the mountain. In springtime, there is often a large bed of pink fawn lilies bordering the left shoulder after the route turns southwest. Chains of sturdy elkhorn moss sometimes form matrixes across bare ground. The forested slopes are steeper on the left, but the healthy mixed forest continues.

On the west side of the peak, a road junction offers short routes to both of Mount Octopus's peaks. The road to the left has road signs labeled 4404 and 4406, and leads to the lower peak, several communication towers, and two DNR sheds sometimes left open to provide shelter from the weather.

The main road leads to the slightly higher peak, the site of a 1914 survey marker, and the site of the long-gone Mount Octopus fire lookout tower. Neither peak measures the 2486 feet recorded in the 1980s inventories. It is likely that both sites were lowered to their current elevations when the ground was flattened to support communication facilities after the fire lookout tower was removed; 2444 feet is the highest elevation on either peak now.

Classic artifacts of a 40-foot fire tower and cabin have not yet been found on the site. One story told is that the tower was removed in the 1980s so its cabin could be displayed in a regional museum, but it burned instead.[8] That suggests melted glass and building hardware could still be there. If you find any remains of the wooden fire lookout tower and cabin, burnt or not, please send the news to my website (www.leslieromer.com).

---

[8] http://willhiteweb.com/washington_fire_lookouts/mount_octopus_lookout/forks_155.htm, accessed November 1, 2018.

26. OWL MOUNTAIN LOOKOUTS

RT Distance: 4.5 miles
High Point: 3484 feet
Elevation Gain: 700 feet
Season: Jun-Aug
A Discover Pass is required.

History

There was at least one fire lookout station on or near Owl Mountain at the eastern edge of the Hoh-Clearwater State Forest. The state forest shares its eastern boundary with the Olympic National Park (ONP), within sight of massive Mount Olympus and the true wilderness of the Olympic highlands. Owl Mountain summit, now only a recording weather station site, is a scant mile from the national park boundary. At the border, and several hundred feet above the state forest's boundary road, are a Department of the Interior benchmark and the remains of a cedar-shake Aircraft Warning Service (AWS) building the National Park Service considered nominating as a National Historic Building in 1984. The site elevation in the national park is 86 feet higher than the summit of Owl Mountain.

Owl Mountain AWS Lookout cabin. (Olympic National Park photograph included in a National Park Service "PNRO (Pacific Northwest Regional Office) Inventory" (Form PNR-100 6/82), 1984.

Ray Kresek's seminal fire lookout inventory, first published in 1984, described the building on the summit of Owl Mountain (3398-foot elevation) as a 2-story modified cupola cabin, built in 1941 as an AWS post.[1] Kresek's source for much of his information about the AWS lookouts was his father, Fabian, who maintained radios for the AWS stations near the Washington coast during World War II. In the book's discussion of the

---

[1] Kresek, *Fire lookouts of Oregon and Washington*, 1985, and each edition and *Lookout Inventory* through 2015.

coastal stations, he mentioned, "Owl Mountain required four pack mules to haul the year's supply of radio batteries a dozen miles up its steep narrow path beyond timberline."[2]

An Olympic National Park historical document,[3] and memos between federal AWS offices in Seattle and Portland, state forest managers in Olympia, and forest wardens in the Clearwater area, identify an AWS station location southeast of Owl Mountain. Memos between state and federal officials in June and July 1942 discussed potential AWS sites in the area between the Hoh and the Queets Rivers.[4] They selected a site at the boundary between the Olympic National Park and Clearwater State Forest[5]—although neither land jurisdiction is named in any of the memos. Owl Mountain was described in one memo as one-mile azimuth-300 from the site, identifying the selected site's distance to the southeast of the named peak.

A National Park Service form used for inventorying buildings for potential historic preservation was completed by the Olympic National Park in 1984. It identifies the Owl Mountain AWS Lookout as "one of the few extant AWS lookouts in western Washington."[6] In order to be nominated for the National Register of Historic Places, the building needed to be 50 years old, while this one was closer to 40 at that time. Unfortunately, the building was not maintained and the Owl Mountain AWS building was never nominated for the National Register.

The 1942 memos indicate that the Aircraft Warning Service managers were not particularly concerned with whose land their monitoring stations were built on. The document recording the disposition of AWS buildings at the end of the program in 1944 indicated that Owl Ridge (a name descriptive of the national park location) was on state land, with a pre-existing building which had been winterized. A shake cabin built of native material had been added by the AWS program (this describes the historical building in the national park), and the property was being returned to the state of Washington.[7] This mixture of descriptors indicates the federal AWS program did not know the specific location of the

---

[2] Kresek, *1998*, 112.
[3] Gail E. H. Evans, PNRO Inventory form PNR-100 6.82 for OWL MOUNTAIN A.W.S. LOOKOUT and, Gail E. H. Evans, "Historic Building Inventory Olympic National Park Washington" quoted in http://www.windsox.us/VISITOR/HISTORY_BUILDINGS/HOH_AREA_2.html#EL10.
[4] Six memoranda dated June 10, 1942, through July 18, 1942, found by Eric Willhite in the AWS files of the National Archives in Seattle.
[5] This was the name of the Hoh-Clearwater State Forest in the 1940s.
[6] Gail E. H. Evans, PNRO Inventory form PNR-100 6.82 for OWL MOUNTAIN A.W.S. LOOKOUT.
[7] [US Forest Service] Region 6, "Report of Aircraft Warning Service Stations," May 1, 1944, Sheet #II.

AWS station. The site was considered remote in the 1940s, and remains so today. While the remains of an AWS cabin on Owl Ridge, southeast of Owl Mountain, is easily found, there is also descriptive evidence of a pre-existing state lookout facility on Owl Mountain. A mystery remains.

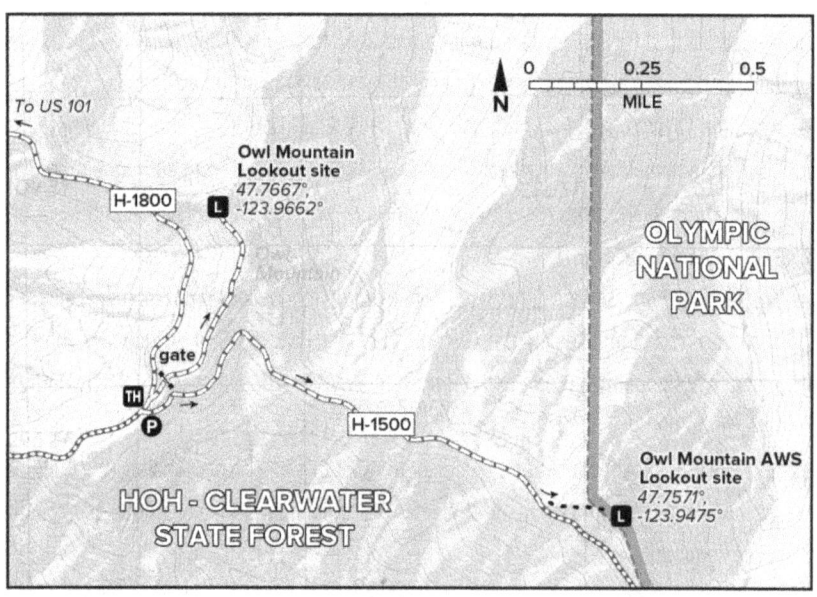

Hike Summary

Hike a short distance on state forest roads to the foot of Owl Mountain Ridge. Take an adventurous scramble to the top of the steep, forested ridge to find the wood-and-metal artifacts of the documented lookout cabin, just inside the Olympic National Park. Return to the junction of H1800 and H1500 and hike the gated road leading to the summit of Owl Mountain. Enjoy broad views in all directions. Note that a gate on the access road is locked September through April, 9 miles from the trailhead.

Getting There

- Drive US Highway 101 between Kalaloch and the Hoh Oxbow. Turn east at milepost 176 on the Hoh Mainline Road toward the Clearwater Corrections Center.
- Drive 7 miles to a junction with H1000. Turn left at the sign: "South Fork Hoh Campground 7.5 miles."
- At 9.4 miles from US Highway 101, turn right at a Y. H1000 continues to the left. The narrow road on the right has a white gate marked DNR-26-11-12. A vertical, vinyl H1800 road sign stands among the vegetation on the right. This road is closed September 1 to May 1 for wildlife protection. The road is usually snow-covered above 2500 feet until late May.
- Starting at about 15.4 miles from the highway, expect to encounter a series of small rockslide areas. The Department of Natural Resources patrols roads in this area after the gates are opened in the spring, but fresh slides continue to occur. I have yet to encounter rocks that could not be easily removed while visiting the area, but you might want to consider hiking from here.
- At 18.4 miles from US Highway 101, park at a wide spot on H1500, around the corner from its junction with H1800.

Hiking Route

Stretch your legs after the drive with a hike northeast on H1500, a dappled road bordered with wildflowers from the moment the snow melts. In early summer, clusters of avalanche lilies bloom on the slopes rising on the left side of the road. Foxgloves and daisies join them as the season progresses.

After 0.25 mile, the road passes over a small creek, turns a corner, and follows a ridge running southeast. At 0.65 mile from the start, pass a side road following a narrow ridge running north. The open space beside the main road is broader now; grassy fields appear first on the left, then the right side of the gravel track.

At 1.1 miles from the car, look for a 10-foot-wide opening in the trees on the left. As the 1984 ONP historical building report mentioned, no clear trail to the Owl Ridge site exists. What remains of the historical route leaves State Forest Road H1500 at these coordinates: 47.7575°, -123.9508°, elevation 3148 feet. Enter the state forest of hemlock and fir trees and turn right in about 20 feet, where a road-width opening between the trees leads gradually uphill.

The lookout site is at the western edge of the ridgetop, about 0.2 mile to the east, at coordinates 47.7571°, -123.9475°. Ascend the ridge until you find metal NPS (National Park Service) boundary markers 5 to 6 feet high on the east side of large conifers, then follow an eastward route, close to the western ridge edge. This avoids a very steep section of the hillside, south and southwest of the fire lookout site. Although the route is almost due eastward, the presence of large trees, downed trees, and thickets requires circuitous routing to reach the intended destination.

Once on the ridge, a last NPS boundary sign on a broad tree trunk welcomes you to the remains of the Owl Mountain AWS Lookout site. Ten feet in front of the tree is a Department of the Interior National Parks Department survey marker, set in concrete at ground level. It is stamped with the location, T26 R10 (Township 26, Range 10) and the date, 1984. Behind the tree are the remains of the cedar-shake building that measured 13×17 feet and one-and-a-half stories tall in 1984. Young trees and shrubs block all views from the building site. Mount Olympus, Mount Tom, and other North Olympic peaks are, however, visible from the north side of the clearing edge, a few feet beyond the survey marker. Explore the Owl Ridge site for other artifacts: a stone foundation, roofing paper, metal washtubs. In late summer, enjoy the many huckleberries on bushes surrounding the site. When ready, descend the steep hillside, avoiding the drop-off directly downhill from the lookout site.

After returning to your parking spot, continue around the corner to the narrow, gated gravel track ascending the hill—Owl Mountain—between roads H1800 and H1500. The road to the summit is 0.4 mile, gaining 300 feet. It leads to a small weather recording station so it has occasional motorized visitors, which keep grasses from covering the hilltop. A square concrete pad, which served as base for a tower, and three galvanized eyebolts to support guy wires sit at the end of the road. Is the site large enough for a cupola cabin?

There are great views to enjoy in all directions on a clear day. A full range of snowy peaks, including Mount Olympus, may be visible to the east. Mount Octopus and the ocean beyond it lie to the west.

Kloochman Rock, site of another contemporary fire lookout station, stands tall to the south, while Colonel Bob and its neighboring peaks are visible to the southeast.

Avalanche lilies beside the route to the Owl Mountain AWS Lookout, June 2018.

Was there a fire lookout station on Owl Mountain itself, or only on the slightly higher ridgetop a mile away? I hope you will make your way to both peaks, draw your own conclusions, and enjoy the adventure.

27. KLOOCHMAN ROCK LOOKOUT

RT Distance: 1.3 miles or more
High Point: 3356 feet
Elevation Gain: 800 feet or more
Season: Late May-Aug[1]
A Discover Pass is required.

History

In *Gods & Goblins: A Field Guide to Place Names of the Olympic National Park*, author Smitty Parratt summarized a Queets tribal legend in which an old "squaw," or klooch, accompanied hunters on a fall hunting trip and got lost in a snowstorm. They looked to the top of the mountain and imagined they could see her form there, so they named the mountain for their klooch. This discussion of the term says "man" was added much later, by European settlers.[2] Several Chinook jargon dictionaries published in the early-to-mid-twentieth century defined kloochman as a Chinook trade jargon word meaning "woman, wife, or female."[3]

Kloochman Rock Lookout, 1940 (Photograph by Byrne, courtesy of Olympic National Park.)

Kloochman Rock Lookout stood on a stone promontory 3000 feet above the broad Queets River Valley and all nearby trees. The site is in the Olympic National Park, but just a few feet from the southern border of Hoh-Clearwater State Forest. Before the national park was established in 1938, the lookout site was in the Olympic National Forest. In 1931, the national forest supervisor H. L. Plumb and an assistant regional forester made an inspection visit to the fire monitoring

---

[1] The forest roads between Yahoo Lake and Kloochman Rock are closed to motor vehicles from early September to late May for elk protection.
[2] Parratt, 71.
[3] See the Chinook jargon dictionaries included in the bibliography.

station. The supervisor wrote in his report, "The lookout had to live in a tent about 1000 feet from the peak. A house should be built on the rock, but the State should contribute, as it covers a good deal of their territory in the Clearwater [State Forest]."[4]

The state did not contribute, but the top of the rock was blasted off in about 1932 to provide a 20-foot-wide, level building site. The blasting was done by Wilbur Northrup, a member of a local pioneer family, who also worked on the cabin construction in 1932, served as the fire lookout at Kloochman the next year, and took his bride, Louise, there for a honeymoon in September 1934.[5]

The Kloochman Rock lookout cabin was a summer observation station in the Aircraft Warning Service (AWS), 1942 to 1944. Although the cabin was considered winterized, AWS staff moved to the Anderson Ranch, down in the Queets Valley, for the cold winter months.[6]

In his 1968 hiking guide to the Olympic National Park trails, Robert Wood remembered the view of the cabin from below: "near the base of the rock mass capping the peak, one can glimpse through the trees the lookout cabin, perched atop the summit rocks like a tiny bird cage, and anchored by cables for protection against the shock of winter storms. The final ascent is via wooden ladders up the steep rock face, and caution must be exercised because the timbers have rotted."[7] Hikers no longer follow Wood's route, which climbed the tall cliff from the Queets River. The current trail approaches from the north. Ray Kresek is generally supported in listing the Kloochman Lookout cabin as removed in 1957,[8] despite Wood's publication a decade later.

Hike Summary

This hike starts in the Hoh-Clearwater State Forest and ends in the Olympic National Park. The route to Kloochman Rock combines a variable-length road hike with an adventurous 0.5-mile trail and a 50-foot vertical rock climb assisted by fixed ropes to reach the lookout site. The rock climb is not recommended for hikers without climbing experience.

---

[4] Memorandum of Inspection dated February 5, 1932, signed by Forest Supervisor Plumb. The original is held in the National Archives in Seattle; a copy was provided by Olympic National Park Archives, Port Angeles.
[5] Parratt, 71.
[6] http://willhiteweb.com/washington_fire_lookouts/aircraft_warning_service/andrews_ranch/queets_valley_105.htm, accessed January 12, 2021.
[7] Robert L. Wood, *Wilderness Trails*, 139.
[8] Kresek, *1985*, 114.

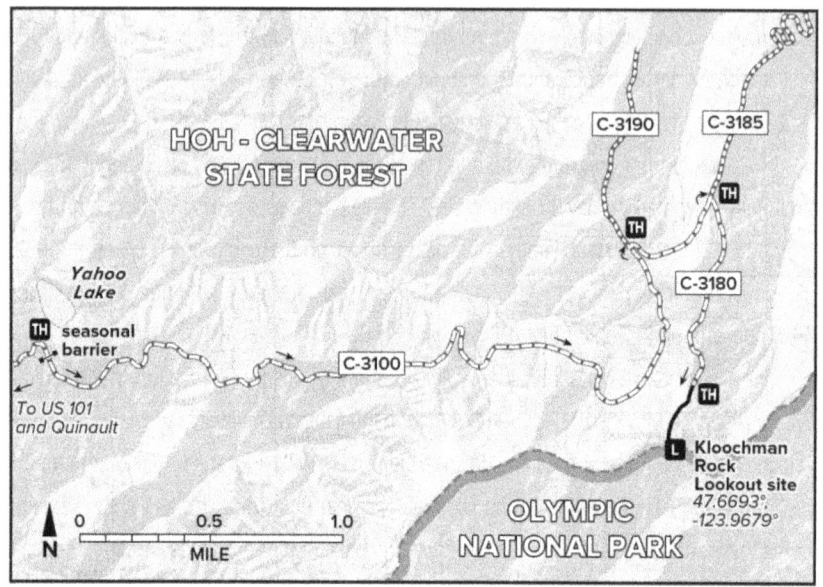

Getting There

- From US Highway 101 between Lake Quinault and Queets, turn east on the Clearwater Road at milepost 147, a short distance north of the Queets-Clearwater School.
- At 8.4 miles, keep left on the Clearwater Road.
- At 13.4 miles, turn right onto paved Road C-3000. A sign says 10.1 miles to Yahoo Lake, which is on the route to Kloochman Rock.
- At 17.4 miles, keep right on the mostly paved Road C-3100.
- At 20.7 miles, the pavement ends. Keep right. Sometimes a directional sign to Yahoo Lake stands at the junction.
- Continue driving 2.7 miles on Road C-3100 to the Yahoo Lake trailhead sign. Park here September through May, and for a 10-mile-plus hike. In summer months, driving farther is allowed, but roads may be blocked by fallen rocks. When the roads are clear, the hike can be started from any of several starting points suggested in the hike description.

Hiking Route

As this is a combined road-and-trail hike, the length of the outing depends on how much walking you choose to do. The road is often rough driving, with occasional big boulders on or beside the route where they have fallen from unstable slopes. Much of the road is on a high ridge, offering intermittent narrow views into the broad valley of the Solleks River to the north and the Queets River Valley to the south and east. The healthy mixed forest bordering the road is dominated by hemlocks.

Park by the big sign at the Yahoo Lake trailhead for a roundtrip hike of 10.7 miles, with a 1400-foot elevation gain. Common roadside flowers border the route to the final footpath: daisies, fireweed, long-stemmed dandelions, foxgloves, and pearly everlasting brighten the summer landscape with their lavender, pink, white, and yellow highlights.

There are several small clearings beside the route, offering opportunities to park and begin the hike from a variety of starting points. Two road junctions, both without identifying signs in summer 2017, are additional places to park and start hiking. Each junction requires a right turn to continue toward Kloochman Rock. The first junction is labeled on state forest maps as the meeting of C-3100 with C-3190 running north. The second is the junction of C-3185 headed east and C-3180 going south. Hiking from the C-3190 junction offers a 3.0 mile RT hike with 1000 feet elevation gain. Hiking from the start of C-3180 provides 2.1 miles RT with an 800-foot elevation gain.

Wherever you start walking, follow C-3180 south to its end. At the far side of the road-end clearing, turn right to the unsigned but obvious trailhead into the forest. No signs identify the builders of this 0.5-mile trail, which is such an asset for hikers. I was told in 2005 it had been built by local Boy Scouts whose leader worked for the Washington Department of Natural Resources. I don't know if the trail receives official maintenance, but it has been easy to follow whenever I have visited.

Most of the fairly steep route—it has a 500-foot gain in just under 0.5 mile—is easy to see on the floor of the forest and is marked with distinctive blue vinyl diamonds high on the trees beside the path.

Sections of the route that lack diamonds are well marked with pink survey tape on tree or shrub branches. There are a few trail sections where alternate routes are offered; I recommend following the diamonds where they are visible. The well-designed trail leads through the initial thicket of chest-high salmonberry bushes, across open forest traverses bordered with wide colonies of oxalis with distinctive shamrock leaves, over thick logs with steps carved in their tall flanks, and zigzags up to the high ridge marked with National Park Service boundary signs. The ridge summit, Kloochman Rock, and the airy space on the other side of the ridge are inside the Olympic National Park.

Follow the trail left across the ridge and turn the corner at the eastern end. A weather-beaten tree stands between you and the Queets River Valley 3000 feet below. A rock wall and a thick rope offer the only alternative to sitting down, eating lunch, and returning the way you came.

Here is the 50-foot rock climb. I have always found the rope here sturdy, but cannot offer assurance for the future. In 2017, it was 0.5-inch-thick and tied several times around a well-rooted tree about 12 feet up the hill. In the protection of trees and shrubs, ascent of a wall with good footholds is feasible if you can get a secure grip on the rope for insurance. If you cannot get a strong grip on the rope, you have gone far enough. The rest of the way involves a couple more ropes, traversing a curve while looking over the edge of the precipice, climbing a 45-degree slope that offers no encouraging footholds, another steep climb with footholds, and finally clambering onto a 10×10-foot wooden platform with no railings. A solar panel hangs off one corner and a waist-high, rectangular lockbox supporting a short antenna anchors another corner of the slatted wooden structure. A folding camp chair graced the platform in 2017.

The square wooden floor with its steel-beam supports was built on bare rock after the lookout cabin was removed. It was used as a helipad for some years, but is not currently marked for identification by aircraft.

A few recognizable artifacts of the earlier lookout cabin can be found near and under the wooden deck. Shards of window glass sparkle on the rock surfaces close to the structure. Look for bolts permanently fastened into the rocks. They may have anchored the cabin that sheltered fire observers here, watching over the forests.

The panoramic views are certainly spectacular. The Pacific Ocean is 20 miles away and easily visible in clear weather. The Queets River meanders through its long valley below, but few details are recognizable from this high perspective. Snow-clad Olympic peaks are often visible to the northeast.

Enjoy it all from one of the best vantage points the west Olympics have to offer.

28. FINLEY PEAK LOOKOUT

RT Distance: 21.0 miles
High Point: 3421 feet
Elevation Gain: 4950 feet
Season: Jul-Oct
Wilderness Camping Permits are required here, but not an entrance fee.

History

The first forest fire lookout in the Olympic Mountains was built in 1916, not on the high point of Finley Peak, but on its ridge, far above the north shore of Lake Quinault. The land was in the young Olympic National Forest, first established as a Forest Reserve by President Grover Cleveland in 1897. Historical photographs show a rustic, one-room cabin with cedar-shake siding and a steep, peaked roof. This image includes a thick pole taller than the cabin beside it, where an observer could stand on a small platform for wider views.

C. P. Cockrell at Finley Peak Lookout, 1920. (Courtesy of Irene Potter.)

Two of the first people to work at this lookout station were women: Mavie Olson and C. P. Cockrell. Local schoolteacher Mavie spent several summers there in the 1920s, alone with her dog and her rifle.[1] The Olson family were Quinault Valley pioneers and early owners of the Quinault Lodge on the shores of the lake with the same name.

When President Franklin D. Roosevelt signed legislation creating the Olympic National Park in 1938, this section of the national forest was included. The lookout was staffed into the 1930s and removed in 1947, after World War II.[2]

---

[1] Agnes Lockhart Hughes, "A Girl Who Lives Very Much Alone," *American Magazine*, March 1921, 53-54.
[2] Kresek, *2015*, 22; Spring and Fish, 197.

28. FINLEY PEAK LOOKOUT · 157

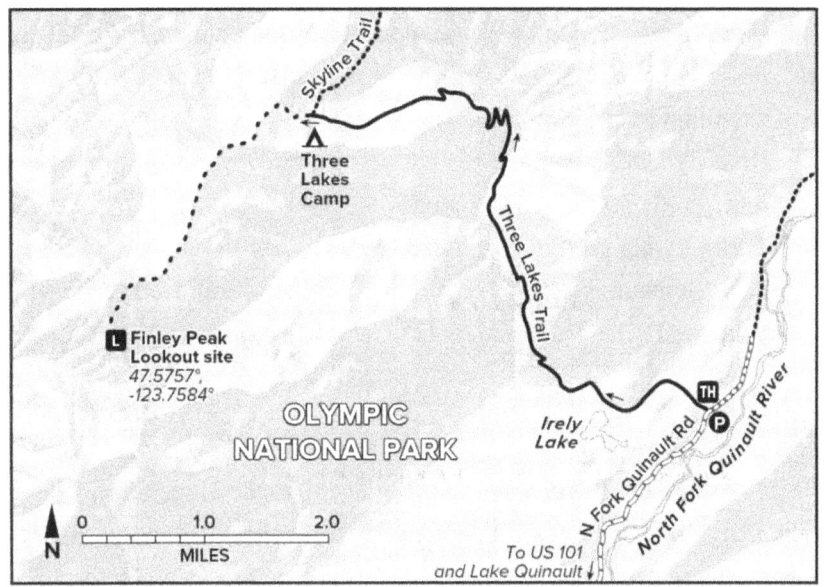

Hike Summary

The hike to the Finley Peak Lookout site is no mere adventure, it is the most challenging in this collection. My very experienced companions on my first attempt to reach the site labeled the hike as a "ten, on a difficulty scale of one to five." Although the mileage and elevation gain may seem feasible for a shorter trip by strong hikers, navigational issues encourage reserving a full day for exploring the abandoned trail between the Three Lakes Camp and the lookout site below Finley Peak, thus making a visit to Finley Lookout site a three-day outing with two nights camping in the Olympic National Park backcountry.

Getting There

- Drive US Highway 101 to the Lake Quinault South Shore Road.
- There are separate entries from US Highway 101 to the South Shore Road from north and south. It is 2.4 miles from the highway to the ranger station from the north and 2.2 miles to the ranger station if coming from the south. Obtain your Wilderness Camping Permits

at the ranger station for $8 per person per day.[3] No other permits or passes are required for entry or parking at the trailhead for this hike.
- Continue on the South Shore Road for 11.5 miles to the Quinault River Bridge. Pavement gives way to gravel in this section of the route, and potholes slow the pace.
- Turn left and cross the bridge, then turn right on the bumpy North Fork Quinault Road. Continue for 2.9 miles to trailhead parking on your right. The Three Lakes Trail starts across the road.

Hiking Route

The first segment of the route is the 7-mile trail to the Three Lakes Camp. The first 4 miles of this are a popular day hike. Beautiful scenery is present from the beginning, with giant cedars and hemlocks all around. The trail is bordered with a wide variety of wildflowers blooming early spring through summer. The route features all types of trail surface, with little recent maintenance beyond occasional brushing and removal of downed trees. Much of the trail looks like a narrow, rocky streambed. It is often damp or has water running through it. In the latter case, foot traffic on the trail verge can mash the vegetation into a green mat.

The hike has a short, steep hill near the start, followed by a long, flat area laced with wetlands and creeks. An old boardwalk tries to keep hikers above wet soil, but its cracks often catch trekking poles and toes of boots. At 1 mile, a left branch splits off to visit Irely Lake, which appears as more of a broad meadow than pond by midsummer.

The trail continues with a series of short climbs and descents punctuated by small streams, trending upward toward Big Creek. The elevation gain in this section of the trail is a moderate 850 feet in 4 miles.

As it approaches the broad creek, the trail drops and rises again steeply on the other side of a narrow side canyon. Crossing Big Creek itself is fairly easy during most summer months. With low summer stream flow, pools, a sandy beach, and large tree trunks close to the

---

[3] This reflects the 2018 wilderness camping fee for this area.

crossing, the area is attractive to day-hikers and through-hikers alike. It is a good place for a rest before the serious switchback work begins.

The total distance and elevation gain to Three Lakes Camp is 7 miles and a 3000-foot ascent, with less than a third of the elevation achieved before Big Creek. Winter storms bring down trees and hillsides along the upper trail each year, so be sure to review trail reports on https://www.wta.org/ and the Olympic National Park website for recent information before planning a trip here.

The pathway to Three Lakes becomes steeper and rockier after Big Creek, with few streams crossing the trail. The old-growth forest has more exotic wildflowers in its understory as it gains elevation—beargrass and avalanche lilies among them. At 5 miles, pause to admire the nation's largest yellow, or Alaska, cedar tree.[4] It has an impressive girth and lack of bark on its lower trunk, but foliage on top demonstrates the resilience that has enabled its long survival.

At 7 miles, the Three Lakes Camp has tree-shaded tent sites scattered throughout its 5 acres. The "lakes" range from a pretty pond to a boggy meadow with several rushing creeks and surprisingly few insects. Bear wires are centrally located a short distance from the "throne" toilet—a basic household toilet seat on a box, surrounded by a wooden fence for privacy.

Beyond the Three Lakes Camp, follow old trails that no longer appear on national park maps and are largely unknown to current park staff. Because of their long use, the trails still exist as beaten ground, hidden by high huckleberry bushes that do their best to conceal the historical trail. The route is very occasionally obscured by fallen trees. A bigger challenge is to follow the old paths on ridges that rise and fall several hundred feet every 0.5 mile, and to keep going, knowing the destination is not on a high point but on a narrow, protected saddle a couple hundred feet below the ridge's closest peak.

---

[4] "Alaska cedar," https://af-legacy-prd.americanforests.org/big-trees/alaskacedar-cupressus-nootkatensis/

Leave the Three Lakes Camp at the bear wire near the "lakeshore."[5] Head west, crossing the meadow, noting the unusual wetland wildflowers: marsh marigold, bog orchids, asters, and tall, unknown blossoms, dark red or white, blooming as summer's end approaches. A trail emerges on the far side after the route crosses both the marshy shore and a clearing covered with talus. Follow it to the edge of a grassy field, then up to the ridge on the right. At 0.25 mile, it merges with a slightly better established north-south footpath. At 0.4 mile, the Tshletshy Creek Trail descends to the right. When scouted in 2016 and 2018, a short signpost supported the two pieces of a sign for this historic trail. The route to the Finley Lookout site follows the narrow trench that remains of the old Tshletshy Creek Trail from the south side of the Three Lakes Camp (trailhead at 47.6013°, -123.7247°) to the ridge west of the camp. The path then continues southwest on an increasingly obscure way-trail for about 3.5 miles.

After a short distance, a broad, sloping meadow appears on the east (left) side of the trail. This was the site of a popular trail shelter, apparently removed decades ago, but fondly remembered by hikers who had come this way in years past. Beyond this point, huckleberry shrubs hide the route, branches meeting and overlapping from the hiker's knee to chest, while boots continue to confirm that a beaten trail continues unseen, below.

Once you find the Finley Ridge trail, it can be followed most of the way to the fire lookout site. There are a couple of high points on the ridge that the trail avoids climbing, which should be your inclination as well. About 3 miles from camp, at 3450-feet elevation and coordinates 47.5825°, -123.7550°, follow the trail as it leaves the ridge and parallels it at about 3400-feet elevation. The route gradually descends to a damp wetland. Continue southwest at the foot of the ridge, on the perimeter of the wet meadow. As it approaches the end of the ridge, follow the

---

[5] When I have been here, this lake has been a meadow, quite stable and dry enough to cross in hiking boots.

trail rising from the meadow, onto a narrow neck of land between higher ridges.

Toward the end of this bench between ridges, you will find the Finley Peak Lookout site at these coordinates: 47.5757°, -123.7584°. Most noticeable are large pieces of an old cast iron woodstove, then sparkling pieces of window glass. That the glass is several inches across attests to the small number of visitors that reach this site. Please leave it for others to discover—more popular hiking destinations have only shards of glass remaining. Close examination of wood scraps on the site reveals straight edges of very old, dimensioned lumber. If you discover more, be sure and share your findings.

During two scouting trips here, we found scraps of survey tape along our route, and occasional blazed trees as well. Historical photos show large hiking parties of The Mountaineers ventured here to visit the lookout and view Lake Quinault from high above in the 1920s. These blazes could well have shown them the way. The survey tape was left much more recently. Much of it was bright when seen during the scouting trips mentioned above.

Blogger Eric Willhite took another rough route, bushwhacking up from the North Shore Lake Quinault Road on an extended day hike in May 2018.[6] He left a visitor register in a jar at the Finley Peak Lookout site. In August 2018, my party was the next to sign in.

On your return trip, watch for a turn that is easy to miss. At these coordinates: 47.5984°, -123.7353°, turn north (left) and follow the trail a short distance downhill and then right, to continue northeastward toward the Tshletshy Trail sign and the Three Lakes Camp. Have a wonderful adventure!

---

[6] He discussed his cross-country trip with me via email and posted site photos and a route description on a webpage: http://willhiteweb.com/washington_fire_lookouts/finley_peak_lookout/lake_quinault_305.htm.

29. HIGLEY PEAK LOOKOUT

RT Distance: 1.0 mile
High Point: 3025 feet
Elevation Gain: 250 feet
Season: May-Oct
No pass or permit is required.

History

Higley Peak, high above the north shore of Lake Quinault, was named for a pioneer family in the Quinault Valley that crossed the Olympics from Hoodsport at the beginning of the twentieth century. Father and son, Alfred and Orte Higley, were well known in the community for running a sawmill and delivering weekly mail to the valley residents.[1]

Higley Lookout cabin, 1940s. (US Forest Service photograph found in National Archives, Seattle, courtesy of Ron Kemnow.)

In the early 1930s, the Forest Service built a simple cabin for a fire lookout station on the peak. Observation staff climbed a steep trail from the lake to get there, at least through World War II. It was one of eight fire lookouts Wes and Winona Harner of Montesano worked in as Aircraft Warning Service (AWS) relief staff, 1942 to 1944. Excerpts from Winona's journal and photos are included in *Frontier Legacy: History of the Olympic National Forest*. Her snapshot of the square cabin with a tall chimney at Higley Peak accompanies a brief report on their trip up the trail from the lake. "Left Quinault at 8:30 started hiking at 10 to 9. Arrived at Higley Peak at about 12:00 . . . Jumped an elk on the climb up. What a climb too. Started raining at about 3:15 visibility nil."[2]

---

[1] Parratt, 54, 59.
[2] Rooney, 69-70.

The Forest Service continued to staff and periodically remodel the Higley lookout, adding a 40-foot tower in 1957 and rebuilding the cabin and tower in 1964.[3] In 1973, the tower and lookout cabin were removed. There are two versions of the story—that the cabin and tower were lifted by a helicopter and dropped in Lake Quinault when a cable broke[4]— or that it was successfully moved to the Snohomish County Airport.[5] Current researchers are looking for a conclusive answer.

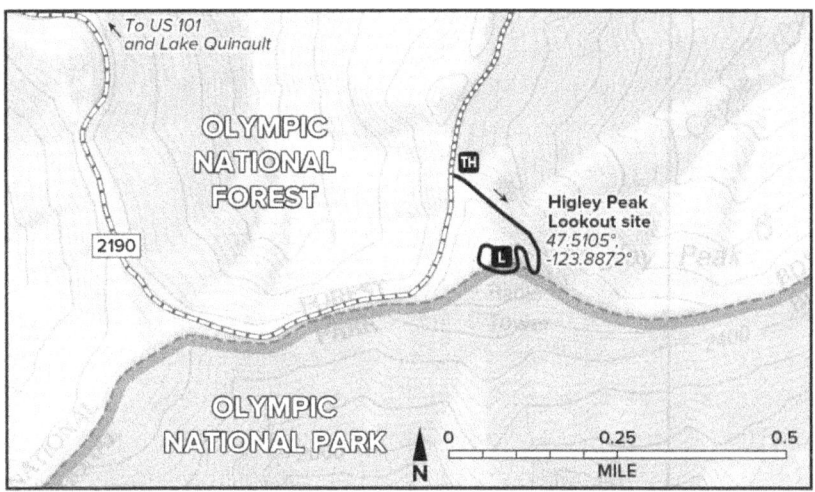

Hike Summary

This is a beautiful, short hike in the Olympic National Forest above Lake Quinault. The long views are gone, but the 0.5-mile trail quickly spirals up the small peak in old-growth forest. In late spring, the display of pink fawn lilies and white oxalis blossoms is outstanding.

---

[3] Spring and Fish, 94. Kresek, *1998*, 114.
[4] Kresek, *1998*, 114.
[5] http://willhiteweb.com/washington_fire_lookouts/higley_peak/lake_quinault_258.htm, accessed November 2019.

Getting There

- From US Highway 101, north of Lake Quinault and a short distance north of milepost 130, turn east on Prairie Creek Road, Forest Road (FR) 2190.
- Drive 9.7 miles on FR 2190, passing FR 2140 on the left.
- After driving briefly on a ridge with distant views through the trees on both sides, come to an open space 50 feet wide, with parking room on both sides of the forest road. Higley Peak is on top of the knob to the right.

Hiking Route

When the trail is not maintained, the trailhead and its dilapidated sign hide in a thicket of salmonberry bushes on the south side of the road and the ridge. Once the shrubs have been penetrated, the trail appears as a boot-wide trace of soft duff cut through a wide carpet of shamrock-leaved oxalis under tall firs and hemlocks.

The path traverses a narrow bench on the south side of the Higley Ridge, where winter storms sometimes bring down broad trees. In 2016, there were about six tree trunks to step or climb over in the first section of the trail, in among the big old trees and the many small plants at their feet. At a quarter mile, the trail turns north, offering occasional glimpses toward the ocean to the west. In another tenth of a mile, it turns again, offering views down the north slope of Higley Ridge. The forest is more open on this side. Paths on the slope below suggest possible alternate routes down the hill. The uphill route turns twice more, in increasingly tighter curves.

The last section of the trail leads west into the lookout clearing. There are four footing blocks standing in a square that look too small to support even the "short tower" built here in 1964.[6] Not far from them sits a 4×4×16-inch concrete rectangle with a similar sized board bolted to the ground about 8 inches away. One might be a door threshold, but what is the other?

---

[6] Spring and Fish, 94.

30. HUMPTULIPS RIDGE LOOKOUT

RT Distance: 4.0 miles
High Point: 1760 feet
Elevation Gain: 1000 feet
Season: Mar-Dec
No pass or permit is required.

History

The place name, Humptulips, came from the band of the Chehalis Tribe who lived in this area. The word means both "hard to pole" and "chilly region" in their Salish language.[1] The two phrases offer reasonable descriptions of the Humptulips River and its valley between the slopes of the Olympic Mountains and the Pacific Ocean.

There were three lookouts on the west slopes of the Olympics with the name Humptulips between 1942 and 1970. The earliest was located west of Highway 101, near the village of Humptulips. It sheltered year-round World War II airplane monitors in two portable 8×16-foot buildings. They stood on private land, leased from 1942 to 1944, the years the Aircraft Warning Service (AWS) was active.[2]

The moveable lookout cabin used at Humptulips Ridge and Humptulips Auxiliary Lookouts. (This US Forest Service photograph appeared in an undated Olympic National Forest building inventory in National Archives-Seattle, and posted on www.washingtonlookouts.weebly.com/humptulipsridge.html, courtesy of Ron Kemnow.)

The other two Humptulips lookouts were on the west and east slopes of the ridge between the west and east forks of the Humptulips River. The only map documentation of a Humptulips Ridge Lookout on the west side of the ridge is a US Geologic Survey Lake

---

[1] Phillips, 64.
[2] [US Forest Service] Region 6, "Report of Aircraft Warning Service Stations," May 1, 1944, Sheet #III.

Quinault map created in 1955.[3] The square-mile section the lookout station was located on is shaded differently than the Olympic National Forest sections that surround it on that map. This indicates different land ownership; in this case, state forestland within the Olympic National Forest.

The 1985 Kresek lookout inventory says the State Division of Forestry, and later Department of Natural Resources, had a cabin here in 1950 and a trailer on the site in 1964, but no lookout station here in 1970.[4] Later, Kresek inventories say the cabin was there in 1942.[5] It appears now that the 1942 cabin was built at the Humptulips AWS station 11 miles southwest, and the trailer was more likely located at the Humptulips Auxiliary Lookout site (see chapter 33) in 1964. Ron Kemnow posted an undated Olympic National Forest photograph of an attractive, moveable, square cabin on Humptulips Ridge on his web page for that lookout.[6] The following eyewitness story dates the transfer of the moveable cabin from Humptulips Ridge in spring 1958.

Sandy Floe, who grew up at the Snider Ranger Station north of Forks, was the first staff at the Humptulips Auxiliary Lookout. In a 2018 email to Eric Willhite, Floe reported "The 10×10-foot building was moved from the first location in the spring of 1958 to the location on USFS ground where I served."[7]

Since the photograph was taken by the US Forest Service, and the Forest Service moved the house to Olympic National Forest land, it is most likely the Humptulips Ridge Lookout station was a federal fire watch location, despite being located on state forest land. In a 2020 conversation, Floe said he had not known when he worked there that the former site was state forest land, or why the small lookout cabin had been moved from one location to another.[8]

---

[3] The 1955 USGS map was also distributed as 1957 and 1962 editions. The information also appears on a 1962 Metsker map.
[4] Kresek, *1985*, 114.
[5] Kresek, *Fire Lookouts of the Northwest; Lookout Inventory, Revised 2019*, 23. (Hereafter cited in notes as Kresek, 2019.)
[6] Kemnow found the photo in the Olympic National Forest files at the National Archives in Seattle, according to a 9-1-2020 email exchange with the fire lookout historian. The photo was accessed earlier at https://washingtonlookouts.weebly.com/humptulips-ridge.html.
[7] Excerpt from email texts Eric Willhite shared with me in September 2020.
[8] Telephone conversation with Sandy Floe, October 6, 2020.

30. HUMPTULIPS RIDGE LOOKOUT · 167

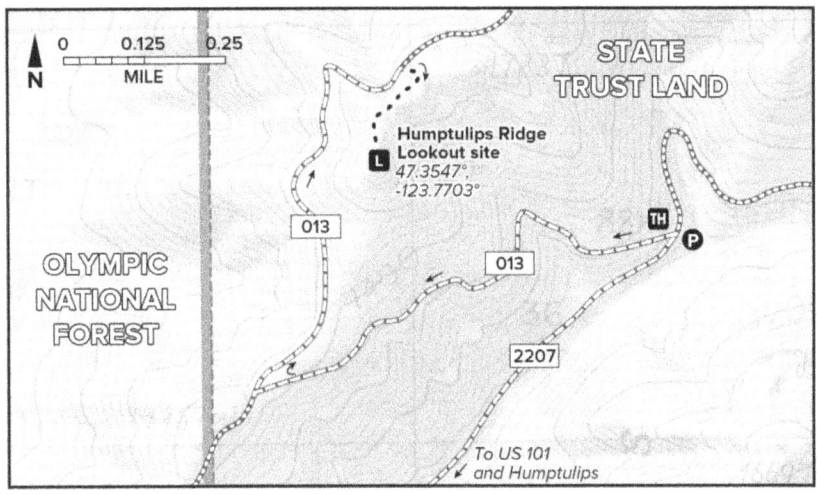

Hike Summary

This is a road and bushwhacking adventure hike. The site is little visited and trees, shrubs, and blackberry vines grow enthusiastically over the last 0.25 mile of the historical route, eliminating the views that qualified the site for a lookout. Enjoy panoramas from the lower route. Geographic coordinates are included in this hike description to assist navigation through the young forest that obscures the original path.

Getting There[9]

- Drive US Highway 101 to milepost 112, a few miles north of Humptulips.
- Turn east on the Donkey Creek Road at signs for the Wynoochee Lake Recreation Area.
- At 8.3 miles, turn left on Forest Road (FR) 2204. There is a wide clearing on the right side of the main road at the junction.
- At 9.2 miles, turn right on FR 2207.

---

[9] This lookout can also be approached from the Wynoochee Valley Road and the eastern end of the Donkey Creek Road/Forest Service Road 22.

- At 11.2 miles, park on the side road on the right, within sound of the Donkey Creek. The hike route starts on road 013, on the other side of FR 2207.

Hiking Route

Thick vegetation and trees border both sides of road 013. A narrow, vertical vinyl sign about 20 feet up the right side of the gravel track confirms the road number, but may hide in tall sword ferns. Foxgloves, daisies, blackberries, and huckleberries all thrive under tall firs and hemlocks. The route gains elevation steadily at about 100 feet per tenth of a mile as long as it remains under the trees.

At 0.4 mile, the road takes a bend to the left where a small creek burbles through a culvert under the road and continues its downhill run on the left. Emerge from the tall trees as the shoulder becomes a narrow strip above a steep downward slope. The route is now on a one-lane-wide bench above a deep valley. The road snakes up around Humptulips Ridge as it ascends.

A 2015 timber harvest on the state forestland in the southern half of this square mile section revealed views across the Donkey Creek Valley to the southeast, and the broader West Humptulips River Valley, slightly farther west. It provided a panoramic landscape of rounded green pyramids in all directions except two shorn hillsides across the immediate valley to the southeast.

At 0.8 mile from the start, the hike route takes a sharp right at a junction with a road headed southwest. Continue hiking around the ridge, with the forested summit coming into view about 0.25 mile away to the northeast. Pass a gravel pit and bare ground around it on the right, and enjoy the conifers and undergrowth that now border the route on the left. This area marks the end of the 2015 tree harvest, which was not expected to resume in the near future.

An old road continues beyond the gravel pit, but has a history of filling in with saplings unless regularly traveled. Vegetation in this area has a way of quickly obscuring little-used paths.

Continue north for 0.6 mile from the road junction at the point. The old roadbed route then turns east. Follow it for 0.1 mile, keeping an eye out for a side road on the right, leading uphill. Recognizing the potential for rapid tree growth in this area, map coordinates are provided for the rest of the hike to Humptulips Ridge Lookout site. Make the turn on the side road at 47.3567°, -123.7697°. Continue a short distance east to 47.3566°, -123.7690°. The forest is relatively open this far.

Go briefly south, then southwest to 47.3563°, -123.7694°. Hemlock and blackberries have been working to reclaim the roadbed this century. Continue on the old route following the land contours to avoid drop-offs to 47.3556°, -123.7705°. This will lead to the road-end clearing where the Humptulips Ridge Lookout cabin was located, at 47.3547°, -123.7703°. There has been a distinctive clearing at this site since my first visit to Humptulips Ridge in 2003. It was a hunters' camp then, and continued use as a campsite will certainly help maintain the cleared area.

A twisted cable planted in the ground at the edge of the clearing is the easiest artifact to find. Any building here when the ridge was tree-less could have made good use of such a guy wire.

Panoramic views from this ridgetop above the Humptulips River were overgrown long ago. Consider the contrasts between healthy forest and recently harvested land, and vegetation's ability to regain dominion when left in solitude.

31. CHESTER RIDGE LOOKOUT

RT Distance: 2.5 miles
High Point: 1384 feet
Elevation Gain: 500 feet
Season: Mar-Dec
No pass or permit is required.

History

Many of the land features in the Olympics were labeled by Olympic National Forest Supervisors early in the twentieth century. Chester Ridge and the nearby creek were named for Chester Wilson, who came to Quinault as a child with his widowed mother in 1895. They were cousins to the Quinault area resort developers, the Olson family. As a young man, Chester Wilson worked in the area forests for the Forest Service, before marrying a teacher and settling down as a dairy farmer.[1]

In November 1956, the District Ranger for the Quinault region of Olympic National Forest announced Chester Ridge would be logged for the first time in summer 1957 to provide funds and a site for a forest fire lookout. The construction was planned for 1958.[2] The lookout station was a 20-foot-tall timber tower with a flat-roofed cabin on top.[3]

One of Chester Ridge Lookout's first staff was Wes Harner. He was a well-known WWII Aircraft Warning Service (AWS) plane spotter who teamed with his wife, Winona, as substitute staff for eight Quinault District AWS stations. When the AWS program ended in 1944, Wes went to fire training school and worked many summers in national forest fire lookouts. In 1958, he moved to Chester Ridge Lookout when the Burnt Hill Lookout was transferred to state forestry management.[4]

Little more is known about the fire tower on Chester Ridge. It continued to be identified as a fire lookout station on district fire management maps for 1959, 1960, and 1965.[5] It was destroyed in 1972.[6]

---

[1] *Lake Quinault Museum Newsletter*, Fall and Winter 2013, 1. Accessed at https://www.lakequinaultmuseum.org/pdf/2013-FALL-AND-WINTER-Landscape.pdf.
[2] *Port Angeles Evening News*, November 14, 1956, quoted in https://washingtonlookouts.weebly.com/chester-ridge.html.
[3] Kresek, *2015*, 22.
[4] Handwritten note on a copy of an excerpt from Winona Harner's *Journal* in Ray Kresek's research notes.
[5] US Forest Service Olympic National Forest Quinault Ranger District, *Plans 1959 Seen-Area Composite*; Fireman's Map 1960, Fireman Map 1965.
[6] Kresek, *2015*, 22.

31. CHESTER RIDGE LOOKOUT

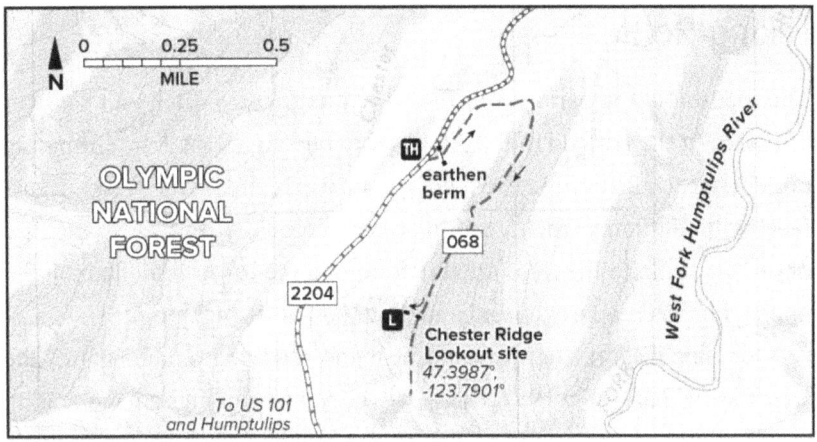

Hike Summary

Here is a short hike in pretty forest on a clear route most of the way to a lookout site with a nice array of artifacts. Hike 1 mile on a gravel road, leaving it for a short search through logging debris to find concrete and metal remains of the old lookout tower.

Getting There

- Drive US Highway 101 to milepost 112, a few miles north of Humptulips.
- Turn east on the Donkey Creek Road (FR 22) at signs to Wynoochee Lake Recreation Area.
- At 8.3 miles, turn left on FR 2204. There is a wide clearing on the right side of FR 22 at the junction.
- Drive north on FR 2204 until 12.2 miles from US Highway 101, where FR 2208 turns right and 2204 becomes a gravel road, continuing straight. Stay on FR 2204, cross the short, narrow Elk Creek bridge, then the high, impressive bridge over the West Fork Humptulips River. Pass the Newberry Creek Road, FR 2020, on the left; it is a potential shortcut to US Highway 101.
- Approximately 14.4 miles from US Highway 101, watch for a side road on the right, your hiking route. It is wide but little used as it is blocked with an earthen berm. Park at the start of this road.

Hiking Route

The road-blocking berm is reinforced with a shallow ditch on its downhill side. At the left end of the ditch is the road sign 068. A tree-thinning project here in 2014 replaced a cushioned moss and oxalis walking surface with a lumpy rock road that has gradually settled in.[7] Close observers will see the trees are thinner along the lower road than on the upper ridge as it approaches the lookout site at its high point.

Occasional large stumps stand near the road edge, remnants of the area's initial harvest in 1957. Foxgloves and alder saplings are reclaiming the road median smoothed in the 2014 road grading. Scotch broom is forming a hedge in sunnier sections of the shoulder. In the shade, oxalis, huckleberries, and ferns are recovering from the loggers' disruption.

The route generally takes the shape of a backwards letter "C," starting north, turning a corner toward the east, and curving south until it reaches the spur road leading to the lookout site. After 1.1 miles, the main road continues south into the forest and the curving spur runs around the south side of Chester Ridge's high point. Prior to the thinning project, the curving track led directly to the lookout site, but it is now covered with logging debris. Cross-country travel is easier than maneuvering through the bulldozed tree limbs and stumps that conceal the old roadbed. Follow game trails and your intuition through young trees to the high point on the ridge. Keep your eyes open for concrete blocks. Trees will grow to conceal them, but sharp eyes should find them at 47.3987°, -123.7901° and 1384-feet elevation. Three concrete footing blocks have been pushed together and one is buried to its top about 20 feet to the north, with the stub of a steel support beam sticking above the ground's surface.

These findings are much more satisfying than the piece of old cable at Humptulips Ridge. If the Humptulips Ridge Lookout trip left you frustrated, a visit to Chester Ridge should improve your mood.

---

[7] These changes were recorded in my trail notes for visits in 2015 and 2017.

32. COLONEL BOB LOOKOUT

RT Distance: 8.2 miles
High Point: 4492 feet
Elevation Gain: 3450 feet
Season: Jul-Sept
A Northwest Forest Pass or another federal lands pass is required.

History

Colonel Bob Mountain was first climbed in 1893 by Clark Pealer and brothers J. N. and Robert Lick. They left a cairn on the summit, naming the peak for a famous nineteenth century orator and Civil War veteran, Robert G. Ingersoll.[1] Colonel Bob Ingersoll was a champion of free speech, honest talk, and the separation of church and state.[2] The cairn was discovered by local climbers in 1930, and the US Geographical Naming Board made the name official in October the same year.[3]

Colonel Bob Lookout, 1943. (US Forest Service photograph.)

A 1931 newspaper article provides the first documentation of the lookout cabin's existence. In August that year, a Portland newspaper article described the Colonel Bob Lookout cabin and its contents in the National Forest while it served as a honeymoon setting: "They live in a glass house and enjoy real privacy. And at night they never bother to pull down the blinds." It was described as equipped with a telephone, Osborne firefinder, and windows all around. It was the husband's first season at Colonel Bob Lookout, suggesting the cabin construction could have been completed that year.[4]

---

[1] Harry M. Majors, *Exploring Washington*, Seattle, Van Winkle Publishing Co., 1975, 72.
[2] Susan Jacoby, *The Great Agnostic: Robert Ingersoll and American Freethought*, New Haven, Yale University Press, 2013.
[3] "Geographic Names Decisions," *Washington Historical Quarterly*, Vol. 22 No. 1, January 1931, 77.
[4] *Sunday Oregonian*, August 30, 1931, and [Albert Lea, Minnesota] *Evening Tribune*, August 11, 1933, quoted in https://washingtonlookouts.weebly.com/colonel-bob.html.

The two inventories of fire lookouts in the Northwest[5] and a book on Olympic National Forest history[6] record it as built in 1932 or 1933. An official Forest Service Structural Inventory listed it as built in 1934.[7] Regardless of its precise construction date, the 14×14-foot cabin stood on the rocky peak of Colonel Bob for more than thirty years. It was staffed in the summers until 1967. Spring and Fish report that it was damaged by heavy snow, then burnt that year.[8]

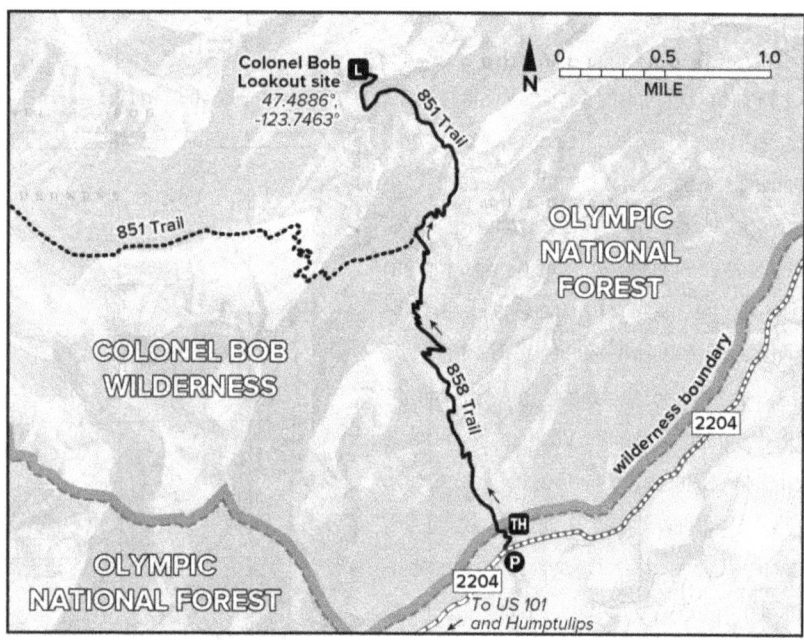

Hike Summary

This is a challenging hike in the Colonel Bob Wilderness of the Olympic National Forest. Aversions to the steep and rocky trail are tempered with an impressive variety of wildflowers. The bare rock lookout site on the summit offers amazing views of Lake Quinault, the Olympics, and the Pacific Ocean.

---

[5] Kresek, *1998*, 114; Spring and Fish, 197.
[6] Rooney, 39.
[7] It was quoted in https://washingtonlookouts.weebly.com/colonel-bob.html.
[8] Spring and Fish, 197.

Getting There

- Drive US Highway 101 to milepost 112, a few miles north of Humptulips.
- Turn east on the Donkey Creek Road (FR 22) at signs to Wynoochee Lake Recreation Area.
- At 8.3 miles, turn left on FR 2204. There is a wide clearing on the right side of FR 22 at the junction.
- Drive north on Forest Road 2204 for 10.8 miles, coming to the end of the paved road after 3 miles, shortly after FR 2208 turns right. There are signs pointing toward Pete's Creek Trailhead at junctions of the gravel road.
- Park on the right at Pete's Creek Trailhead.

Hiking Route

As there are two trails leading away from the Pete's Creek parking area, be sure to start on the north side of the road, headed uphill. Immediately enjoy the big trees and varied shrubs in the old wilderness forest. The trail is fairly soft underfoot and starts climbing gradually. The wildflower display begins with yellow monkeyflowers, white oxalis, and May lilies beside the narrow path. It crosses two creek beds—both dry when visited in August 2017, but known to surface some years. Farther along are actual metal mile markers high on left-hand trees, identifying 1 and 2 miles achieved. You are not alone if you feel you must have come a longer distance when you reach these signs.

At 2.4 miles, the two lower trails headed toward Colonel Bob from north and south meet. This provides some satisfaction, as do the views over the lower forest to the south. A signpost at the junction points to campsites at Mulkey Shelter (left, toward Lake Quinault) and Moonshine Flats (right, toward the summit). You have accomplished half the elevation gain by this junction too.

The trail zigzags in a northwesterly direction to this point. Now it starts a long curve northeastward before turning northwestward again to reach the summit. Very gradually, the tread becomes rockier and steeper. The need to take large steps is noticeable, both uphill and down. Flower varieties change as the elevation increases; bright white avalanche lilies appear where the snow has recently melted; beargrass plumes stand tall above long-leaved hummocks; tiny Merton's bluebells dot dense, chest-high shrubs.

Trail reports suggest many people climb up Colonel Bob before snow has left the area. It is likely that early-season hikers have cut the many trails near Moonshine Flats trying to find their way. Someone else fortunately added orange trail arrow signs high on a few trees to reduce confusion. Let them guide your route to the tarn that marks the start of the last 1000-foot gain to the summit.

In this last section of the trail, the Colonel Bob Wilderness reveals its panoramic potential. Occasional views between trees and at cliff edges show off dramatic rocky peaks nearby, as well as distant forested ridges. Flowers, like the vivid rosy penstemon, grace the trail edge. Near the top, the path takes a sudden turn to the west. This is the final approach. Ascend the rocky cap on steps cut roughly in basalt. The summit has little vegetation, but low, natural rock walls offer a little shelter from the chill winds that often sweep these heights. The views from the site are spectacular: to the north, Lake Quinault and Mount Olympus crown verdant forest landscapes, while Mount Rainier and higher Cascades grace the eastern horizon.

Aside from the stone steps carved in the last rise, only a bronze US Coast and Geodetic Survey marker near the northern edge of the summit remains from human structures that once stood here. The metal has been scuffed by long years of wear, but its date, 1952, and the letters stamped into its surface—COL—are still legible for exultant visitors to the 4492-foot peak today.

33. HUMPTULIPS AUXILIARY LOOKOUT

RT Distance: 6.0 miles
High Point: 1690 feet
Elevation Gain: 350 feet
Season: All Year
No pass or permit is required.

History

This was the last of the three fire lookouts named for the nearby Humptulips River. An Aircraft Warning Service (AWS) Humptulips lookout was the earliest. It was located just west of Highway 101 from 1942 to 1944.[1] We know now that a small moveable cabin was placed on the Humptulips Ridge Lookout site (on state forestland on the west side of Humptulips Ridge) sometime in the 1950s (see chapter 30) and moved to this site in the Olympic National Forest in 1958.

The Humptulips Auxiliary Lookout was located on the east side of the Humptulips Ridge, above the east fork of the Humptulips River. This fire watch station was unknown to most twenty-first-century fire lookout enthusiasts until Ray Kresek included its location as an undated "patrol point" in his 2019 fire lookout inventory.[2]

The flattened outhouse, downhill from the Humptulips Auxiliary Lookout site, 2018.

---

[1] See Chapter 30, "Humptulips Ridge Lookout," for more information about the three Humptulips Fire Lookouts.
[2] Ray Kresek, *2019*, 23.

Despite being lost to lookout historians for several decades, the auxiliary lookout was known to at least some national forest staff near the end of the twentieth century. In the 1990s, a forest ranger told hiking friends of mine there had been a fire lookout site at the end of Forest Road 2205-053. They found an outhouse standing a short distance downhill from the landing at that road end, but nothing more. My friends called the site "Humptulips—Joe's Lookout" for the location and the ranger who had told them where to find it.

In 2015, Forest Service staff at the Quinault Ranger Station were intrigued enough by my questions about this seemingly undocumented fire watch station to do some research. They said they were confident no lookout building had been constructed on the site, and they had no record of the outhouse. They did find three Quinault Ranger District Fire Management maps,[3] each with a slightly different label or icon on the fire lookout site on the east side of Humptulips Ridge. It was called Humptulips Auxiliary Lookout in 1959, Humptulips Ridge in 1960, and Humptulips Ridge Lookout (moveable) on the 1965 map. The symbols on the map legends indicate that it was considered a lookout station in 1960 and an auxiliary lookout or fireman's station in 1959 and 1965. With this lookout site generally unknown, it was reasonable for Ron Kemnow and other historians to attribute related records they discovered to the other fire watch station on Humptulips Ridge. For a decade or more, at least two popular websites attributed all "Humptulips Lookout" history to one station, rather than three.[4]

Sandy Floe wrote to blogger Eric Willhite in 2018, letting Willhite know he was the first person to staff that building at the Humptulips Auxiliary Lookout site, in spring 1958. Floe had grown up in a US Forest Service family at the Snider Ranger Station in the north Olympics. He was happy to share his experiences at the last Humptulips Lookout, and clarify the relationship between the two fire stations on the Humptulips Ridge.[5]

It is clear now that "moveable" on the 1965 fire management map referred to the portable ground house, or to a trailer driven to the road end for lookout use at times of high fire danger. As the better known Humptulips lookout site is named Humptulips Ridge, I will consistently include "Auxiliary" in this fire lookout station's name.

---

[3] Deborah McConnell and a coworker were my helpful contacts in the Quinault District office.
[4] https://washingtonlookouts.weebly.com/humptulips-ridge.html; http://www.firetower.org/lookout/us/wa/humptulips-ridge-lookout-site/.
[5] Eric Willhite shared the emails with me, and I followed up with a phone conversation with Mr. Floe.

33. HUMPTULIPS AUXILIARY LOOKOUT · 179

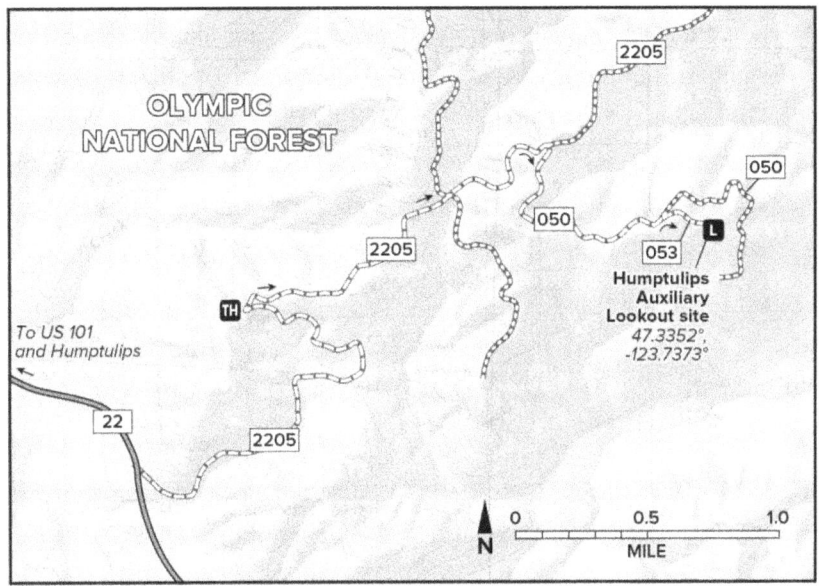

Hike Summary

This is a pleasant, mostly shady road hike with ridge views in the Olympic National Forest. Only a brief excursion to see the flattened outhouse requires leaving the gravel roads rebuilt in 2016. Signs posted on trees in the area indicate this section of the forest experienced a "heavy thinning" at about the same time. The thinning followed a severe winter windstorm that flattened many trees and the historical outhouse.

Getting There

- Drive US Highway 101 to milepost 112, a few miles north of Humptulips.
- Turn east on the Donkey Creek Road (Forest Road 22) at signs to Wynoochee Lake Recreation Area.
- At 8.3 miles, pass the junction with Forest Road (FR) 2204. There is a wide clearing on the right side of the main road at the junction.
- At 8.9 miles, make a left turn onto FR 2205, angling uphill. It has a small road sign on its right shoulder, near the intersection.

- At a four-way intersection with a gated road at a cleared area on the right, go left uphill to a lopsided T intersection at 10.7 miles from US Highway 101. The right branch, FR 2205, continues as the main road, while a less-traveled road goes left. Park at the broad T intersection for a 6-mile RT hike and great views into the West Humptulips Valley along the way. Alternatively, drive an additional 0.7 mile to park in a small, abandoned quarry for a shorter hike.

Hiking Route

The elevation at the T intersection is 1250 feet. Hike the forest-bordered road, enjoying views into the broad West Humptulips River Valley in the first 0.5 mile. The route gains a few hundred feet elevation along the way. At 0.7 mile from the T, pass an old quarry on the left. In a short distance, bypass spur roads that take off from both sides of 2205, which continues eastward.

The thinning project in 2016 trimmed trees close to the gravel road, as well as removing storm debris and fuel for wildfires. This improved views into densely wooded valleys to the north and up the slopes that dominate the right side of the road.

At 1.6 miles, there is a four-way intersection with FR 050. Turn right onto FR 050. The route to the lookout site is up spur road 053, which leaves 050 just before the larger track turns steeply downhill.

There have always been a couple of spur roads on the right side of 050, between the junction and FR 053. Two of them were rebuilt in the 2016 project, and should be easy to spot. The third is fading into the landscape.

At 2.6 miles, hike up FR 053. Large root balls with stumps have blocked its entrance to motorized visitors since the thinning project. The spur road's full name, 2205-053, appears on a wooden survey post on the right. The number 053 has been spray-painted on the uphill side of one broad stump as well.

Follow the gray gravel road to its end at 3.0 miles from the car, gaining 100-foot elevation on the 053 spur. At the end of the track, the hillside slopes down from the road surface to a natural bench, losing about 20 feet from the highest elevation of this eastward pointing ridge. The thinning did not improve the views from here, so the forested valley below can only be imagined.

Look carefully down through the trees at the end of the road. About 90 feet away is the flattened wooden outhouse, held in place by braided guy wires. The wires suggest that even the bench below the ridge end was windy, requiring tethers to keep the privy in place.

Enjoy the historical remains left on site by a modern forest management practice that restored the route to this old fire lookout, while protecting the forest from contemporary fire danger.

34. TWIN PEAK LOOKOUT

RT Distance: 8.0 miles
High Point: 1340 feet
Elevation Gain: 1250 feet
Season: All Year
No pass or permit is required.

History

This long-forgotten fire lookout site is located between the East and West Forks of the Humptulips River, south of the Olympic National Forest. It was not included in the inventories published in the twentieth century, but first surfaced on Eric Willhite's website in 2018. Eric originally found it on a 1930 Olympic Trail Guide map.[1] After Willhite's discovery, I found Twin Peak Lookout on several Olympic National Forest and Park maps dated as late as 1938.[2]

Every map that includes the Twin Peak Lookout also shows the better known Burnt Hill Lookout. Burnt Hill was located near the northwest corner of Township 21N Range 9W (a township is a 36-square-mile area), while Twin Peak Lookout was closer to the center of that township, in Section 22. From their consistent appearance together on federal forest maps, it is fair to conclude that both of these fire watch stations served the Olympic National Forest during the 1930s, although neither of these fire lookouts was within the national forest borders. Burnt Hill had a building, and was fairly close to US Highway 101, so it was retained through World War II as an important Aircraft Warning Service station. No record or remnant of a building at the Twin Peak site has been found, nor has it appeared on any maps after 1938.

After the war, the lack of a fire lookout between the forks of the Humptulips River probably contributed to the decision to build the Brittain Fire Lookout, a state forestry fire watch station[3] built in 1946 near the southeast corner of the same township, in Section 35.

---

[1] http://willhiteweb.com/washington_fire_lookouts/twin_peak/humptulips_204.htm.
[2] Olympic National Park and Olympic National Forest maps, 1930, 1934, 1938.
[3] The Burnt Hill and Brittain Lookouts are well documented, but their sites are located on private forest land requiring Rayonier Inc. access permits, so their histories and hike descriptions are not included in this collection.

34. TWIN PEAK LOOKOUT · 183

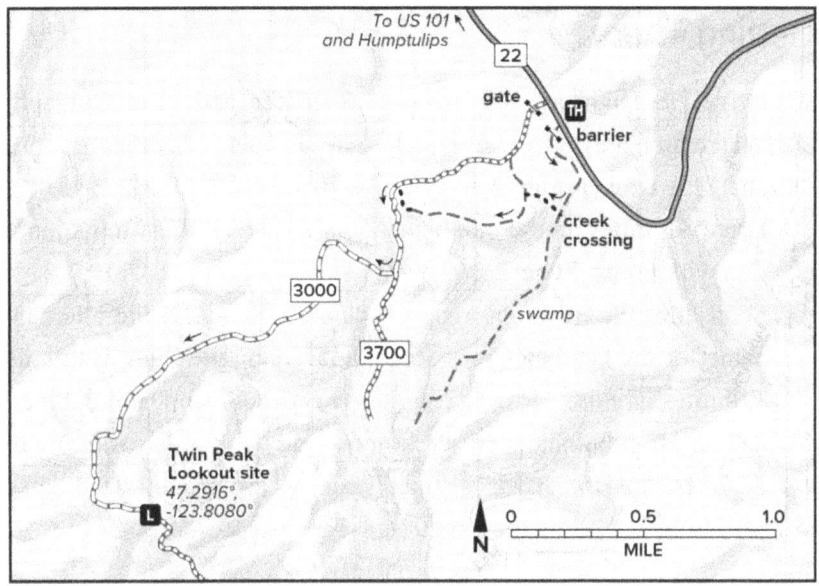

Hike Summary

This is an 8-mile hike in rolling countryside above the Humptulips River Valley, on a combination of abandoned private forest roads and well-maintained roads within the Grays Harbor County Timberlands. Start at a Green Diamond sign that welcomes non-motorized recreation use on its jersey-barrier-closed road. Accessing the county timberlands via this route requires an adventurous mile of hiking on untraveled roads, a narrow creek crossing, and 0.25-mile forest bushwhacking.

View of the Humptulips River Valley along the way to the Twin Peak Lookout site.

Getting There

- Drive US Highway 101 between Aberdeen and Lake Quinault. Watch for a brown Donkey Creek Road sign between mileposts 112 and 113. Turn east on Donkey Creek Road.
- Drive 8.3 miles on the old, paved Donkey Creek Road to its junction with Forest Road 2204 on the left.
- Soon after the junction, a sign for Forest Road 22, the alternate name for the Donkey Creek Road, appears on the right. Continue 1.6 miles on Forest Road 22, to a barricaded Green Diamond road and an informational sign. Park here. One-tenth mile earlier there is American Timber Management gate, where unauthorized entry is forbidden. Follow the directions on the signs.

Hiking Route

The narrow Green Diamond forest track parallels the paved national forest road for 0.25 mile before turning southwest. The road was closed late in 2018 and has rarely seen motorized traffic since. Between tall trees, all varieties of vegetation cover the road base. Wildflowers appear in small clusters throughout the hike. Coltsfoot and swamp lantern appear in early spring, followed by yellow violets, salmonberry, and trillium. Fat, ripe, evergreen blackberries and pearly everlasting brighten the understory in late summer.

At 0.4 mile, the gravel road turns left, while a low, overgrown earthen berm and a thick, fallen tree block the abandoned track ahead. Go straight—follow a narrow trail at the left end of an abandoned vinyl culvert, and descend a 15-foot hill to a narrow creek.

Cross the creek on convenient stepping-stones and find your way up the other bank. Go to the right and follow a broad track up a rise covered with vines for a few hundred yards. The track narrows, passing an abandoned recliner and stroller, then widens and meets a drivable road with a grassy median at 0.6 mile. Check landmarks here so you can recognize this junction when you return.

Turn left and continue to the end of the road. Enter the forest, following a trail that initially trends left, marked with pieces of red-and-blue or orange flagging tape. The red-and-blue flagging marks the northern boundary of the Grays Harbor County Timberlands in this section of the forest.

At 47.3081°, -123.7877°, turn right and follow a trail in a cut bank, heading north. This bushwhacking connector avoids the section of Road 3000 in the private timberlands managed by American Forest Management. This cross-country route is only 0.25 mile, but potentially challenging. Follow it downhill to a well-maintained, two-lane gravel road at coordinates 47.3089°, -123.7882°—close to two Grays Harbor County Timberland signs and orange stripes on roadside trees.

The forestland south and west of this sign—and the coordinates—are within public land, so hikers here should face no complaints of trespassing. Turn left on the road and continue south.

After another one-third mile the road splits, with Road 3700 going straight and the main road, 3000, turning right. Stay on 3000 as it heads northwest. At 2 miles from the start, pass a mossy side road on the right that immediately splits into two, and follow the Road 3000 as it turns south. There are occasional harvested areas along the road, but the mix of conifers—hemlock, fir, and cedar—provided a tall green wall along both sides of the route during hikes here in 2019 and 2020.

In the next mile, start to enjoy views into and across the broad green valley of the West Fork Humptulips River to the right. First gain filtered views through the trees, then broader perspectives at clearings along the road edge. The Twin Peak that provided the lookout's name appears on the other side of the West Fork of the Humptulips River.

Sun-loving wildflowers appear along the open ridge, too. On the left, you may be able to spot a tall wooden cross, a memorial marked "Eric 7-10-10," standing about 100 feet off the road. Such structures occasionally appear in the forest landscape, always a reminder to proceed with care when enjoying wildlands.

The road ascends about 450 feet in the last mile, providing opportunities for even broader views. Just before the last ascent, the route splits as it rounds a bend to head east-southeast toward the high point on the ridge. The two branch tracks meet again in a short distance, so take your pick. In the last 0.25 mile, the road heads east and tall peaks are visible between deciduous trees on the left side of the route. In spring, Colonel Bob and its sibling peaks at 4500 feet shine with broad patches of snow. They are 16 miles to the north, between the little traveled West Fork Humptulips River Valley in the foreground, and the popular Lake Quinault beyond.

The elevation at the high point of the road is 1340 feet. Scramble a few feet up the rise to the right of the track to visit a small clearing on the highest point in the area. This may well have been the Twin Peak Lookout site.

There are tall trees in all directions now, but the spot would have had grand views of both the west and east branches of the Humptulips River after a timber harvest. Just past the road summit, a side road heads downhill 0.1 mile to a logging landing. The end of this narrow track offers the best panorama of the broad West Fork Humptulips River Valley available on the hike.

Since no one has found physical artifacts from a fire lookout station here, knowledge of how the site was used in the 1930s remains a mystery. Like other early lookouts, it could have been served by a person living in a tent, making his sightings on an Osborne firefinder only supported by unstable posts.[4] Enjoy the views and consider any differences you notice between private forestland and the county forestlands along the route.

---

[4] See the history of the Anderson Butte Lookout, Chapter 48, for a contemporary description of such a fire lookout station.

KITSAP PENINSULA

Hikes accessible from State Route 3
in Mason and Kitsap Counties.

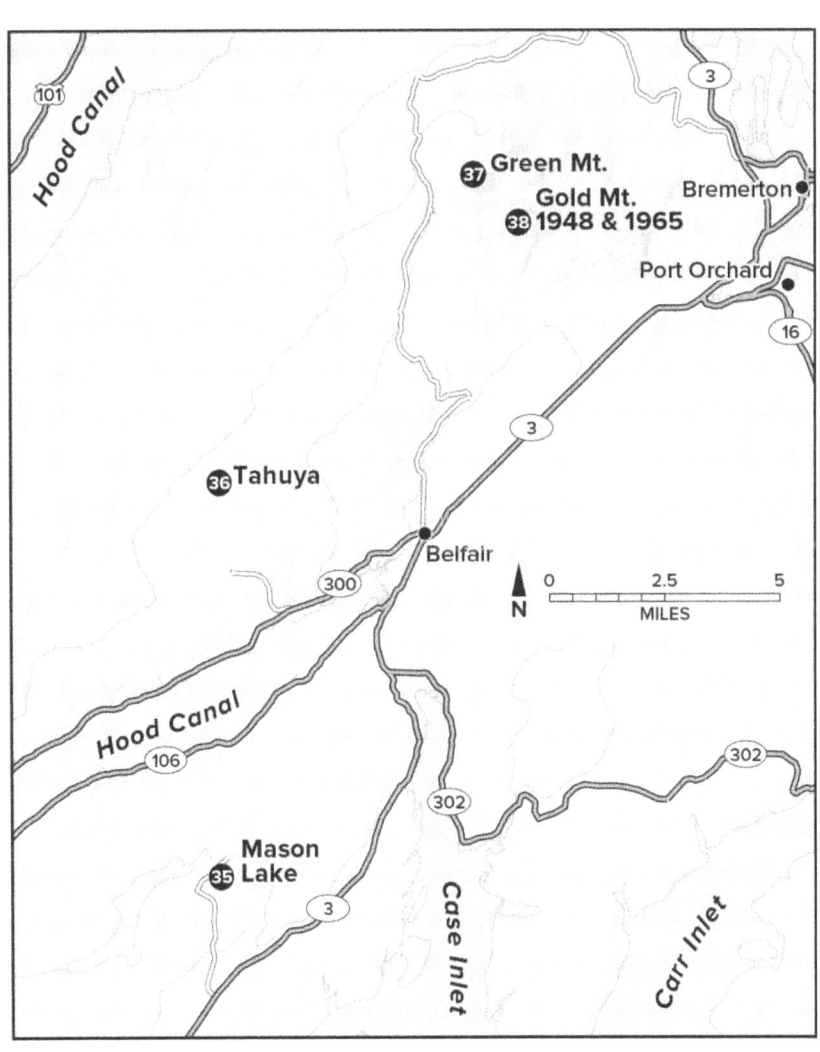

35. MASON LAKE LOOKOUT

RT Distance: 2.8 miles
High Point: 362 feet
Elevation Gain: 400 feet
Season: All Year
No pass or permit is required.

History

When the US military picked locations for aircraft observation stations during World War II, they selected the top of the low ridge east of Mason Lake, a dozen miles north of Shelton. In 1942, the Aircraft Warning Service (AWS) built a 14×32-foot cabin on the private forestland for volunteer plane spotters who worked there for the next two years. When the AWS stations were decommissioned in 1944, the Mason Lake cabin was transferred to the Washington Division of Forestry.[1] The state forestry department used it as a forest fire lookout post until 1961.[2]

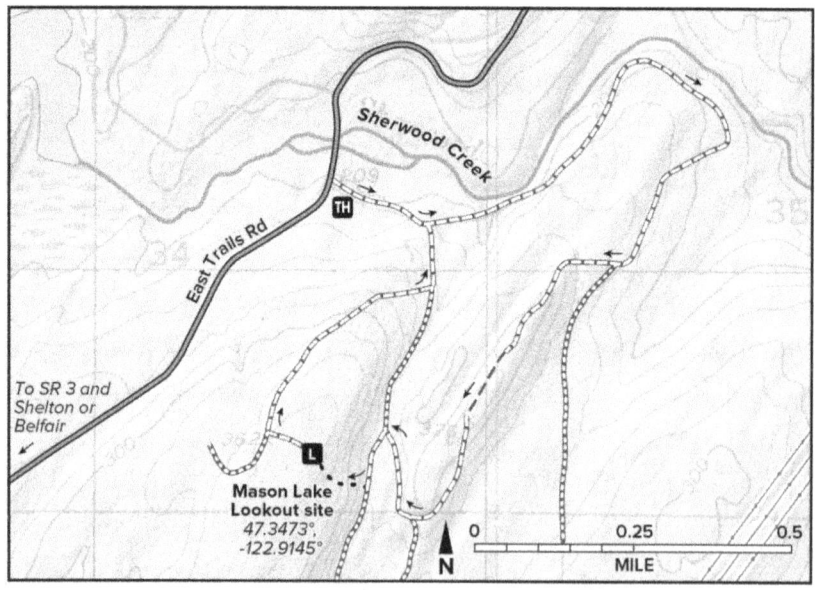

---

[1] [US Forest Service] Region 6, "Report of Aircraft Warning Service Stations," May 1, 1944, Sheet #II.
[2] Kresek, *2015*, 23.

Hike Summary

This is a low-elevation loop hike on a Green Diamond Resource Company tree farm. Follow the gated road along Sherwood Creek, then climb a couple of ridges to the lookout site with views in all directions. Mason Lake is close below but not visible. The Olympic Mountain range to the west, forested coastal ridges to the south, and Mount Rainier in the east are included in broad panoramic views. No artifacts of the lookout cabin remain.

Getting There

- Drive State Route 3 between Shelton and Belfair. Between mileposts 14 and 15, turn west on the Mason-Benson Road E., at a sign for Mason Lake County Park.
- Drive slightly more than 2.5 miles, passing Benson Lake on the left.
- Turn right on E. Trails Road (Mason Lake Road goes left). Drive almost 1 mile, turning right on a gated gravel road.
- Park on the road shoulder, being careful not to block Green Diamond Resource Company's gate, numbered 2385 on its left gate post. Non-motorized recreation is welcome here.

Hiking Route

Start up the moderate slope on the road beside Sherwood Creek. Trees close to the creek remain to protect water quality, offering a healthy mixed forest of cedar, hemlock, and fir to the left of the hiking route. Keep left at the first Y, continuing to parallel the creek, which burbles audibly in winter and spring. Enjoy occasional views of the water, flowing broadly between thick, grassy banks.

The road curves to the right (southeast) at about 0.6 mile, tracing the water course that has gained a swampy patch featuring swamp lanterns (often known as skunk cabbage), before disappearing into dense forest.

At 0.8 mile, our route turns southwest away from the creek. After another quarter mile, take a grassy branch road to the right, continuing the moderate ascent through the tree farm. At 1.33 miles, this road ends on the top of a 260-foot-tall hill. Fortunately, the route's continuation is visible a few hundred yards away on the next small hill to the southwest. This short section of the road was half-heartedly covered with logging debris after the last harvest here, around 2018. Step over the small, downed limbs, and continue your hike. Descending from the second hillock, a crossroad appears in a few hundred yards. When you reach it at 1.7 miles, turn right.

Hikers on the route to Mason Lake Lookout site. (Edythe Hulet photograph, courtesy of the photographer.)

This road curves downhill between two ridges. Another grassy side road appears on the left after one-eighth mile. Hike 100 yards on that road, cross a culvert, and turn right on an old jeep track climbing the second ridge at these coordinates: 47.3464°, -122.9125°. Use the jeep track indentations to guide you up the hill through evergreen huckleberry bushes and young fir trees. Keep to the right as you approach the top of the taller ridge. The goal is to meet an old road rising northwest to southeast from the other side of the hill. If you miss it, you will come to a southwest to northeast road a few hundred feet down the other side of the ridge. From there, you can turn right and find the route to the ridgetop that way.

No artifacts of the old fire lookout building have been found, but the high point of this area is beside the ridge-climbing road, at 365-feet elevation. The high point's coordinates are 47.3473°, -122.9145°. The best views are found here, too. The western horizon features Mounts Elinor and Washington's snowy peaks among the Olympics' rocky skyline. Turn around for a grand view of Mount Rainier and the Cascades.

When satisfied, descend the narrow road and turn right to complete the loop. This road's border includes alder, manzanita, and scotch broom among its fir trees. Bypass a lesser road on the left, headed west, but take the next left turn at a T. In another 0.1 mile, turn left again on the road that runs beside Sherwood Creek. You have completed the loop; the trailhead is just 0.15 mile ahead.

36. TAHUYA LOOKOUT

RT Distance: 6.5 miles
High Point: 443 feet
Elevation Gain: 260 feet
Season: All Year
A Discover Pass is required.

History

The community and river named Tahuya are close to Hood Canal, west of Belfair. An authority on place names says "Tahuya is derived from Twana Indian words 'ta' and 'ho-i,' meaning 'that done,' referring to something notable that happened here long ago."[1]

Only a few clues to this fire lookout's early history remain. A 1944 report of the Aircraft Warning Service (AWS) mentions a 14×32-foot cabin built by the AWS at Tahuya was to be transferred to the state of Washington at the end of that World War II program.[2] Washington Division of Forestry's Annual Report for the same year announced the only fire lookout tower they built that year was at Tahuya.[3] From practices at other AWS stations, we can assume the Tahuya cabin was built at the beginning of the wartime program in 1942. We don't know whether the state forestry tower replaced the cabin or the tower was added to the wartime facilities in what is now Tahuya State Forest.

The Kresek fire lookout inventory reports the tower was abandoned in 1957.[4]

Hike Summary

Trails to the Tahuya Lookout site from the southern edge of the Tahuya State Forest have been designed for motorized trail bikes and ATVs, but are open to hikers and horses as well. Popular with bikers—especially on weekends—some sections evolve into challenging, curvy, angled trails between infrequent regrading. The landscape alternates between open fields offering panoramic views of distant Olympic

---

[1] Phillips, 142.
[2] Washington Division of Forestry, Memo to File: A.W.S. Posts Retained for Use by State Under Cooperative Agreement with the U.S. Forest Service, [June, 1944].
[3] Washington Division of Forestry, *Thirty-Ninth and Fortieth Annual Reports . . . Ending October 31, 1944*, 11, quoted in https://washingtonlookouts.weebly.com/tahuya.html.
[4] Kresek, *2015*, 24.

Mountains over long-limbed rhododendrons, and forest trails bordered with dense salal and evergreen huckleberries. The Tahuya fire lookout site is not this hike's best feature, but offers an invitation to explore interesting state forestland near the southern end of Hood Canal.

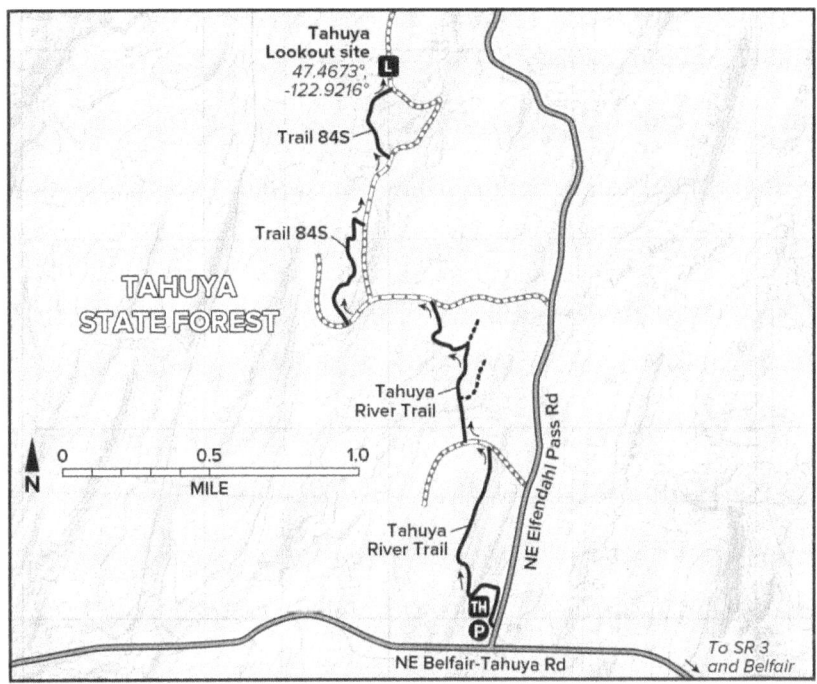

Getting There

- From State Route 3 in central Belfair, follow signs west toward Belfair State Park. After a couple of blocks, the road is labeled State Route 300.
- At 3.2 miles from State Route 3, pass Belfair State Park on the left.
- At 3.6 miles, turn right on the Belfair-Tahuya Road.
- Follow this road uphill and away from the water. At 5.5 miles from State Route 3, turn right on N.E. Elfendahl Pass Road.
- In 100 feet, turn left into the first parking lot and park.

Hiking Route

Leave the north side of the parking lot on the unsigned gravel path that parallels the N.E. Elfendahl Pass Road; follow it until the path intersects the Tahuya River Trail in a short distance. Trees on both sides of the road were harvested in 2015, but the landscape has recovered quickly with shrubs and conifers.

Turn left at the trail junction and see the first of several pairs of 6-foot long fence railings at the edge of the forest intended to limit the width of ATVs using the trail. Signs identify this as the Tahuya River Trail and the fencing as a 48-inch gateway for ATVs. The first of many young pines appear here under tall fir trees. The new forest will be more diverse than earlier tree plantations here.

At one-third mile, the path angles north to traverse a low ridge. In another 0.5 mile, a sign warns of an approach to a stop sign at a road crossing, a reminder that many trail users ride motor bikes. In 2021, a blue-and-white *Trail left* sign at the road crossing guides traffic to turn left and hike this one-lane gravel road for 0.1 mile, then turn right at another Tahuya River Trail sign. This section of trail passes under tall firs that provide a little shade and sometimes share a comfortable breeze. The understory, dominated by rhododendrons, salal, and sword ferns, also includes wildflowers and young evergreens.

A bridge crossing an unnamed creek on the way to the Tahuya Lookout site.

After beginning with common daisies, dandelions, self-heal, and foxgloves near the parking lot, the variety of wildflowers along this section of the trail is impressive. The open fields are highlighted with native rhododendron shrubs, many covered in early summer with the big pink blossoms characteristic of Washington's state flower. Other flowering plants sometimes seen here are tiger lilies, penstemon, lupine, star flower, thimbleberries, and strawberries. The biggest surprise is the sight of tall, creamy beargrass blossoms, either bordering the trail or popping up among the rhododendrons. They represent an Olympic variety that ignores the Cascades' standard of 3000-feet elevation for these distinctive flowers.[5] They provide a special treat for wildflower fans in the lowlands.

At 1.1 miles, cross the little creek on a narrow metal bridge with wooden decking. Continue north toward the Tahuya Lookout site, bypassing a branch of the Tahuya River Trail heading east on the north side of the waterway.

At about 1.3 miles, another stop sign and a wooden gateway alert hikers and bikers to a trail junction labeled with only another *Trail left* sign, and lavender vinyl diamonds fastened to trail-side tree trunks. At about 1.7 miles, turn left on a broader track, which ends in about 0.1 mile, at a road angling left and right. Turn left.

At 2 miles, turn right on a path marked Trail 84S. In about 0.25 mile, take the right branch at a Y. The 84S snakes northward under tall firs in an open forest, with rhodies and foxgloves at their feet. Breaks in the mature forest at the western edge of the younger tree plantation allow occasional views of the snow-peaked Olympic Mountains.

This section of trail ends at a two-lane gravel road. Turn left and walk the road for almost 0.5 mile. To the left of the road are indications of incomplete trail reconstruction after a timber harvest, 2015 to 2018. Pass a road intersection on the right. When the road curves right, turn left into the forest and resume Trail 84S when its sign appears about 100 feet from the road at the edge of thick forest. This section of trail 84S is a braided route, with lavender vinyl diamonds on the trees offering reassurance that we haven't lost the way.

---

[5] Mark Thompson, "Low Elevation Beargrass on the Olympic Peninsula" [thesis], 2015, accessed at: http://depts.washington.edu/uwbg/research/theses/Mark_Thompson_2015.pdf.

At 3.2 miles, the 84S crosses a road and heads northeast. The lookout site is northwest, so turn left and hike on the intersecting road. In a short distance, the one-and-a-half lane gravel route curves north. Very soon—at 3.25 miles from the trailhead—there is a small clearing in the dense forest beside the broader gravel road, just past a side road on the left. This is the location of the former Tahuya forest fire lookout. It has only slightly higher elevation than the surrounding land, 443 feet. The coordinates are 47.4672°, -122.9217°.

I first visited this clearing in 2003 when the fir trees here were thin and the shrubbery, sparse. We found broken concrete and a galvanized iron angle-beam at the site. Now the clearing is surrounded with salal, dense evergreen huckleberry bushes, rhododendrons, and young pines under tall firs. An area across the road has been clearcut at least once since my initial hike here. It is possible that some remnants of the old tower remain somewhere in the dense vegetation. If you search successfully, be sure to share news of your find.

37. GREEN MOUNTAIN LOOKOUT

RT Distance: 7.4 miles
High Point: 1639 feet
Elevation Gain: 1200 feet
Season: All Year
A Discover Pass is required.

History

The high point on Green Mountain, in the Green Mountain State Forest in Kitsap County, once offered a full circle of views from Puget Sound and the Cascades to the Olympic peaks—and forests in all directions. It was for this commanding view the private Washington Forest Fire Association chose the site in 1929 for one of the first four privately funded fire lookout towers in the state. The organization worked with the State Division of Forestry[1] to design and build a 50-foot wooden tower with a ladder for climbing to the viewing platform. The platform had waist-high walls and a roof to give firewatchers some protection. A nearby tent was supplied for overnight stays.[2]

From 1929 to 1963, a total of four wooden towers were built on this viewpoint. The Association's 1931 report mentions the Green Mountain Lookout tower had been rebuilt that year to 94 feet, and was expected to provide wildfire protection to Mason, as well as Kitsap County.[3]

The first Green Mountain Lookout tower, 1929. (From the *1929 Annual Report of the Washington Forest Fire Association*, courtesy of the Washington Forest Protection Association.)

---

[1] Until 1957, state forests were managed by the Washington Department of Conservation and Development, Division of Forestry. It became part of the new Department of Natural Resources in 1957.
[2] Washington Forest Fire Association, *Twenty-Second Annual Report*, 1929, 13-14.
[3] Washington Forest Fire Association, *Twenty-Fourth Annual Report*, 1931, 8-9.

As one of its last projects in Washington State, the Civilian Conservation Corps replaced the fire tower here for the wartime Aircraft Warning Service (AWS) in 1942.[4] That version was 84-feet tall, including a live-in cabin on top. A married pair of plane-watchers occupied it the same year it was built. An AWS inspector reported that they worked very efficiently, but should probably have a ground cabin as well, as the winds in the tower could be strong and noisy, and they would need to stand watch through the wartime winters.[5]

The Washington Department of Natural Resources (DNR) built the last replacement in 1963, after the guy wires supporting the tall tower were removed by boy scouts who thought it had been abandoned.[6] The last tower was 50 feet tall, including a cabin on top. State forestry management decided to replace Green Mountain lookout staff with air patrols in 1969.[7] The tower was removed in 1971.

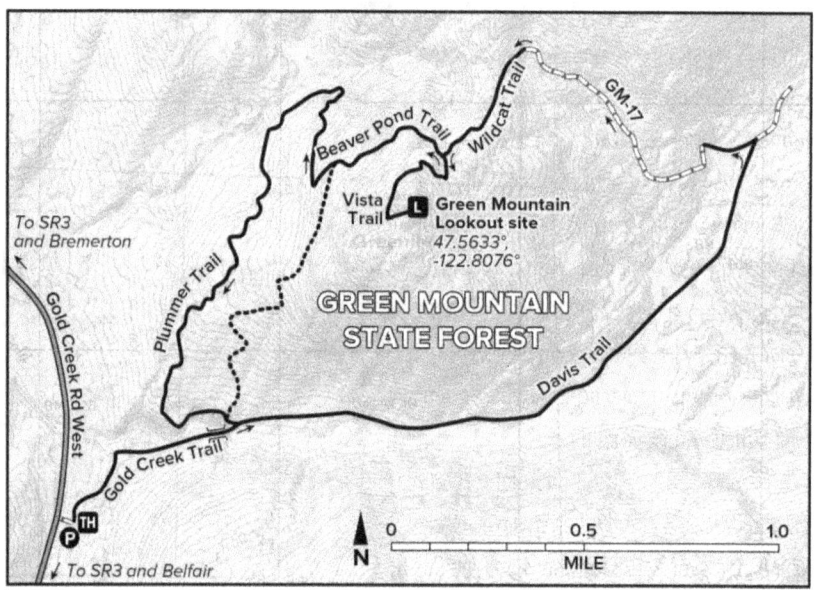

---

[4] Spring and Fish, 199.
[5] AWS Supervision memo, June 16, 1942, accessed at https://willhiteweb.com/Washington _climbing/green_mountain_kitsap/green-mountain-observers.jpg.
[6] http://willhiteweb.com/washington_climbing/green_mountain_kitsap/kitsap_peninsula _hiking_063.htm.
[7] *The Daily Chronicle*, October 6, 1969, quoted in https://washingtonlookouts.weebly.com /green-mountain.html.

37. GREEN MOUNTAIN LOOKOUT · 199

Hike Summary

Green Mountain State Forest offers a maze of trails for hikes, mountain bikes, horses, and motorized trail bikes. Wheeled traffic is often heavy on weekends. The length of this 7.4-mile loop can be adjusted with map study and navigation. Enjoy wonderful views of the forest, water, and mountains—and spectacular rhododendrons in season. *Map Note*: At this time, the only accurate trail-maps for this state forest are available online from private parties, not DNR.

Getting there from Bremerton (coming from the east or north)

- From Bremerton, take Kitsap Way west from State Route 3.
- Drive 1.4 miles and use the left turn lane to take a slight left on Northlake Way NW.
- At 2.5 miles from State Route 3, take a slight left onto the Seabeck Highway NW.
- At 5.5 miles, take the second exit at a traffic circle to NW Holly Road.
- At 9.7 miles, turn left onto Lake Tahuya Road NW.
- At 10.9 miles, turn left onto Gold Creek Road W.
- At 12.8 miles, turn left into the Gold Creek Trailhead parking lot of the Green Mountain State Forest. There is a brown sign announcing the trailhead. Park between the first trailhead and the outhouse.

Getting there from Belfair (coming from the south)

- Follow signs toward Belfair State Park from the traffic light at the junction of State Route 3 and NE Clifton Lane.
- In two blocks, turn right at the stop sign onto NE Old Belfair Highway.

- At 3.5 miles from State Highway 3, turn left on NE Bear Creek/DeWatto Road.
- At 6.6 miles, turn right onto Gold Creek Road W.
- At 9.0 miles, turn right into the parking lot. Small signs just before the entrance announce the approach to Gold Creek Trailhead. Park between the trailhead and the outhouse.

Hiking Route

Start at the Gold Creek trailhead opposite the entrance to the parking lot. After a quarter-mile, the namesake creek appears in a canyon on the left. Small and quiet in summer, this section of Gold Creek features an interesting waterfall tumbling over a jumble of rocks in rainy seasons.

A sturdy wooden bridge crosses the creek at one of its beauty spots, close to the junction of the Gold Creek Trail and the Davis Trail. Follow the Davis Trail across the second bridge and enjoy slow elevation gain as you hike another 1.5 miles through the forest. After the bridges, Gold Creek becomes the domain of beavers, punctuated with beaver dams and cattail-bordered ponds on the right side of the pathway. A few of the ponds feature well-built beaver lodges. The duck and bird populations vary with the seasons, but mallards and red-wing blackbirds are reliable sights most of the year.

A beaver pond beside the hiking route to the Green Mountain Lookout site.

At 2.2 miles, there is a T junction with a stop sign for bicycles just past a small creek crossing; the Davis Trail turns right. Your route turns left and parallels the creek. In another 0.25 mile, the trail emerges onto a drivable road. Turn left and continue north on the woodsy route close to the narrow stream. A nice mixed forest borders the water, with firs, maples, alders, sword ferns, salal, and flowering shrubs offering a full spectrum of the shades of green.

This idyll pauses at a triangle intersection about 2.5 miles from the start. Turn left on the GM-17 route.[8] Forest is on the left and a hillside of young conifers, on the right. The trail starts gaining elevation in earnest here. The harvested areas on higher hills offer views to the east looking out to Puget Sound and the distant Cascade Mountains.

At 3.5 miles, turn left between trees onto the Wildcat Trail and follow it through open forest featuring leggy native rhododendrons. The higher the trail, the denser the rhody population. In late spring, this section of the route offers an amazing display of the big pink blossoms.

After leaving this part of the Wildcat Trail, cross the road that is headed up to the Vista parking lot. The road and trail cross several times, offering a choice between trail and road hiking each time. The road is only open to vehicles in the summer, so hikers really do have a choice most of the year. Follow Vista Trail signs to the broad parking lot with an outhouse, a large map on a signboard, and several picnic tables. The Vista Trail continues uphill beside the map board. Ascend the narrow, rocky trail to the summit ridge, pass a gated road and a couple of picnic tables, and emerge on the rocky top of Green Mountain.

A 1979 guidebook described the fire lookout as being on a "rock-knob cliff-edge site."[9] Four concrete footing blocks surrounding the picnic table on the rocky summit confirm the location where the tower stood. A chain-link fence at the cliff edge protects visitors from falling, although the vegetation and the natural rocky bench a few feet below don't look as precipitous as the old description suggests.

---

[8] A 3-foot-tall-brown vinyl road sign near the junction has reliably identified the route since early this century. On a 2019 visit, it was obscured by tall bracken, but still there.
[9] Harvey Manning, *Footsore 4*, Seattle, The Mountaineers, 1979, 212.

Take a break on top and enjoy the views and the artifacts. The only opening in the forest now is toward the east, but it offers downtown Seattle, Bellevue, Cascades, and Mount Rainier on a clear day. Trees block views to the west, but the return route includes trails that provide panoramas in that direction.

For the 7-mile-plus route, return on the Vista Trail and follow it to a junction with the Beaver Pond Trail. Turn right onto the Beaver Pond Trail; follow it for 0.5 mile, enjoying westward views of Hood Canal, the Olympic Mountains, and little Tahuya Lake. Take a left on Plummer Trail and follow it for a mile. Enjoy the sounds of Gold Creek and its waterfall on your right, about 0.75 mile down the Plummer Trail. Follow that path another one-eighth mile to its junction with the Gold Creek Trail, shortly before the junction with the Davis Trail, between the two bridges.

Turn right and re-cross the smaller wooden bridge over Gold Creek. Follow the trail through the forest about 0.5 mile to return to the trailhead. This is the trail that brought you into Green Mountain State Forest at the start of your hike. Views and perspectives are different coming and going. Can you recognize the trail on the way out?

38. GOLD MOUNTAIN LOOKOUTS

RT Distance: 8 miles
High Point: 1761 feet
Elevation Gain: 1600 feet
Season: All Year
A Discover Pass is required.

History

In 1948, the Washington State Division of Forestry raised a 75-foot Navy surplus steel tower with a small observation cabin on the high point of the long Gold Mountain Ridge. That cabin was too small for staff lodging, so a 14×18-foot ground house was built as well.[1] In 1965, the department replaced the tall tower with a 50-foot wooden tower with a live-in cabin about 0.25 mile away on the eastern end of the same ridge.[2] The terrain suggests the second tower was built to provide clear views of state forests south of the ridge, leaving northern views to the tower on nearby Green Mountain. Historical lookout inventories report the last Gold Mountain Lookout was "destroyed 1972."[3]

A half-dozen television stations and communication companies have erected their relay towers along the 2-mile ridge since that time. Trees have grown tall on the summit, hiding the route foresters took to the first lookout tower. Panoramic views across clearcut patches on the ascent show why Gold Mountain was a good location to watch for fires.

Gold Mountain Lookout tower construction nearing completion, 1965. (Photograph from the June 1965 Department of Natural Resources' *Totem Magazine*.)

---

[1] Washington Division of Forestry, *Forty-Third and Forty-Fourth Annual Reports for the Period Commencing January 1, 1947, and Ending October 31, 1948*, 24.
[2] Kresek, *2015*, 22.
[3] Kresek, *2015*, 22.

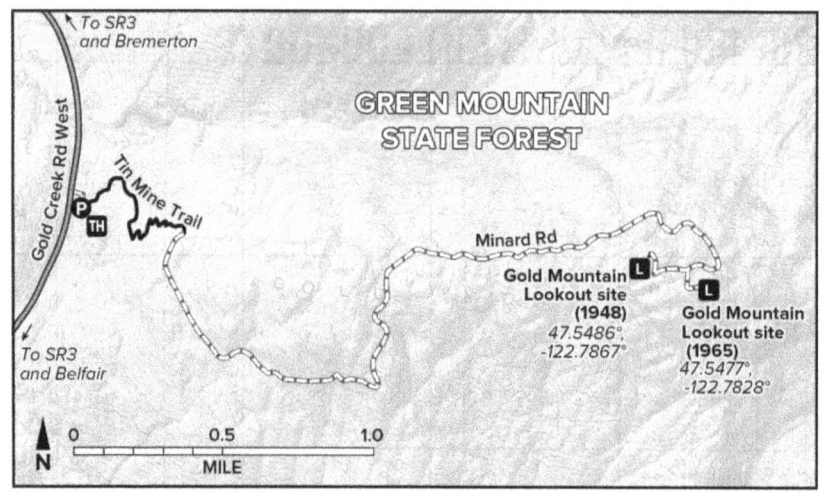

Hike Summary

This hike visits both Gold Mountain Lookout sites. It begins at the Tin Mine trailhead in the Green Mountain State Forest and shares a narrow trail with mountain bikes for part of its ascent. Bikers appear mostly on weekends and are generally courteous. The trail connects with an old forest road crossing the Gold Mountain Ridge on a route that primarily serves the modern communication towers standing tall above the ridge. One lookout site is easily reached by road. Access to the second requires a short, adventurous, cross-country traverse.

Getting there from Bremerton (coming from the east or north)

- From Bremerton, take Kitsap Way west from State Route 3.
- Drive 1.4 miles and use the left turn lane to take a slight left on Northlake Way NW.
- At 2.5 miles from State Route 3, take a slight left onto the Seabeck Highway NW.
- At 5.5 miles, take the second exit at a traffic circle to NW Holly Road.

- At 9.7 miles, turn left onto Lake Tahuya Road NW.
- At 10.9 miles, turn left onto Gold Creek Road W.
- At 12.8 miles, turn left into the Gold Creek Trailhead parking lot of the Green Mountain State Forest. There is a brown sign announcing the trailhead. Park between the outhouse and the picnic tables.

Getting there from Belfair (coming from the south)

- Follow signs toward Belfair State Park from the traffic light on State Route 3 in the center of Belfair.
- In two blocks, turn right at the stop sign onto NE Old Belfair Highway.
- At 3.5 miles from State Highway 3, turn left on NE Bear Creek/DeWatto Road.
- At 6.6 miles, turn right onto Gold Creek Road W.
- At 9.0 miles, turn right into the parking lot. Small signs just before the entrance announce the approach to Gold Creek Trailhead. Park between the outhouse and the picnic tables.

Hiking Route

Follow the Tin Mine Trail marked for non-motorized use that starts to the right of the outhouse. In 2020, this trail name appears on signs in the southern part of this state forest, but not on the Department of Natural Resources' website. That map was dated 2009.

Hike 0.25 mile on a narrow trail through a shady forest to a junction marked with a metal diamond ◊ trail sign on a tree trunk on the left side of the main trail. Take the side trail on the right, which has been designed primarily as a challenge for mountain bikes. The rough path remains in the trees for a few hundred feet, then starts its climb south on the hillside, clearcut in 2019. A lot of logging debris remains, but young conifers and small shrubs—notably sword ferns, Oregon grape, salal, and lupine—have been doing their best to restore the landscape. Views of the Olympic Mountains, Hood Canal, and Lake Tahuya emerge to the north and west as you ascend the hill.

The trail winds steeply up the hill, gaining about 500 feet in 0.55 mile. Signs at the ridgetop indicate the Tin Mine Trail continues to the east from its junction with a one-lane forest road.

Turn right on the road to continue toward Gold Mountain Ridge. The road quickly turns south. On its left side is an abandoned gravel pit. The trees in this area were harvested early in this century, and their replacements are growing quickly. Continue on this track for 0.7 mile. In spring, watch for purple lupine and the bright pink blossoms of native rhododendrons along the roadside.

At 1.5 miles from the trailhead, the track meets the main gravel road on Gold Mountain Ridge. This is Minard Road, a name that appears on historical maps of the route to the Gold Mountain fire lookout. Continue traversing the ridge toward the northeast. This section of forest was harvested between 2010 and 2015. Some of the best views of the hike are gained here, and the best chance of seeing wildflowers. In spring, enjoy early columbine, orange native honeysuckle, and many native rhododendron shrubs with their large pink blossoms—plus the hummingbirds that cavort above them. Mission, Tiger, and Panther Lakes are visible in the foreground, downhill to the southwest. A snippet of Hood Canal can be seen far south of the lakes, large segments of Puget Sound's waters appear to the southeast, with Mount Rainier floating above them all on clear days.

The ridgetop is reached in about 0.25 mile as you pass a gate identifying the large installation down its spur road as belonging to KCPQ, Channel 13. That development includes a tower tall enough to disappear in passing clouds. Something in the complex hums insistently as hikers reach its northern boundary, distracting briefly from forest views and bird songs.

Turn east and continue on the ridge. Pass a gated road on the right that leads to a tower belonging to KTBW-TV, Tacoma. Views emerge on the left as well, of a comparable tower on Green Mountain, a mile or two to the north.

The road continues eastward. At 2.5 miles, keep right at a Y junction. The ridge road reenters the forest where openings allow broad views east and north. After trending downhill, the route circles the eastern end of the ridge. As the gravel track turns south and west to complete the curve, it climbs steeply. At 3.5 miles, the road splits into three tracks.

Native rhododendrons, Washington's state flower, in full bloom along the route to the Gold Mountain Lookout sites.

The paved left spur leads south to a metal tower visible over the trees. Head for the tower, passing between old yellow gateposts, and follow the steep road a short distance down and up the next hill. In the trees immediately north of the securely fenced communication tower, find several concrete footing blocks at 1570 feet elevation. One stands almost 4 feet tall on the edge of the clearing, while others are partly hidden under vegetation and soil. I like to think these blocks supported the 50-foot wooden lookout tower built here in 1965, but their current positions indicate they have been moved. It is also possible that some of these tall blocks supported a different kind of tower, also lost in history.

After considering the site's remains and drawing your own conclusions, return to the main road. Continue west another 0.25 mile to an ungated road on the right. Follow it a short distance to two communication towers. The elevation of the second lookout site is 1761 feet, 20-feet higher. Knowing the Gold Mountain high point is nearby and a little higher, look through the trees to a slightly taller hill to the west.

For a fairly clear route, walk around the fence surrounding the nearest communication tower. The forest has little undergrowth and the 300-foot-wide valley has gentle slopes, providing an easy descent and zigzag up the final rise. Follow open paths to the top and discover an open area on the higher rocky knoll covered with moss. Near the summit, a bronze disc set in concrete crowns the high point. It is engraved *US Coast and Geodetic Survey* and has GOLD HILL 1954 stamped into its surface. About 6 feet to the west a bit of concrete sticks out, with the stub of an angle beam barely visible above the vegetation. I have found three angle beams on this site located just far enough apart to support the original 75-foot steel tower. Perhaps you can find the fourth angle, or the bronze Reference Mark No.1 disc that stood in the center of the tower supports.[4]

You may also meet other explorers while visiting Gold Mountain. This peak is identified on the internet as both the high point of Kitsap County and as a geocache site.

---

[4] US National Geodetic Survey, "Data Sheet PID SY5508 GOLD HILL LOOKOUT TOWER"; https://www.ngs.noaa.gov/cgi-bin/ds_mark.prl?PidBox=SY5508.

OLYMPIC PENINSULA SOUTH

Hikes accessible from US Highway 101
south of Potlatch State Park on southern Hood Canal,
and from the Wynoochee Valley Road in Grays Harbor County.

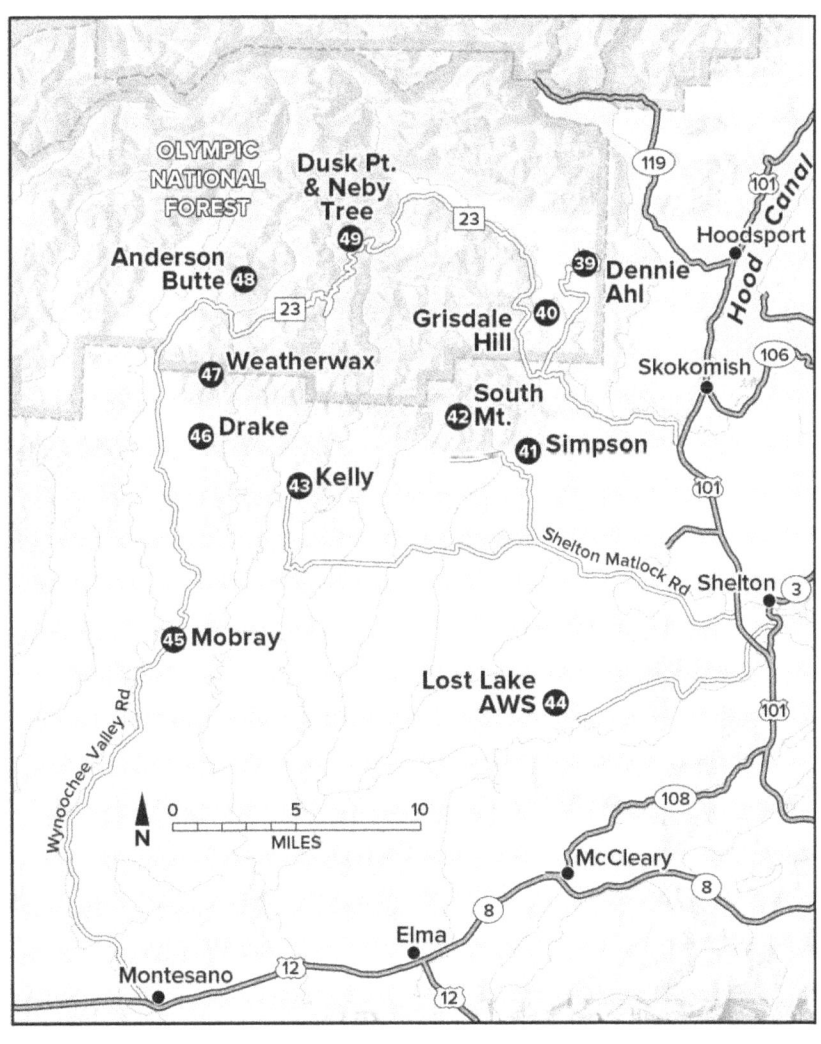

39. DENNIE AHL LOOKOUT

RT Distance: 3.0 miles
High Point: 2004 feet
Elevation Gain: 450 feet
Season: All Year
No pass or permit is required.

History

A 1942 Aircraft Warning Service (AWS) memo states the "Camp 3 lookout" cabin (later known as the Grisdale Hill Lookout) was expected to be moved to Gibbons Ridge, northwest of Dennie Ahl Hill, as some thought this was a better location for plane-watching than the Grisdale Hill location.[1] Despite this plan, the Forest Service built the 30-foot-tall Dennie Ahl lookout tower on a hilltop between two forks of the Skokomish River in 1943.[2]

Dennie Ahl Lookout, 1952, with south Olympic peaks in the background. (Olympic National Forest photograph, curated by Steve Ricketts.)

Dennie Ahl (also known as Denny) had a long career with the Olympic National Forest, and was well regarded by coworkers and his bosses. He started working for the Olympic National Forest as a seasonal forest guard in 1905. By the 1930s, he was known as "one of the region's top logging scalers." After he died of a heart attack while rowing across Lake Cushman to service a fire crew[3] in July 1941,[4] forest administrators

---

[1] July 28, 1942, memo from M. L. Merritt, Liaison Officer, Seattle to Jason Frankland, Portland, found in the Aircraft Warning Service files in the National Archives at Seattle by Eric Willhite, accessed at http://www.willhiteweb.com/washington_fire_lookouts/dennie_ahl_lookout/mason_county_419.htm.
[2] Kresek, *2015*, 22.
[3] Rooney, 10, 31, 91.
[4] "Notice to Creditors by the Administratrix of the Estate of John Dennie Ahl," *Shelton Mason County Journal*, July 31, 1941, 7.

named this lookout in his honor. At the dedication ceremony, "Denny's widow, M Ahl . . . took a silver flask out of her purse and we all had a drink to Denny's memory."[5] In 1957, the Forest Service also gave his name to a tree nursery, the Dennie Ahl Seed Orchard, not far from the lookout.[6]

The lookout tower was used as an emergency fire watch station in the 1950s[7] and taken down in 1971.[8]

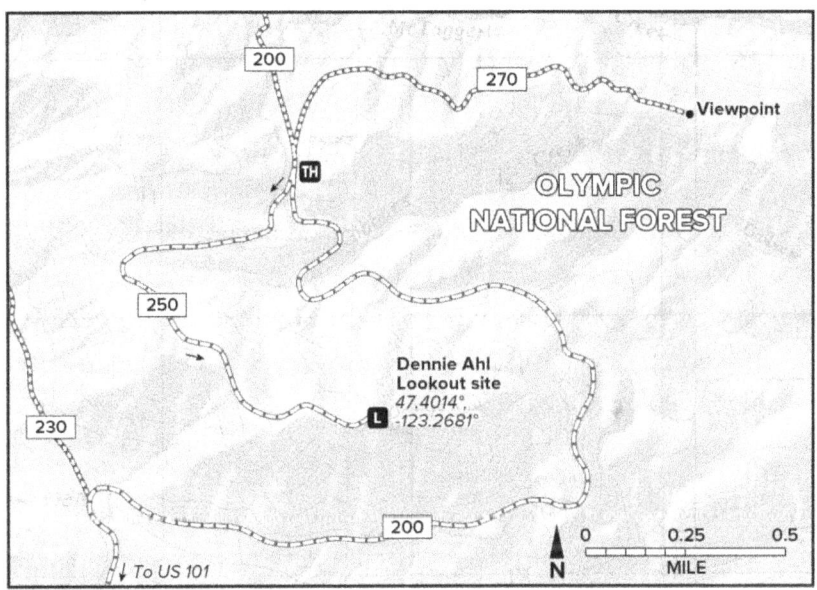

Hike Summary

This short hike uses lightly traveled national forest roads near the South Fork Skokomish River basin. Timber thinning started in the area in 2018, improving views into the Olympics along the ascent. The lookout site has trees obscuring some views but offers a panorama across Hood Canal toward Mount Rainier and the south Cascades.

---

[5] Chriswell, 61.
[6] Rooney, 91.
[7] *Port Angeles Evening News*, May 18, 1956, quoted in http://washingtonlookouts.weebly.com/dennie-ahl.html.
[8] Kresek, *2015*, 22.

Getting There

- At the junction of US Highway 101 and State Route 106, turn west onto the Skokomish Valley Road. This road is famous for the salmon that swim across when the river floods, so be aware of flood warnings, especially after heavy rainstorms.
- At 5.5 miles from US Highway 101, turn right and head uphill on Forest Road (FR) 23.
- At 8.0 miles, take a sharp right turn on FR 2340.
- Cross the High Steel Bridge over the South Fork of the Skokomish River at 10.4 miles.
- At 12.5 miles, turn left on FR 200. (The main road has a sign for FR 2340 near the intersection.) There are minor side roads off FR 200, but none were signed or drivable in 2019.
- Stay on FR 200 until you have driven 17 miles from US Highway 101. At the junction of FR 200 and 250, park on the right shoulder of FR 200 or on the left verge of FR 250.

Hiking Route

The hike starts at the junction of FRs 200 and 250. The route climbs up mossy road 250 in a generally circular 1.5-mile path. The forest here was thinned in 2018, offering views into a healthy, second-growth Olympic Peninsula forest all along the way. Coltsfoot, violets, and oxalis blooms brighten the road edge in spring. Young deciduous trees—big leaf, vine maples, and alders—mix with conifers near the start of the hike. Douglas firs, hemlocks, and cedars dominate the upper forest. The thinning allows occasional views of snowy peaks to the west between the dark trees.

The route ends in a large clearing where a 6×6-foot concrete pad remains. It once held the lookout station's flagpole, southeast of the 30-foot-tall tower and high observation cabin.[9]

---

[9] US National Geodetic Survey, "Data Sheet PID SY1820 DENNIE RESET"; https://www.ngs.noaa.gov/cgi-bin/ds_mark.prl?PidBox=SY1820.

The wooden tower was anchored in large concrete footing blocks. The blocks were moved from the clearing, most likely by bulldozer, when the tower was removed in 1971. They are now located in the forest, northwest of, and a few feet lower than, the clearing. Three are fully visible and one is completely buried, with only a short length of rebar sticking out of the ground.

This hike can be extended by walking north about one-tenth mile on FR 200 to a side road, FR 270, on the right. Hike about 0.5 mile, to where that road emerges from the forest to wide views including Lake Kokanee (a smaller reservoir below Lake Cushman), Hood Canal, and the Cascades. Or drive south of the High Steel Bridge on FR 2340 to add Hike 40, a 4-mile roundtrip hike to Grisdale Hill Lookout, to your day.

40. GRISDALE HILL LOOKOUT

RT Distance: 4 miles
High Point: 1511 feet
Elevation Gain: 800 feet
Season: All Year
No pass or permit is required.

History

The Grisdale Hill forest fire lookout was located above the Skokomish Valley with clear views in all directions. It was initially named for the Simpson Timber Company's Camp 3, which stood at the foot of the hill to the southeast. The Camp existed from 1930 to 1947, and the Camp 3 L.O. appears on the 1930 Olympic National Forest map, but the date of the lookout's construction is not known.

Mr. and Mrs. Floyd Smith enjoyed a tour of the Forest Service lookout at Camp 3 in August 1939. "It proved an interesting visit, as the duties of a lookout scout are quite complicated."[1]

The WWII Aircraft Warning Service (AWS) used the station in 1942 and '43. It was listed among the short lookout towers in the Hoodsport District that were winterized for year-round service by enclosing the open area between their support posts.[2] In 1942, regional AWS management expected the Camp 3 lookout cabin to be moved to "Gibbons," a viewpoint northwest of Dennie Ahl Hill.[3] When the Forest Service completed the Dennie Ahl Lookout tower in 1943, the AWS duties were transferred there.[4]

It is clear that the name of the lookout station was changed after World War II and the AWS program. Grisdale Hill was named for one or both of the Grisdale brothers, George and Bill, who came from Montreal in Canada to work for their uncle, Sol Simpson, at the Shelton-based Simpson Timber Company in the late 1890s. At least one of them spent his entire working life with the Simpson Company.

---

[1] *Shelton-Mason County Journal*, September 3, 1939, as quoted in https://washingtonlookouts.weebly.com/grisdale-hill.html.
[2] Chriswell, 53.
[3] Memorandum from M.L Merritt, Liaison Officer, Seattle to James Frankland, Portland, dated July 28, 1942.
[4] The transfer is shown with an arrow on the *Olympia Filter Station Map*, October 1943, accessed at http://willhiteweb.com/washington_fire_lookouts/aircraft_warning_service/locations_091.htm.

Ray Kresek's fire lookout inventory reports the US Forest Service built a tower here in 1946.[5] It was likely a replacement structure, following a large wildfire that occurred that year at Camp 3. During that era, the site offered a clear view of the famous High Steel Bridge over the Skokomish River (built in 1929 by the Simpson Timber Company), as well as its current panoramic views of the Olympics and South Puget Sound.

No date has been identified for the removal of the Grisdale Hill Lookout. A 1953 Olympic National Forest map marks its location within the national forest as a "permanent fire lookout station." A 1961 Olympic National Forest map has no lookout station symbol for the Grisdale Hill Lookout, and the land no longer is within the national forest.

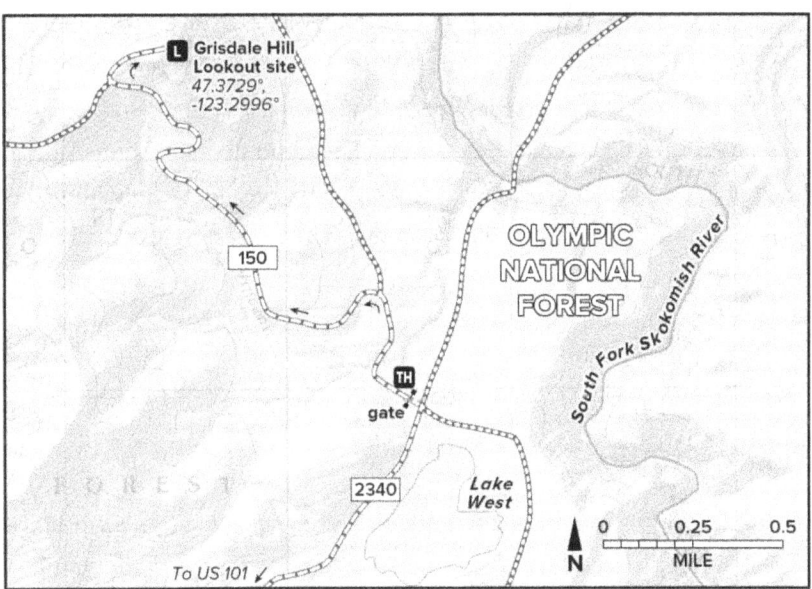

Hike Summary

This is a short hike with enough elevation gain to get your heart pumping, as well as grand views of the peaks and valleys of the south Olympics. It is located on Green Diamond Resource Company forestland, which is open to non-motorized recreation unless extreme fire hazard or active logging is present. In fall and winter, check for floods of the Skokomish River, which can close the access roads to this hike.

---

[5] Kresek, *2015*, 23.

Getting There

- At the junction of US Highway 101 and State Route 106 north of Shelton, turn west onto the Skokomish Valley Road. This road is famous for the salmon that swim across when the river is flooding, so be alert for flood warnings after especially rainy periods.
- At 5.5 miles from US Highway 101, turn right and uphill on Forest Road (FR) 23.
- At 8.0 miles, take a sharp right turn on FR 2340.
- At 9.7 miles, you may catch a glimpse of Lake West through the trees on your right (easier to spot in cooler seasons, when there is less foliage). Very shortly—at about 9.8 miles—turn left at an unsigned road that intersects FR 2340 just north of the oft-hidden lake. That road is gated and has a Green Diamond Forestry status sign to the right. The big red dot is accompanied by text explaining that non-motorized visitors are welcome on the forest roads during daylight hours.
- Park on the rough ground adjacent to the side road. Do not block the gate.

Hiking Route

This hike begins as a pleasant walk on a gravel road curving through a forest of hemlock and fir. The roadway even trends slightly downhill to cross the Vincent Creek at the first curve. After 0.4 mile, turn left. The only road sign on the entire route appears on a tree beside the continuing road, labeled 150.

Continue in the trees on a fairly level track for another 0.33 mile. The total elevation gain at the next junction is only 75 feet. If this feels too easy, you are correct.

The road separates into two tracks that are nearly parallel. Follow the one on the right, going slightly uphill. As the path rises, look south across the forested Skokomish Valley to a ridge of mountains including tall South Mountain—considered the southernmost of the Olympic peaks, with over 3000-foot elevation. The ridge on the right side of the gravel track is punctuated twice by gravel pits. The route steepens as it gains elevation. As you reach the top of each rise, another bit of road appears ahead—until you can see over the other side.

Grisdale Ridge is reached in 1.8 miles from the trailhead. Five hundred feet of elevation are gained in the process, and the payoff is in the views. Arrayed ahead are all the Olympic Mountains visible from this southeastern corner of the peninsula. The ribbon of the South Fork Skokomish River flickers on the valley floor to the north, but your quest is not complete.

Views to the west and northwest were opened by logging on the west end of the ridge in about 2015. That harvest opened a roadway to the south and a spur to the southwest, as well as restoring views of Mount Washington and the curves of the big river below.

South Fork Skokomish River Valley with early snow on the peaks. The photograph was taken from the hike route to the Grisdale Lookout site.

Follow the old road to the right as it gains a little more elevation in the last 0.25 mile. Loggers' bulldozers were used to reshape the hilltop into two hillocks. A search in the foliage on the north side of the eastern summit reveals two square concrete blocks, one with a protruding galvanized metal post. These are the remnants of the footings that supported the sturdy wooden legs of the lookout tower above.

Grisdale Hill's views remain for all to enjoy. To the east and south, the broad hook at the southern end of Hood Canal, the hills and mountains of surrounding South Puget Sound, Mount Rainier, and the south Cascades all fill the panorama. One sunny day in May, both white and yellow swallowtail butterflies soared overhead, performing mating ballets while hunting nectar—and entertaining hikers while we ate lunch and enjoyed the extensive view.

This hike can be extended by exploring other road spurs from the ridgetop junction. It can also be combined with a visit to the Dennie Ahl Lookout (Hike # 39) several miles farther north, or to the High Steel Bridge, a short distance north of the Grisdale Trailhead on FR 2340.

41. SIMPSON LOOKOUT

RT Distance: 3.6 miles
High Point: 1240 feet
Elevation Gain: 950 feet
Season: Oct-Dec
No pass or permit is required here during autumn hunting season dates.[1]

History

The Simpson Timber Company, parent of the Green Diamond Resource Company of Shelton and Seattle, grew from the small S. G. Simpson Company founded in 1890 by Sol Simpson, a Canadian immigrant. His son-in-law, Mark Reed, joined the company in the late 1890s and took on executive roles after Simpson died in 1906.[2] Reed was a very successful businessman and longtime state legislator. The company grew to be the second largest timber company in Washington state after Weyerhaeuser, with its most concentrated land holdings in the northwest quarter of the state.

The Simpson Lookout was located on a bench below the top of 1370-foot-high Simpson Hill,[3] eleven miles northwest of Shelton and about three miles southeast of South Mountain. The State Division of Forestry (SDF) built the 40-foot wooden observation tower with a cabin at ground level on Simpson Timber Company land in 1936.[4] In 1947, the Simpson Company magazine included an article about honeymooners who staffed this fire lookout that summer. "Lloyd and Sedate Bretthauer enjoyed being up in the air so much they stayed in the tower night and day . . . Groceries and firewood were raised forty feet from the ground by rope and pulley."[5]

In 1956, SDF replaced this monitoring station with a lookout on the significantly taller (3070-foot) South Mountain. The Simpson tower and its ground cabin were removed in 1961.

---

[1] Visit Green Diamond web pages for details: https://greendiamond.com/recreation/washington-lands/ and https://www.greendiamond.com/news/.
[2] "Simpson Logging Company History," *International Directory of Company Histories*, vol. 17, Saint James Press, 1997, accessed at https://www.fundinguniverse.com/company-histories/simpson-investment-company-history/.
[3] R.M. Beeman, [Fire Lookout Site Evaluation] "Simpson State Tower (and hill above)," Sept. 11, 1938; Document 22-16.01, National Archives in Seattle.
[4] Washington Division of Forestry, *Thirty-first and thirty-second annual reports for the Period Ending November 30, 1936*, 14.
[5] "Honeymoon on Simpson Lookout," *The Simpson Lookout*, September 1947, 8.

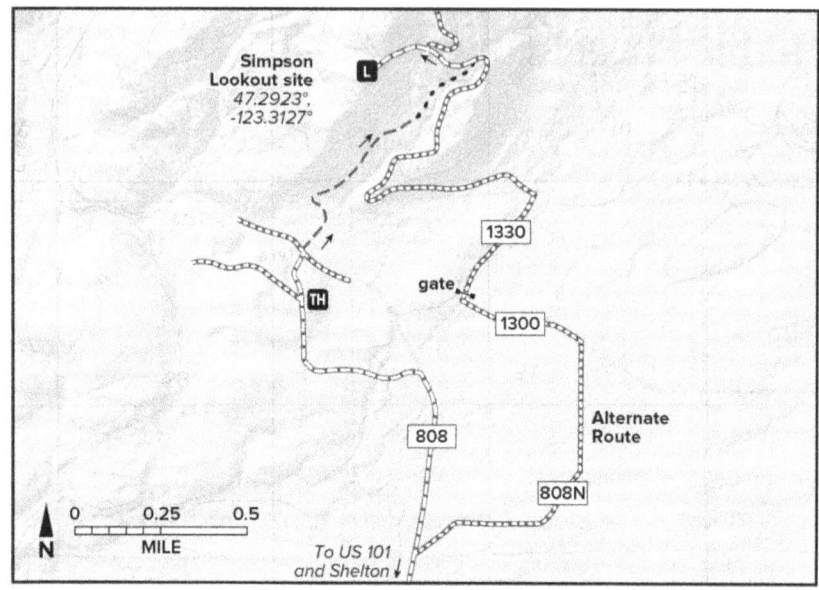

Hike Summary

The route provided here is short but interesting. It starts at the unsigned junction of Forest Road 808 and an unlabeled road running north. The 1.8-mile route uses both gravel roads and a jeep track through a young tree plantation for a short, adventurous route to reach the summit. An alternate route of variable length is offered at the end of this hike description.

Getting There

- Drive west on the Shelton-Matlock Road from US Highway 101 at Shelton.
- Pass through the village of Dayton, and notice big Green Diamond Resource Company signs as you pass a large log-sorting yard on the right side of the road.
- At 9.7 miles from US Highway 101, turn right at the third Green Diamond tree farm sign, between mileposts 10 and 11. Roads from here to the trailhead are generally well-maintained gravel. Drive a

short distance to a T and turn left. Pass through an open gate with a Green Dot sign. Forest maps identify this road as Forest Road (FR) 808.
- At 13.4 miles, pass a junction with Forest Road 1600 on the left. Pass a series of minor side roads on the right, most of which have numbers in the 800s.
- At 13.6 miles from US Highway 101, the main road, FR 808, takes a sharp turn to the left while a narrower road disappears into the trees straight ahead/north. Park at this junction to hike to the Simpson Lookout site.
- This junction is wide enough to park safely anywhere on the outside of the curve. Logging trucks do, however, steam past at full power, so park beside the widest part of the intersection to avoid flying gravel.

Hiking Route

Start north on the evergreen-bordered road, which soon twists left and steeply downhill. At 0.25 mile, it emerges in a narrow, clearcut valley with a distinctive wooded summit to the north-northwest: Simpson Hill.

Cross a narrow east-west track that ends as a blocked, decommissioned road a few hundred yards to the east, and start uphill on another serpentine stretch of gravel. About 0.5 mile from the hike's start, the road ends abruptly. The surrounding landscape is dotted with seemingly randomly planted trees, approaching 3 feet in height in late 2016. They are surrounded with bare earth, occasional native plants eager to reestablish themselves, and small pieces of branches and chunks of timber—minor logging debris. At the edge of the forest on a ridge straight ahead, spot another gravel road. Looking more closely at the young tree plantation surrounding you, notice an old jeep track climbing across the tree planting toward the upper road.

Some hikers think walking gravel roads and clearcuts is not much fun, but following a jeep track on uneven terrain can provide an interesting challenge and lead to interesting discoveries. After completing the one-third mile traverse, the gravel road is substantially more attractive. Turn left, then raise your eyes from the ground and appreciate your elevation gain and views now available to the south. Lake Nahwatzel appears as a bright blue patch of water against the dark green forest in that direction.

Animal tracks are recorded on the road when the ground has a carpet of snow. There may be mountain bike tire tracks or a snowshoe track on the upper, snow-covered road, but animal prints dominate. Deer, large cat, and tiny mammal tracks often crisscross the snow on the upper part of the route.

Initially, there are trees only on the higher side of the road, allowing wide views to the south and east. After turning the corner toward the south, forest on both sides restricts views to the sky, the ground, and the next bend in the road. Several Ss take us the rest of the way to the top. Long views are lacking, but there may be remnants of the old tower hiding in the understory at the left side of the road. Only one old concrete block has been found there in recent years. The tower was located on a bench of land below the summit, so the location of the find is plausible, with little currently known about the interim history of the site.

Alternate Route

As mentioned earlier, the alternate is a variable length hike, depending on how much of the following route you drive or hike.

- The alternate starts at the junction of the main line road driven to the hike route described above, FR 808, with FR 808N, about 0.5 mile south of the starting point of that route.
- Follow road 808N through a tree plantation to a junction with FR 1300 in a little less than 1.0 mile.
- Turn left and continue 0.67 mile to FR1330 as the route gradually leaves the area of young trees and enters mature forest. A gate at the start of FR 1330 may be closed.

- Hike an estimated 1.7 miles on FR 1330 as it winds uphill through forest and joins the hiking route described above. Before joining the recommended route, FR 1330 borders a wooded ravine with a creek running through it. Trees close to the creek have been left standing during timber harvests to protect water quality and wildlife habitat. All of the 950-foot elevation gain of the alternate route is achieved on FR 1330.

42. SOUTH MOUNTAIN LOOKOUT

RT Distance: 8.0 miles
High Point: 3040 feet
Elevation Gain: 2450 feet
Season: Oct-Dec
No pass or permit is required here during autumn hunting season dates.

History

South Mountain is the southernmost peak of the Olympic Mountain Range. Its high ridge has two distinct summits about 1.75 miles apart. The lookout cabin was located on the slightly higher western point, at 3070 feet[1] elevation. It was constructed in 1956 to replace a lower state forestry lookout on nearby Simpson Hill.[2] Both locations are within a large Green Diamond Resource Company tree farm, Green Diamond being the most recent reorganization of the company started in 1890 as the S. G. Simpson Company.

The State Division of Forestry (SDF) built a standard lookout cabin[3] with windows all around, placing it on top of one story of enclosed storage. The windows were covered with shutters in winter, providing protection from the deep snow common on the top of the peak.

South Mountain stood as the highest in the network of state fire lookouts in Mason County for about 20 years. Staff there checked in by radio with fire monitors at Dow Mountain above Lake Cushman to the north, and at the Dayton Lookout,[4] a few miles away, and south of the Matlock Road. The Department of Natural Resources (which replaced SDF in 1957) decided in the '60s that planes were a more efficient way to monitor forest fires. The South Mountain lookout cabin was removed in 1976.

During a visit to the lookout site in January 2017, my companion and I met two workmen in the communications control building. One told us about his experience on the

---

[1] Historical records state the elevation for this lookout site as 3070 feet, but the elevation was brought down when the site was prepared for a communication tower in 2003. Current topographic maps indicate the elevation is now 3040 feet.
[2] Articles published June 29, 1956, in *The [Centralia] Daily Chronicle* and July 2, 1956, in the *Port Angeles Evening News* are quoted in https://washingtonlookouts.weebly.com/south-mountain.html.
[3] Louise Hartley, "Lookout's Job Big Part of Conservation," *Shelton-Mason County Journal*, estimated publication date: August 15-18, 1959.
[4] Hartley, "Lookout's Job . . ."

construction crew for the communication tower and its support buildings in 2003. They first removed the 12×12-foot foundation of the lookout building, then lowered the elevation of the summit hill by 15 feet.[5]

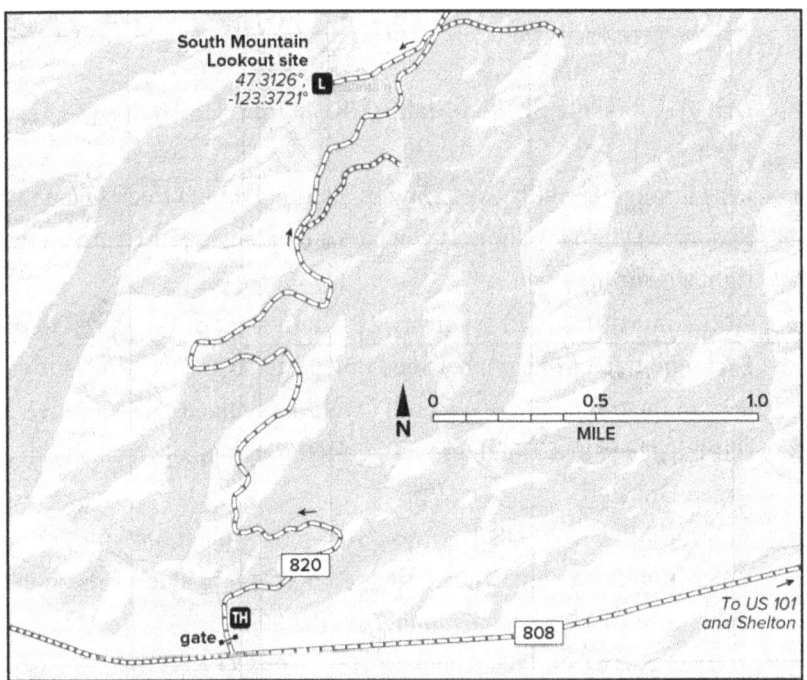

Hike Summary

The hiking route to this lookout site is on forest roads within the Green Diamond Resource Company tree farm, west of Shelton. The company opens the roads for hunting and recreation purposes each autumn, closing the main gates again in early January. Visit their website to see the latest press release on public access. Other routes to South Mountain are described on the internet and in old guidebooks, including access from the north via national forest roads in the Skokomish River Valley. Unlike those routes, the driving and hiking routes described here are well-maintained and consistently accessible on a published schedule.

---

[5] A friend and I hiked to the South Mountain Lookout site through foot-deep snow, January 5, 2017. Unfortunately, I did not record the name of the longtime employee we met that day.

The perspectives are ever-broadening as the route gains 2450-foot elevation in 4 miles. At the summit ridge, enjoy the panoramic views fire lookouts experienced daily.[6]

Getting There

- Drive west on the Shelton-Matlock Road from US Highway 101 at Shelton.
- Pass through the village of Dayton and notice big Green Diamond Resource Company signs as you pass a large log sorting yard on the right side of the road.
- At 9.7 miles from US Highway 101, turn right at the third Green Diamond tree farm sign, between mileposts 10 and 11. Roads from here to the trailhead are generally well-maintained gravel. Drive a short distance to a T and turn left. Pass through an open gate with a Green Dot sign.
- At 13.4 miles from US Highway 101, pass a junction with Forest Road 1600 on the left. There are a series of minor side roads on the right, most of which have numbers in the 800s.
- At 13.6 miles from US Highway 101, the main road takes a sharp turn to the left, while a minor road goes straight ahead. Stay on the main road.
- At 14.8 miles from US Highway 101, turn left at a big junction with an *Evacuation Route* sign. Pass through another open gate with a Green Dot sign and cross over a bridge.
- At 17 miles from US Highway 101, turn right on FR 820. Park at a wide spot beside the road between the intersection and the closed gate.

---

[6] Visit Green Diamond web pages for details: https://www.greendiamond.com/recreation/washington-lands/ and https://www.greendiamond.com/news/.

Hiking Route

With over 600-foot elevation to gain in each mile, there is little surprise the route starts uphill immediately after the gate. The hiking surface is level gravel, bordered on both sides by tall hemlocks that block views and most sunlight not shining directly on the road. The route snakes up the hill for 0.5 mile, then emerges above a young tree plantation on a steep slope, looking down the 300 feet already gained.

Mount Rainier across the Puget Sound lowlands from the route to South Mountain.

For the next 0.5 mile, there are improving views from the slope edge: first, a landscape of treetops, then, rounded gray peaks in the mid-distance. The Cascades appear on clear days, with Mount Rainier, Mount Adams, and Mount St. Helens prominent above the local hills.

At 1 mile, turn a corner and lose the long view to a narrow, uphill perspective. The trees are almost all hemlocks, although small groves of alders provide the contrast of smooth gray bark and a spreading growth pattern against the dominant dark evergreens. Sword ferns and salal stand at their feet, but few other plants are noticeable in the well-groomed forest.

Soon, a cascade plummets down the steep slope at a bend in the road to catch the eye. Flowing water is occasionally heard along the route, but this is one of few opportunities to see and enjoy the motion. A few turns later, a side road heads downhill on the left. The main road up South Mountain has few junctions and its side routes generally go downhill, keeping decision-making simple.

At 2.5 miles and 2240-foot elevation, reach a major junction and viewpoint. The side road on the right heads downhill through a clearcut that offers views of the Skokomish River Valley to the north and the South Cascade Mountain range and forested lands to the south. When the sun shines, the views to the east are amazing: Cascade summits from

Glacier Peak to Mount St. Helens line the eastern horizon. In all weather, silver ribbons of creeks and rivers glint below among the green swath of forests. The track continues steadily upward until it reaches 3.2 miles. There, the route flattens to gentle rises and declines, gaining only 100 feet or so in the next 0.5 mile.

At 3.75 miles, emerge on the summit ridge at a road junction on a broad flat shoulder of South Mountain. There are big views to the north and west. On clear days, snowy peaks of the Olympic Mountains can be seen in all their glory. The apparent main road continues straight ahead and slightly uphill, but another well-maintained gravel road turns left and distinctly uphill.

The South Mountain Lookout site is on the western and tallest peak on the ridge. Thus, the left turn is the route to our destination. Three peaks now serve as locations for relay and repeater towers on the ridge, so sighting them is not particularly helpful for navigation.

After ascending 0.25 mile, the road goes halfway around the top of the west summit. Above are footpaths to concrete block buildings and a tall steel tower, with guy wires often whistling in the winds sweeping across the peak.

Until 2003, the lookout building's foundation remained on the highest point of South Mountain as an artifact of the peak's historic fire lookout. It was removed as part of the site preparation for construction of the tower and other facilities now standing there. Almost all remnants of the South Mountain fire lookout station were removed then, although a rough set of old concrete steps remain on the east side of the modern communication tower, unattached to any modern structure.

During your visit, check out the 360-degree panorama. Consider the vantage of the southernmost Olympic Mountain and look for the linked peaks, Eleanor and Washington, a few dozen miles to the northeast. Beyond them stand The Brothers, and far distant Glacier Peak and Mount Baker in the northern Cascades. Your viewpoint is not as elevated as the South Mountain lookout tower in the mid-twentieth century, but offers a rare view in all directions. Enjoy!

43. KELLY LOOKOUT

RT Distance: 1.6 miles
High Point: 880 feet
Elevation Gain: 330 feet
Season: All Year
No pass or permit is required.

History

Until a few years ago, the history of this fire lookout station was a complete mystery. Hikers would ask why the popular Metsker maps identified the lookout at Kelly's location as Simpson Lookout. Then, Eric Willhite found a 1940 State Division of Forestry (SDF) memo saying "Simpson L.O., located [in Kelly Lookout's map location] was formerly a national forest lookout, but is now abandoned with a 14×14-foot standard house remaining on the site."[1]

The remains of the Kelly Lookout cabin in 2000. (Irene Potter photograph, courtesy of the photographer.)

In 2019, I found a 1938 lookout site evaluation prepared by National Forest Ranger R. M. Beeman, for the same location. He identified it as "Simpson Lookout (abandoned)" as he considered the location for US Forest Service use. He described the building as having six broken windows, and more importantly for his purposes, "7 miles from Weatherwax (West)—7 miles from South Mtn. Covers most of their mutual blind spot, along boundary. Good emergency fireman lookout station."[2]

---

[1] Carroll E. Brown, Memorandum for the Files, January 12, 1940. Posted at http://willhiteweb.com/washington_fire_lookouts/kelly_hill_lookout/satsop_river_304.htm.
[2] R. M. Beeman, [Fire Lookout Site Evaluation] "Simpson Lookout (Abandoned)." Sept. 10, 1938; Document 22-16, National Archives in Seattle. The boundary he refers to is most likely the southern border of the Olympic National Forest.

The lookout appears with other Forest Service lookouts on Olympic National Forest maps published in the 1930s, but it was not located within the national forest boundaries.[3] It is now in a Green Diamond Resource tree farm. It was known as the Simpson Lookout then, presumably named for the Simpson Timber Company (predecessor to the Green Diamond Resource Company), the largest timber company in the east Olympics at the time.

In 1936, 2 years prior to Beeman's evaluation, the State Division of Forestry (SDF) built another fire lookout station about 10 miles east-northeast and called it Simpson Lookout.[4] The author of the 1940 SDF memo was aware of the two fire lookout stations named Simpson.[5]

Although none of the historical documents found to date says so, it is apparent the abandoned lookout station was at some time transferred to SDF management. As the story below indicates, it was reactivated and given the name Kelly, presumably for its location near the Grays Harbor County road, also named Kelly.[6] That road now ends at the gate of a very pretty farm, about 2.5 miles south-southwest of the lookout site.

When fire lookout enthusiast Irene Potter first heard about the Kelly Lookout in the 1990s, she went to Matlock and asked about it. She met an older woman named Maggie Ogg who was part of the local Kelly family who had a farm beside Kelly Road. Mrs. Ogg shared a childhood memory of joining her siblings in taking their dad's lunch to him when he staffed the lookout. "It was over five little humps to the north on the trail."[7] Unfortunately, there were no dates attached to the story.

Hike Summary

Park beside a Green Diamond Resource Company gate on a wide forest road and hike 0.8 mile to the lookout site. The ascending route is through a healthy tree farm that opens onto a clearcut landscape and territorial

---

[3] Maps I examined at the National Archives in Seattle in 2019.
[4] Washington Division of Forestry, *Thirty-First and Thirty-Second Annual Reports for the Period Commencing December 1, 1934, and Ending November 30, 1936*, 14.
[5] Carroll E. Brown, Memorandum for the Files, January 12, 1940. accessed at http://willhiteweb.com/washington_fire_lookouts/kelly_hill_lookout/satsop_river_304.htm.
[6] The road name appears on some maps as "Kelly" and as "Kelley" on others.
[7] In an email received from Irene Potter, April 2, 2019.

views a short distance before the few remains of the lookout cabin. If a longer hike is wanted, forest roads continue in several directions.

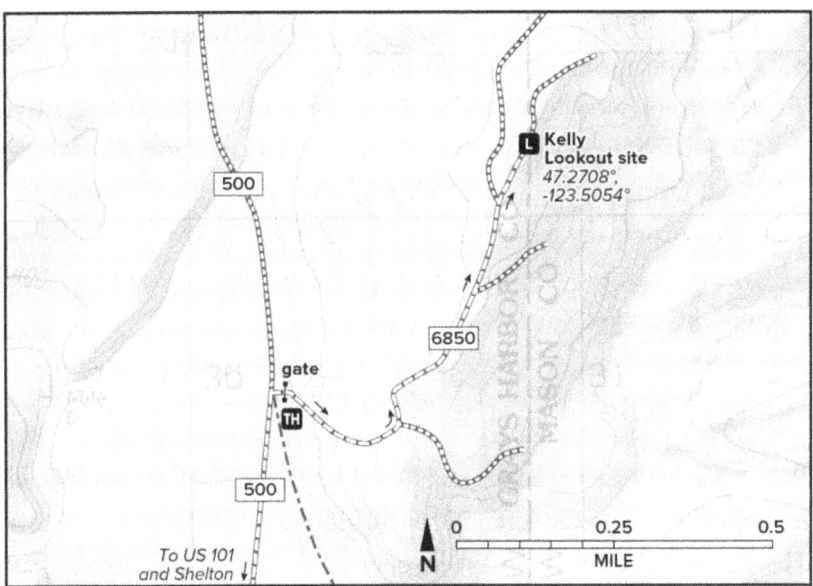

Getting There

- Drive west on the Shelton-Matlock Road from US Highway 101 at Shelton.
- Drive through the hamlet of Dayton; pass pretty Lake Nahwatzel, then tiny Matlock. The road jogs left at Matlock and then right in a short distance.
- At 16.7 miles from US Highway 101, the road name changes to Deckerville Road.
- Just before the road turns left, pass a sign welcoming travelers to Grays Harbor County. The road name changes to Boundary Road.
- At 20.8 miles from US Highway 101, turn right on Kelley Road. The first half-mile of this road crosses a beautiful section of the Middle Fork Satsop River and has a wonderful border of tall, mossy bigleaf maples between it and the river's lowlands.
- At 1 mile from the Boundary Road, turn left on narrow Forest Road 500. This gravel route has a small, white sign on a tree beside the

road, and no gate. Continue on this road for 0.3 mile and turn right, staying on FR 500—now only indicated by a small sign on the other side of the road.

- Here, Forest Road 500 is a broad, two-lane thoroughfare, looking capable of carrying speeding log trucks in both directions. Drive FR 500 for slightly more than 2.1 miles to its junction with a mossy, gated farm road and FR 6850. FR 6850 is a Green Diamond Resource Company road, where non-motorized visitors are welcome whenever active logging is not present and there is no significant wildfire danger.

Hiking Route

Walk past the forest road gate and head uphill on the well-maintained road that curves to the left as it passes through healthy mixed forest. There are occasional glimpses into open glades, but mostly dense forest on both sides. The understory is a familiar mix of salal, sword ferns, and Oregon grape, with small beds of yellow violets and white oxalis blossoms in spring.

Pass two roads on the right. They offer only short views of downhill, forested land before they turn corners and disappear.

At about 0.75 mile, approach a Y junction. The road on the left goes downhill, while the road straight ahead climbs steeply through dense forest for a short distance. At the junction is a blank signboard, no longer sharing information. Directions from old friends and some maps available on the internet suggest the lookout site was on the forested first high

Hikers enjoying the landscape surrounding the Kelly Lookout site.

point on the ridge. Searches of that area have not found any recorded artifacts.

As you continue on the ridge, the world opens before you. The rest of the ridge and much of the narrow valley below have been clearcut. Panoramic views are available in all directions. Can you pick out South Mountain and its radio towers to the east? Is Minot Peak visible to the south, on the other side of State Route 8? Can you spot Weatherwax Ridge or Anderson Butte to the west? These small peaks all hosted forest fire lookout stations during Kelly Lookout's active years. On clear days, Mount Rainier and its snowy friends in the Cascades, as well as a jumble of Olympic peaks to the north adorn the horizon, drawing surprised exclamations from the unsuspecting.

Continue the short distance to the second crest of the ridge. A game trail on the left offers an easy route to the high point. Mature trees have been removed and the young replacements are spaced widely enough to allow a pretty mixture of salal, Oregon grape, and sword ferns to grow at their feet. A stump carved with a chainsaw sits near the high point. South of it is a shallow jumble of old lumber. Prodding the wood reveals that one or two edges of each piece still holds old green paint. A few green-tinted shingles lie not far away.

Friends who visited Kelly Lookout in 2000 took photos of a damaged Kelly green cabin, a much deeper shade than the paint on the wood fragments remaining today.[8] Here's hoping all visitors will leave these historical remnants for future visitors to enjoy. The site sits on the county line and offers grand views over private timberland in both Grays Harbor and Mason Counties. Enjoy the perspective!

---

[8] The green building appears in the 11/17/00 trail notes of Olive Hull and the photographs of Irene Potter.

44. LOST LAKE LOOKOUT

RT Distance: 5.2 miles
High Point: 860 feet
Elevation Gain: 530 feet
Season: All Year
No pass or permit is required.

History

This plane and fire watch station was built on a low peak west of Lost Lake in southeastern Mason County. Not included in the twentieth-century fire lookout inventories, it was first noticed on the lists and maps documenting the World War II Aircraft Warning Service (AWS) stations in Washington discovered in the twenty-first century.

These documents did not identify the specific location of the Lost Lake AWS station, but there was only one road in the square mile section west of Lost Lake in the early 1940s. It ran from the Highland Road to the westernmost of the three hilltops in that section. The high point was often labeled as White Star Peak on twentieth-century maps,[1] named for the White Star Lumber Company, which operated from 1908 until about 1930 in the area between Elma and Shelton.[2]

The reasons this site was picked for an AWS station were not recorded, but the AWS did pay for the 14×32-foot "standard house" built here. It was on private land but was one of the World War II AWS posts managed by the US Forest Service transferred to the Washington Division of Forestry in May 1944, when the federal AWS ended operations.[3]

A record of the Lost Lake lookout being staffed after the war has not been found. The AWS' record of this station's assignment at the end of the AWS program says, "retain for the State of Washington."[4] A 1950s aerial map of this peak shows a broad open area and

---

[1] Eric Willhite discovered the existence and location of this observation site in 2020, and shared his early findings via email in December 2020.
[2] Photo Collection 516, University of Washington Libraries Special Collections. Accessed Jan 16, 2021, at https://digitalcollections.lib.washington.edu/digital/collection/clarkkinsey/id/1565/.
[3] Washington Division of Forestry, Memo to File: A.W.S. Posts Retained for Use by State Under Cooperative Agreement with the U.S. Forest Service.
[4] [US Forest Service] Region 6. "Report of Aircraft Warning Service Stations," May 1, 1944, Sheet #II.

44. LOST LAKE LOOKOUT · 235

likely buildings.[5] So the possibility of this location continuing as a private forestry lookout site has not been ruled out.

It is known that the first building on Washington Division of Forestry's Dayton Fire Lookout, a few miles to the northeast, came from the Lost Lake AWS station. A handwritten state forestry document dated a year after the federal AWS report includes the note that this building "moved to LO Mt. Kennedy."[6] Kennedy was the name given to one of the peaks of Dayton Mountain.

This record aligns with the memories of Jerry Needham, who was the first person to staff the Dayton Lookout. He described the lookout building he moved his family into in May 1945 as a "two-room A.W.S. building . . . The six of us were right real cozy—that's for sure. Stephie did all her good pastry and bread baking on a small Lang wood burner, got sorta warm in here during the hot August days."[7]

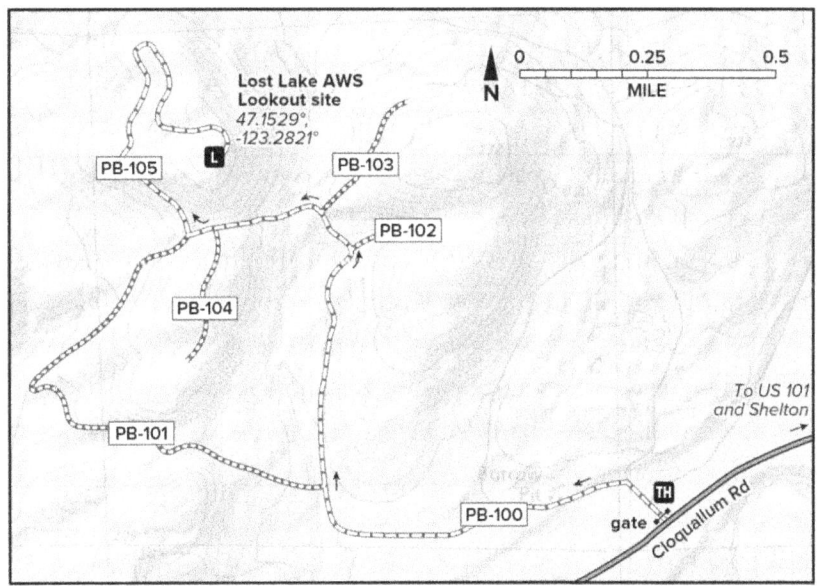

---

[5] An aerial map image was provided by Eric Willhite, December 2020.
[6] Washington Division of Forestry, Memo to File: A. W. S. Posts Retained for Use by State Under Cooperative Agreement with the U.S. Forest Service.
[7] '"Hello" from SH-40,' *Olympia District's Ten Eight*, July 1963, [3].

Hike Summary

This is a pleasant road hike over the rolling hills of a Port Blakely tree farm. There are great views of forestlands in Mason and Grays Harbor counties from a viewpoint 0.5 mile from the lookout site. On clear days, the panorama even includes the cooling towers of the abandoned Satsop nuclear plant.

Getting There

- From US Highway 101, exit to State Route 3 on the south side of Shelton.
- Drive into Shelton and turn left on Arcadia Avenue.
- In less than 0.5 mile, Arcadia Avenue ends at a T. Turn left onto Cloquallum Road.
- At 1.35 miles, this road crosses US Highway 101 on a high overpass.
- At 2.7 miles, drive past Lake Isabella on the left, and at 10 miles, pass the Lost Lake Road on the right.
- Between mileposts 10 and 11, and 10.7 miles from State Route 3, turn right on a Port Blakely Tree Farm access road. Parking is allowed on the roadsides approaching the tree farm gate, as long as logging and forest management traffic can access the gate. Additional parking is available on a road stub, 0.1 mile east, on the south side of Cloquallum Road.

Hiking Route

As long as most of the road signs on this tree farm continue to stand, it will be easy to find the way to the Lost Lake Lookout site: just follow road PB100. At the beginning, the route seems obvious because PB100 is clearly the main road, but some of the side roads are numbered and some are not.

For the first 0.8 mile, hike through a young tree plantation, enjoying views of the surrounding forested hills. The route then takes a turn northward; the more heavily traveled forest road goes west, and is signed PB101. Continue on the northward route, on an unsigned road with a grassy median. This quickly becomes a narrow, two-track road surrounded by forest. Narrow creeks slip under the track in hidden culverts. Moss, Oregon grape, and sword ferns border the roadway.

In another 0.6 mile, the route turns west at a junction with PB102. This section crosses two or three ridges, with more significant creeks crossing under the road. Look for beaver activity in the roadside ponds. Small birds are fond of the flowing water, chattering their appreciation as they flit among the shrubbery.

Emerge from the thick forest and lightly trafficked track at a junction with PB104, which heads south and uphill. Enjoy the broader views west, continuing another 0.1 mile on the more heavily traveled main road. Turn right on PB105 and start uphill toward White Star Peak. In 0.2 mile, reach the best viewpoint of the hike at an open corner. It is a great place for lunch, whether ascending or returning from the lookout site.

The route to the Lost Lake Lookout site on a sunny spring day.

The forest road narrows and loses its tire tracks as it continues uphill. Branches reach out from nearby shrubs and trees, and blackberry vines catch on passing boots. The hindrances are not constant, but do repeat along the almost-mile track to the top. The one side road branching from PB105 leads temptingly uphill. Do not follow it. Continue south, following the main route all the way to the old road's high point. At 2.6 miles from the gate, you will reach the forested summit of White Star Peak and the site of the Lost Lake AWS station. The road is a little wider here, still ready to accommodate a 30-foot-long building, just as it did during its plane-spotting days, in the 1940s.

Exploration of this lookout site started in December 2020. No artifacts of the long-removed buildings have yet been discovered. If you find remnants of more than hunting camps, be sure to share your discoveries.

45. MOBRAY LOOKOUT

RT Distance: 0.5 mile
High Point: 656 feet
Elevation Gain: 50 feet
Season: All Year
No pass or permit is required.

History

The Washington State Division of Forestry built a 12-foot wooden tower on a high point of rolling hills close to the Wynoochee Valley Road, northwest of Montesano, in 1937.[1] In 1942, when western Washington was alert for Japanese air attacks, the original tower was replaced with a 32-foot wooden tower topped with an 8×8-foot cabin.[2] Keith Hoofnagle, who spent several summers working on the Weatherwax Lookout a few miles to the north, remembered a woman from Shelton who had worked on Mobray at the same time. "She lived in a ground house and went up in the tower during the day. The ground house stood there by the road after the tower was taken down."[3] The tower was removed in 1963.

The Mobray Lookout tower, 1950s. (Courtesy of the Alta Bailey Moore Collection.)

The family name, Mobray, appears repeatedly in the local Montesano newspaper, *The Vidette*, in the 1920s and 1930s. "The Wynooche [sic] Valley folks held their usual community picnic in July at the grove on the Elmer Mobray Farm. A good time and a sumptuous dinner with ice cream to spare was enjoyed by the large crowd in attendance."[4] This suggests the fire lookout was sited on the Mobray Farm, or at least named for the popular family. The site is within a Green Diamond Resource Company tree farm now.

---

[1] Kresek, *1998*, 115.
[2] Kresek, *1998*, 115.
[3] Interview with Keith Hoofnagle, November 2017.
[4] *The [Montesano] Vidette*, July 7, 1922, 3.

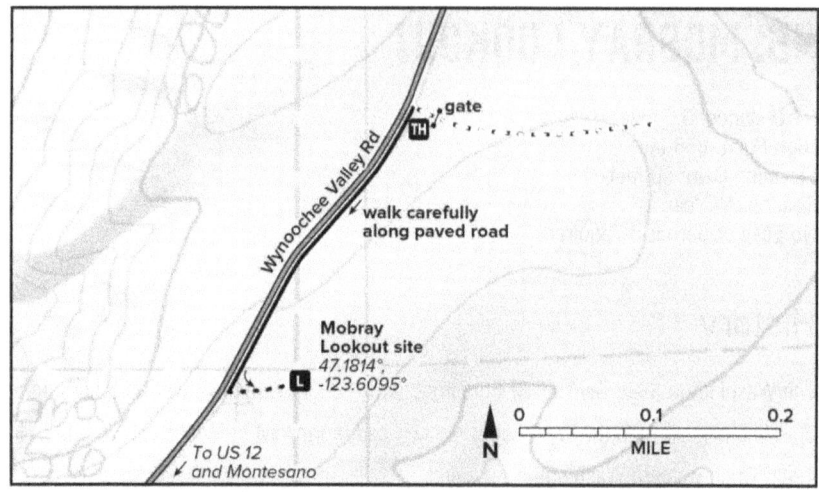

Hike Summary

This hike is short enough to include in the category of "drive-by"—worthy only as a supplement to a longer hike and a different destination. Green rolling hills dominate the views in all directions except north, where the snow-peaked and rocky-sloped Olympics rise above the forest. It is located in a tree farm where hikers are welcome when active logging isn't present and there is no significant wildfire danger.

Getting There

- Driving west on US Highway 12, take the Devonshire Road exit, just west of Montesano and milepost 10.
- At the four-way intersection at the end of the exit ramp, angle left to the Wynoochee Valley Road.
- Drive 18 miles through the broad river valley, which starts with farmland and transitions to a commercial tree farm full of young conifers.
- Two-tenths of a mile past milepost 18 is a gated road on the right with a Green Diamond Resource Company sign. Park here if you can avoid blocking the gate, or park across the paved road on the short road stub there.

Hiking Route

Walk 0.25 mile south, passing milepost 18 on the same side of the paved route as the gated forest road. As you reach the high point on the road, approximately 650-foot elevation, look for a game trail or narrow path into the young trees planted close to the road in 2010. A tree line of older, taller trees starts about 200 feet south of the Mobray Lookout site.

Enter the young trees, wade through knee-high salal when necessary, and head east about 200 feet from the road. If you have a GPS, head for these coordinates: 47.1815°, -123.6093°. Natural openings in the trees caused by hard-packed soil from human habitation will also help you find the artifacts of the lookout tower and cabin removed more than fifty years ago. You should find two or three concrete footing blocks. Two are close together under leggy hemlocks at the coordinates.

A Mobray tower support, in the midst of a vibrant green forest.

46. DRAKE LOOKOUT

RT Distance: 8 miles
High Point: 1443 feet
Elevation Gain: 750 feet
Season: All Year
No pass or permit is required.

History

The Drake forest fire lookout tower was built on a broad promontory above the Wynoochee River Valley known as Reed Hill. Mark Reed and George Drake were Simpson Timber Company managers in the first half of the twentieth century.[1] Reed was a member of the Simpson family and a widely respected state legislator. Drake, a professional forester, also served as president of the Western Forestry and Conservation Association in the 1940s.[2]

During World War II, this plane-watching station was identified as Reed on the 1942 and 1943 Aircraft Warning Service (AWS) maps.[3] An Aircraft Warning Service report, issued when that federal program ended in 1944, described this AWS station as "a private station operated for fire detection by the Simpson Logging Company . . . in cooperation with the State of Washington."[4]

Despite the expectation at the end of its AWS service that it would be retained by the owners, management of the station was assigned to the State Division of Forestry (SDF), and the lookout became known as Drake. Ray Kresek's fire lookout inventories describe Drake as "SDF 1940s: live-in tower."[5]

In the early 1950s, regional newspaper reports announced September closing dates for some state forestry lookout stations. In 1951 and 1952, they included the names of the women who staffed Drake. In September 1952, the reason for ending the season early at that lookout was "ocean fog making the station useless."[6] The tower was taken down in 1963.[7]

---

[1] The company reorganized and became the Green Diamond Resource Company in 2004.
[2] Rooney, 79.
[3] Aircraft Warning Service Olympia Filter Center maps, accessed at http://www.willhiteweb.com/washington_fire_lookouts/aircraft_warning_service/olympia-filter-center.JPG.
[4] The report is quoted in https://washingtonlookouts.weebly.com/drake-reed-hill.html.
[5] Kresek, *2019*, 22
[6] *[The Centralia] Daily Chronicle*, quoted in https://washingtonlookouts.weebly.com/drake-reed-hill.html.
[7] US National Geodetic Survey, "Data Sheet PID SY1828 DRAKE RM 1"; https://www.ngs.noaa.gov/cgi-bin/ds_mark.prl?PidBox=SY1828.

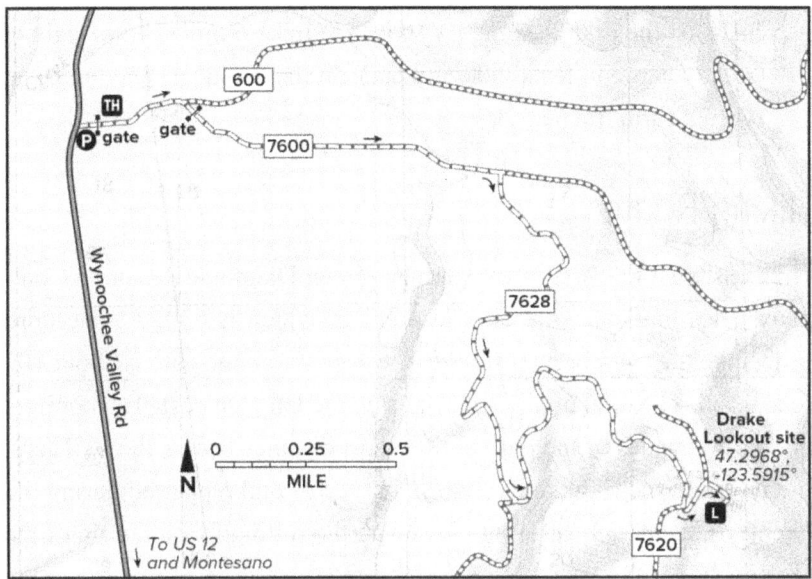

Hike Summary

This is a pleasant road hike over rolling hills in private forestland. Most of the route follows a serpentine road through tall trees, emerging on a ridge with views in all directions, a short distance from the fire lookout's historic location. Ancient stumps and minor logging debris are most of what remains where the tower once stood.

Getting There

- Driving west on US Highway 12, take the Devonshire Road exit, just west of Montesano and milepost 10.
- At the four-way intersection at the end of the exit ramp, angle left onto the Wynoochee Valley Road.
- Drive past milepost 28 on the Wynoochee Valley Road through varied farms and landscape to the southern foothills of the Olympic Mountains.

- Just past the orange sign, "Wynoochee Lake 6 miles," turn right at Green Diamond Road 600 and park on the shoulder, leaving room for tree-farm traffic.

Hiking Route

Hike east past the first of two orange Green Diamond Resource Company gates marked with its road number, which is 600. At one-third mile, take the right branch at a Y. The second orange gate is about 100 feet ahead. The road number, 7600, is on the left gate post. Tall conifers border both sides of the road until a short distance before the Y. There, the forest on the right side has been harvested and replanted during the twenty-first century, offering views into the rolling forest terrain of the Wynoochee Valley.

From the Y, the road heads southeast and is soon bordered with hemlocks, firs, and cedars. Hike on a well-maintained gravel road, passing 3 mossy side roads on the right. At 1.0 mile, the hiking route passes through two wetland areas, featuring a roadside fringe of common reeds, with narrow flags of foliage, 3- to 5-feet tall. Mixed forest—alders among tall hemlocks, cedars, and water-tolerant deciduous shrubs—has been left in these wet areas dedicated to maintaining water quality.

In a short distance, angle right at another Y. The other branch road, little traveled now, could become the main road the next time the timber in this area is harvested.

At 1.3 miles, turn right (south) on Road 7628. This road number sits beside the road on a 3-foot post. In 2019, an area on the north side of the intersection was harvested, leaving 100-foot-tall hemlocks and cedars along the road borders. The clearing provides views up to the eastern end of Weatherwax Ridge, location of the Weatherwax Lookout site.

Until this point, the road segments have run in fairly level, straight lines. Road 7628 rises moderately, following the contours of the landscape in graceful curves. After hiking 2 miles, the elevation gain is only 200 feet.

At 2.66 miles, 7628 reaches its southernmost point at an X junction. Keep to the left to continue on the same road. The next 0.5 mile goes steadily northeast, then turns southeast and carves Ss on the landscape until it reaches a junction with Road 7620 at 3.75 miles and 1370-foot elevation. A young tree plantation on the west side of the road offers views across the Wynoochee River Valley. The dark green lines below indicate older trees left beside streams to protect water quality and salmon habitat. The taller hills and mountains of the Olympic National Forest rise to the north.

After admiring the panorama, turn left on road 7620 and continue about 0.25 mile to the northeast. Pass one road on the left. At the second spur on that side, turn right on a narrow, dark-gravel track. Trees on this side of the road were harvested in the second decade of this century.

Ascend the 3-foot bank to your right and look around. On a clear day, you can see Mount Rainier above the forest to the east, as well as forestlands to the horizon in all directions. Foxglove, fireweed, and other small, native plants make their home among tree seedlings and the scraps of timber that litter the landscape among broad, tall stumps from twentieth-century harvests and the stumps of smaller trees more recently cut close to the ground.

The huge old stumps here are a testament to an older style of logging, when springboards were inserted a few feet off the ground to support men with double-handled felling saws, cutting through trees up to 8 feet thick.

The landmark stump identifying the Drake Lookout's historical location.

Find your way to a very large, cable-wrapped stump close to the gravel track. At some point in its history, someone wrapped a long logging cable around this tree remnant several times and tossed the remaining length on top. It is a popular spot for snapshots. Concrete and metal artifacts of the long-ago tower and its cabin lie partially buried, about 40 feet south of the large stump.

An artifact not found here is a National Geodetic Survey marker reported in the site records as recently as 1986.[8] My friends and I have searched for it several times, but have not found the bronze disc. Let me know if you have better luck!

---

[8] US National Geodetic Survey, "Data Sheet PID SY1828 DRAKE RM 1"; https://www.ngs.noaa.gov/cgi-bin/ds_mark.prl?PidBox=SY1828.

47. WEATHERWAX LOOKOUT

RT Distance: 8 miles
High Point: 2640 feet
Elevation Gain: 1950 feet
Season: May-Nov
No pass or permit is required.

History

Weatherwax Ridge is on the southern border of the Olympic National Forest at the north end of the Wynoochee River Valley. The ridge shares its name with a high school in Aberdeen; both honor a local nineteenth-century civic leader, John M. Weatherwax.

In the late 1930s, the east and west ends of the ridge were considered for national forest fire lookout stations. Ranger R. M. Beeman visited a site near the western end of the ridge in 1938, but thought a higher site on the eastern edge could be better. In 1939, he reviewed the information available and changed his mind, deciding the site at the western end should be preferred.[1] Much of the land on the western ridge is privately owned, which may have contributed to the national Forest Service never building a fire lookout station on the ridge.

Linda Lookout was created in the Weatherwax Lookout tower in 1962. (Courtesy of the artist, Keith Hoofnagle.)

The Grisdale Logging Camp, one of the best organized and most famous of western Washington's many camps, stood at the western foot of the ridge from 1946 until the 1980s. It has been reported that a treetop on the ridge was used as an emergency fire watch station in the mid-1940s.[2] In 1956, the Washington State Division of Forestry

---

[1] R.M. Beeman, [Fire Lookout Site Evaluations]: "Weatherwax Ridge (East)," Feb. 6, 1939; Document 25-16.16 and "Weatherwax Ridge (West)," Aug. 30, 1938; Document 26-16.17, National Archives in Seattle.
[2] This early lookout is mentioned without documentation at https://washingtonlookouts.weebly.com/weatherwax.html and http://willhiteweb.com/olympic_mountains/weatherwax_ridge/lookout_site_041.htm.

erected a 40-foot wooden fire tower topped by a 14×14-foot live-in cabin with an innovative (for the time) aluminum roof on one of Weatherwax Ridge's eastern high points.[3]

In 1960, The Washington Department of Natural Resources (DNR)[4] hired Keith Lundy Hoofnagle, an 18-year-old lookout enthusiast, for fire watch duty at the Weatherwax Lookout. He was surprised to discover he was the one young male on DNR's Montesano district lookout crew. One couple and four older women he thought of as grandmotherly staffed the other five lookout stations. He spent three summers on Weatherwax. When not watching for fires, he created a cartoon series called "Linda Lookout" that was published in the DNR lookout staff newsletter, *Olympia District's Ten-Eight*. After his summers on Weatherwax, Hoofnagle went on to watch for fires in Yellowstone National Park and continued his cartoonist career working for the National Park Service.[5] The Weatherwax Lookout was taken down in 1968, after DNR's decision to replace most of their stationary lookouts with spotter plane patrols.

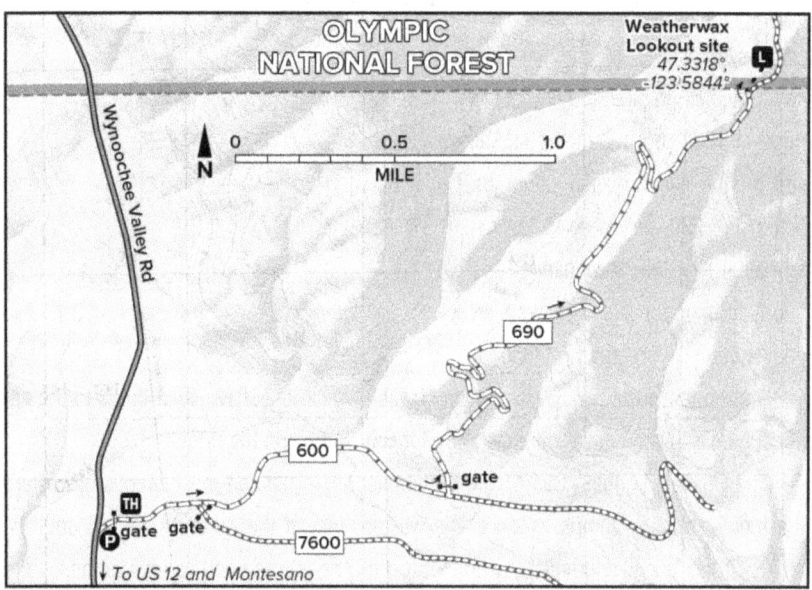

---

[3] Washington Division of Forestry, *Fifty-first and Fifty-second Annual Reports, for the Period . . . Ending June 30, 1956*, 34.
[4] The Department of Natural Resources was established in 1957, absorbing the Washington Division of Forestry.
[5] Keith Lundy Hoofnagle, *The Story of Linda Lookout*, Happy Camp, CA; Naturegraph Publishers, 2015, 5.

Hike Summary

Hike through a Green Diamond Resource Company tree farm on gravel roads to the border of the Olympic National Forest. The first 1.25 miles are almost flat, then the route turns a corner and ascends a serpentine road to the national forest boundary. Enjoy views down into the forested Wynoochee River Valley and east to Mount Rainier along the way. At 4 miles, leave the road for a faint track into the Olympic National Forest and continue a short distance to the high point and an interesting variety of artifacts.

Getting There

- Driving west on US Highway 12, take the Devonshire Road exit, just west of Montesano and milepost 10.
- At the intersection with the frontage road, angle left and continue north on the Wynoochee Valley Road. The roadside sign says "Lake Wynoochee 35 miles."
- Drive 27.8 miles on the Wynoochee Valley Road through varied farm and forest landscape to the southern foothills of the Olympic Mountains. (Long time visitors to the area may remember the 20-mile drive on bumpy gravel that was finally paved in 2012.)
- Just past the orange sign, "Wynoochee Lake 6 miles," turn right at Green Diamond Road 600 and park on the shoulder of the gravel road outside the gate. Leave plenty of space for log truck traffic.

Hiking Route

Walk around the yellow gate and follow the track east. Start out on the floor of the Wynoochee River Valley in a mixed forest of 50-foot-tall hemlock, fir, and alder. The road curves slightly to the left, then splits at about one-third mile. Keep left at the Y.

At 1.25 miles, pass the number 22 on a yellow vinyl sign attached to an old stump on the right. Turn left on gated road 690. The road starts to climb, linking straight stretches with four or five horseshoe bends that offer panoramic views as you stride around each curve. A short distance up the hill, pass a small gravel pit on the right, as well as an uphill side road on the left. It is notable as one of few ascending branch roads on this route, but don't be tempted. It is not headed for the top of the ridge.

An old Simpson Timber Company map of the area revealed several unusual place names not found on other maps. The north-south ridge leading to Weatherwax is labeled Haywire Ridge, while a creek running southeast is called Devils Club Creek. On the west side of Haywire Ridge is the mysteriously named, but better known, Save Creek.

A little more than 2.5 miles from the start, a broad curve offers great views of Mount Rainier while you are facing east. The elevation here is 1780 feet, reflecting the steady ascent. The intermittent views improve as the climb continues. At 3.5 miles, an especially clear day can offer views of Mounts Adams and St. Helens, as well as Rainier. Additional gravel tracks going downhill on both sides of Road 690 were used to access tree harvests earlier in this century. Views to the west allow glimpses of the communication towers on the west end of Weatherwax Ridge, across the Save Creek Valley.

There is fairly steady elevation gain on the way to the Weatherwax Lookout site.

At 4 miles, a distinctive Green Diamond Resource Company sign is posted on a tree to the left. It is not identified as a property boundary marker, but it's in the right location for one. It would be helpful if there were an Olympic National Forest boundary sign nearby, but there is none. Enter the forest here, following a trail that starts a few feet beyond the green-and-white sign. Follow the old roadbed as it gently rises uphill about 15 feet, stepping over small, downed trees as you go. To the right is a white-painted 4×4-inch post with an X cut into its angled top. This is a section marker, presumably marking the boundary of the Olympic National Forest.

Continue uphill another 20 feet and bear left when the roadbed disappears under dense shrubbery. When I found the site in September 2017, the 100-square-foot clearing under tall trees contained pieces of window glass, the galvanized metal cap of a woodstove chimney, and a few pieces of old lumber coated with faded green paint. On the north side of the clearing stood a bronze US National Geodetic Survey benchmark—the azimuth marker for the Weatherwax survey station—located 0.5 mile to the northwest. The bronze disc sits on a 12-inch post with a yellow federal government property sign posted above on a tree trunk. No one has found the footing blocks for the 40-foot tower, although another nearby opening in the tall trees supports only shallow roots of shrubs and saplings. These conditions suggest it could have been the building site.

Please do not take souvenirs; leave the remnants of the old lookout station for others to find as they are. And, of course, please share the news of any discoveries you make on the site.

48. ANDERSON BUTTE LOOKOUT

RT Distance: 7.0 miles
High Point: 3358 feet
Elevation Gain: 2300 feet
Season: Jun-Nov
No pass or permit is required.

History

Anderson Butte is a forested ridge southeast of Lake Wynoochee near the southern border of the Olympic National Forest (ONF). The ridge has a rocky promontory on its western end, and an equally high summit on a secondary ridge running northeast. The people compiling inventories and collecting the histories of Washington's forest fire lookouts in the 1980s thought that the Civilian Conservation Corps (CCC) built the precariously sited fire lookout cabin on the rocky promontory in 1937 and that one of the construction workers had fallen off the butte to his death.[1]

The Anderson Butte Lookout, 1950s. (US Forest Service photo, curated by Steve Ricketts.)

The first clues that this might not be an accurate story appeared on the website of Oregon fire lookout historian Ron Kemnow. He briefly quotes the *Memoirs* of Harold C. Chriswell as saying the Anderson Butte fire lookout staff lived in a tent in 1942, and two government reports saying the lookout cabin was built with Aircraft Warning Service (AWS) funds in 1943 and retained by the Forest Service at the end of its AWS service.[2]

---

[1] Kresek, *2015*, 22, 113; Spring and Fish, 104, 198.
[2] [US Forest Service Region 6], *Lookout Station—Structural Inventory*, 1944 and [US Forest Service] Region 6, "Report of Aircraft Warning Service Stations," May 1, 1944, [Sheet no. missing].

Until I read the Chriswell *Memoirs* myself, I thought the 1937 building might not have been sturdy enough for year-round AWS use, and had been replaced in 1943, but Ranger Chriswell's details changed my thinking.

He arrived in western Washington to become the District Ranger at Hoodsport in March 1942. He stopped to meet his new boss in Olympia on his way to his assignment. He learned about Anderson Butte at that first meeting: "Anderson Butte L.O. . . . was a big rock that jutted out over solid, heavy timber covering the Satsop and Wynoochee River valleys . . . The lookout lived in a tent down in a saddle and climbed the rock hanging onto a piece of Number 9 telephone wire. The firefinder was mounted on three wobbly sticks with no room to get around it without knocking it out of adjustment or falling off the butte."[3]

"By God, if you don't get another thing done, I want that thing brought up to standard!"[4] were the boss's final words on the subject.

The project had all sorts of difficulties, according to Chriswell. Reaching the site required hiking a 3.5-mile trail with a 25 percent grade. Making the butte big enough to support a 14×14-foot cabin required flattening the rock with dynamite. Construction delays led to the discovery that the foreman could not read blueprints. Then, the cook, who refused to go up and down the steep trail more than once, fell from the butte one weekend and died, while the rest of the workers took their time off elsewhere.[5] The young construction crew (16- and 17-year-olds during the war years) were so upset by his death, they all went home, at least temporarily.[6]

My curiosity about the two stories of workers falling off the butte led me to send a query to the National Archives for the CCC, located in Bethesda, Maryland. I asked if their records showed any CCC deaths in this area in 1937. An archivist responded that there were no work-related Civilian Conservation Corps deaths reported in Washington state during the years 1933 to 1942.[7] The combination of Chriswell's memories and the CCC archival record settled the matter for me.

---

[3] This statement in 1942 indicates that the site was used as a fire lookout without benefit of a building until the project discussed here.
[4] Chriswell, 52.
[5] Letter from Dale G. Rogers to Ray Kresek, dated Mar. 11, 2002. Mr. Rogers identified himself as one of the teenaged crew members who remembered the accidental death of their crew cook, Mar, as a "terrible accident and very sobering!"
[6] Chriswell, 58, 60.
[7] Email query and response, November, 2018.

When AWS funds became available in 1943, the butte was flattened, and a cabin was built and staffed year-round during the war. It served the AWS—without and then with a cabin—1942 to April 1944, when the AWS program ended. The US Forest Service continued to assign fire lookout staff on the butte through 1964, at least.[8] The cabin was removed in 1968.

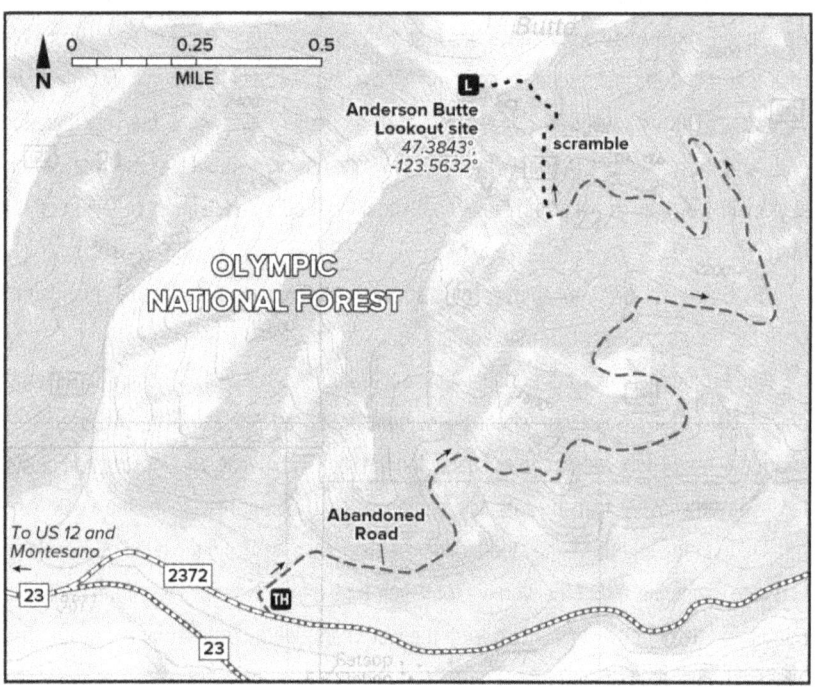

Hike Summary

This is an adventure hike from several perspectives. The first 3 miles of the route are on decommissioned roads that Mother Nature replants more rapidly than light hiking traffic can suppress. Leave the old road at a notable rock outcrop where the lookout route scrambles up a ridge on a steep track usually easy to follow. After one-third mile, turn left, clamber over a half-dozen large tree trunks, and go around a large, smooth boulder on a very narrow track to gain Anderson Butte's stanchion-studded promontory.

---

[8] *Shelton-Mason County Journal*, September 17, 1964, reported in https://washingtonlookouts.weebly.com/anderson-butte1.html.

48. ANDERSON BUTTE LOOKOUT · 255

Getting There

- Driving west on US Highway 12, take the Devonshire Road exit, just west of Montesano and milepost 10.
- At the four-way intersection at the end of the exit ramp, angle left onto the Wynoochee Valley Road. Follow signs toward the Wynoochee Dam. (Long time visitors to the area may remember the 20-mile drive on gravel that was finally paved in 2010.)
- About 30 miles from US Highway 12, entry signs for the Olympic National Forest and signs for Forest Road 22 appear on the right shoulder.
- At 32.7 miles, turn right onto Forest Road 23. Forest Road (FR) 22 turns left here, heading west toward Wynoochee Dam and Donkey Creek Road. FR 23 is a gravel road.
- At 33.6 miles, turn left on Forest Road 2372. Park on the wide shoulder at 34 miles from US Highway 12, or in the field a little farther along the road.

Hiking Route

Hike from the north side of the forest road on a rough spur that leads to a water tank hidden in the forest. After one-tenth mile, the little-traveled track turns left toward the tank and an unsigned trail leads to the right. Some ONF Pacific Ranger District maps show the trail as Forest Road 040, a road decommissioned decades ago. After the road was closed, a couple of shallow ditches were dug in the first 0.25 mile to discourage motor vehicles. More recently, a winter storm redirected a stream to cut a deeper channel through one of the ditches. Navigating these obstacles provides distractions from the healthy forest landscape at the start of the route.

The old road followed the contours of a bench on the ridge, curving to the northeast in a serpentine path. The route is generally through tall trees, with an often rocky slope rising on the left and a drop-off to the right, disappearing into dense forest. There are three notable clearings in the first 2 miles, each at an eastward curve, offering openings between the trees and views into the Satsop River Valley and forested hills on the other side.

A variety of vegetation and wildflowers grow underfoot and along the trail. Moist areas are marked with spongy moss. Leaves of low-growing wildflower plants like the heart-shaped yellow violet and larger, leathery wild ginger border the path. Hemlock, fir, and cedars provide shade for this understory in all seasons.

After the third corner, the trail parallels a canyon on its right with a burbling stream at its foot. At 2.3 miles, the path turns left, and then left again, and starts to gain a little more elevation as it heads south.

After gaining a short rise, the trail turns west and passes through an alder grove and a small field where large rocks have fallen from the slope to the right. At an opening between trees, the route ahead is clearly visible, curving to the right, above a steep drop-off. At the end of the curve, a prominent rocky point overlooks the Wynoochee Valley. The scrambling route to Anderson Butte turns north from the abandoned roadbed at that point, coordinates 47.3806°, -123.5597°.

Anderson Butte is the knob at the left high point on the ridge. The scramble route starts in the foreground.

Take a break when you reach the rocky prominence. Panoramic views into the Satsop and Wynoochee Valleys are available to the south. A patchwork quilt of multi-aged forest spreads out below, with the site of the historical Weatherwax Lookout tower on the next ridge south. The rocky viewpoint sits in full sun and supports an amazing array of wildflowers in early summer: little twinflower, violets, and owl's clover, along with taller bleeding heart, columbine, penstemon, paintbrush, lupine, tiger lily, arnica, valerian, yarrow, and beargrass. Plump salmonberries are sometimes ripe while these wildflowers bloom.

If you are a hiker, this can be quite a satisfying destination. You have come 3 miles or more and gained about 1700-foot elevation. If you look to the northwest, the bald, rocky knob at the end of the ridge is the Anderson Butte Lookout site. The route from here qualifies as a scramble, using Wikipedia's simplest definition: "a walk up steep terrain involving the use of one's hands."[9]

The scramble comes in two sections. The first section goes directly north about 0.4 mile on a 20-foot-wide ridge, while gaining 620-foot elevation. It has a fairly well-established trail, has had flagging added repeatedly in this century, and only requires a hand for balance or climbing an occasional rock to reach the upper ridge at 47.3842°, -123.5605°.

The second section is a little trickier because there are routes to two different destinations from this east end of that ridge. Some peak baggers head for the 3381-foot summit of Anderson Butte, which is on a spur running north. The Anderson Butte Lookout site is southwest from the east end of the upper ridge. To reach the lookout site, cross the narrow ridge on the south side of its crest. Unfortunately, a major winter windstorm earlier this century brought a half-dozen very thick fir trees down on the route to the lookout site. Clamber over these obstacles, resisting the attractively flagged route to the more northerly summit. While crossing the ridge, check your compass or GPS regularly to confirm you are not being drawn toward the wooded promontory to the north.

Sight of a 50×50-foot boulder, hiding among trees at the end of the ridge, is the sure sign you are approaching the Anderson Butte Lookout site. A short, narrow trail on the boulder's north side allows passage

---

[9] https://en.wikipedia.org/wiki/Scrambling. The entry cites the *Oxford New American Dictionary*, 2016.

alongside the big rock. Once past that, the steep, bald promontory appears, with its narrow, rocky trail and the metal posts being all that remain of the sturdy cable that once promised a safe ascent to the lookout cabin.

If you are game for the short scramble to 47.3842°, -123.5629°, there is room for a dozen people to cluster together on top, eat lunch, and take in views in all directions. Lake Wynoochee sits 2500 feet below to the northwest, calm blue and sparkling on a summer day. Snow-capped Olympic peaks stand regal to the north, and the south Olympic forests offer dark green velvet all around.

There are flat concrete blocks set into the level summit here, remnants of the foundation blocks that supported the small cabin that stood here for 25 years, from 1943 to 1968. Small, rusty old nails and sparkles of window glass also remain as artifacts. Please leave them for others to appreciate.

49. DUSK POINT LOOKOUT AND NEBY LOOKOUT TREE

RT Distance: 6.7 miles
High Point: 3240 feet
Elevation Gain: 1200 feet
Season: Apr-Oct
No pass or permit is required.

History

These two lookout sites sit on the high point and on one of the ridges south of Dusk Point, a 3240-foot peak between the Canyon and Satsop River Valleys. US Forest Service Ranger R. M. Beeman's 1938 field report described the Neby Lookout Tree as a "70 ft. tree—seat on top . . . Tree can be climbed without spurs." It also said the "top of mtn., ½ mile north, is logical site for permanent improvement, because much wider coverage."[1] A separate evaluation written the same day considered Dusk Point "good coverage—but Satsop Peak better."[2] The Neby Lookout Tree site was located "a 15 min. walk—¼ mile—by way trail from summit horse trail & telephone line."[3] The dotted line route on the maps accompanying the evaluation forms is presumably the summit horse trail mentioned in the reports. It is close to the current route of Forest Road (FR) 23 through the area.

Dusk Point is listed in both of the published historical inventories of Washington fire lookouts. Kresek says it was established in the 1930s, while Spring and Fish only states it appears on a Forest Service map.[4] The only map I found showing the symbol for a forest fire lookout at the summit was an Olympic National Forest/Olympic National Park map published in 1977.

Retired Forest Ranger Stan Graham remembered Dusk Point was used as an "as-needed" lookout without a building in the 1960s.[5] A short article on the use of house trailers by the Olympic National Forest in 1956 suggests one was probably located on

---

[1] R. M. Beeman, [Fire Lookout Site Evaluation] "Neby Lookout Tree," Aug. 31, 1938; Document 17-14-7, National Archives in Seattle.
[2] R. M. Beeman, [Fire Lookout Site Evaluation] "Neby Mtn. Dusk Point," Aug. 31, 1938; Document 6-5.5, National Archives in Seattle.
[3] Beeman, [Fire Lookout Site Evaluation] "Neby Lookout Tree." The only trail shown on the accompanying maps follows the current route of Road 23.
[4] Kresek, *1998*, 114; Spring and Fish, 198.
[5] Personal conversation, March 2018.

Dusk Point that year. It says a trailer was "delivered to the Shelton Ranger District [for fire lookout use] on the Canyon River drainage."[6] Dusk Point is the only known Forest Service fire lookout station in that District to have had views of the Canyon River watershed.

The only physical signs of long-term use of the site are a likely outhouse hole and scraps of cedar shakes that still appear beside the old road leading to the Dusk Point Lookout site.

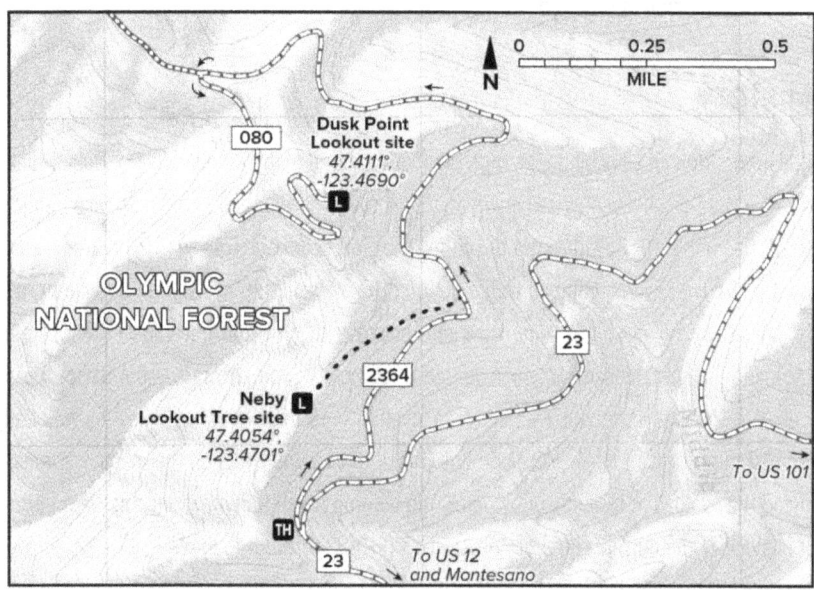

Hike Summary

This hike uses Forest Road 2364 and a little-traveled spur road to reach the Dusk Point Lookout site. The route provides panoramas into the Olympics and the forested landscape to the east as it spirals toward the summit. The high point offers territorial views from southeast to northwest, including snow-topped Cascade peaks in clear weather. An abandoned forest track offers an opportunity to explore for the Neby Lookout Tree site on the return trip.

---

[6] E. C. DeGraff, "House trailers for detection of forest fires," *Fire Control Notes*, Vol.19, no.1, 19-21.

Getting there from US Highway 101

- At the junction of US Highway 101 and State Route 106, turn west on the Skokomish Valley Road. Set your trip meter to 0.
- At 5.7 miles, turn right and uphill on FR 23. The road passes through private forestland on a heavily potholed gravel road.
- At 8.0 miles, keep left on unsigned, but mostly paved, FR 23. Pass the side road to the Brown Creek Campground.
- At 15.1 miles, keep left and go uphill on FR 23.
- At 19.5 miles, keep left at a Y. There may be an informal "Lake" sign on a tree. The pavement ends here.
- At 23.3 miles, pass FR 2350. Spider Lake is hidden in the trees to the east; there are often cars parked along the road here.
- Drive a few winding miles on what is usually the roughest part of the road. At 26.0 miles and FR 23's junction with FR 2364, park in a wide spot.

Getting there from US Highway 12 and the Wynoochee Valley Road

- Driving west on US Highway 12, take the Devonshire Road exit, just west of Montesano and milepost 10.
- At the four-way intersection at the end of the exit ramp, angle left onto the Wynoochee Valley Road. Follow signs toward the Wynoochee Dam.
- At 30 miles from US Highway 12, signs for the Olympic National Forest and Forest Road 22 appear on the right shoulder.
- At 32.7 miles, turn right onto FR 23. FR 22 turns left here, heading west toward Wynoochee Dam and the Donkey Creek Road. The paved road ends here.
- FR 2372 goes left in just under a mile.
- At 34.5 miles, keep right on FR 23 as you pass signs toward the Satsop Center.
- At 36.1 miles, continue straight.

- At 42.3 miles, take a sharp left turn. There is often no sign here, but FR 23 turns left and the road ahead is FR 2368, which is usually potholed.
- At 45.9 miles, keep left, resisting attractive FR 2365.
- At 46.3 miles, park in a wide spot on the right side of FR 23. The hiking route, FR 2364, angles off to the left, starting its spiral ascent to Dusk Point.

Hiking Route

There are one or more signs at this junction identifying the ascending road as FR 2364. I have always been curious about the road's destination beyond Dusk Point, but map research has given few clues.

The road climbs steadily, revealing larger and larger views of Olympic forests as it curves around the north side of Dusk Point. Typical Olympic mountain wildflowers border the road and ascend the rocky walls beside the route. Yellow violets, bright orange paintbrush, deep pink bleeding heart, and tall, white beargrass pompoms follow a profusion of trilliums in spring. A little later in the season it is easy to tell the creamy goat's beard blossom from the similar flower on ocean spray shrubs while ascending the road. Sunshine here also encourages a proliferation of tiger lilies not often seen on shady Olympic trails.

Dusk Point as seen from below.

There are few side tracks to distract from the route. At 2.0 miles, reach an intersection with Forest Roads 080 and 100—heading off to the left and right, respectively. Since 2018, a big plywood sign with hand-painted lettering has appeared high in a tree on the right side of the intersection. Its arrows indicate *Squid Peak* is straight ahead and *The Real Dusk Point* is to the left. The official road signs are overgrown now, but older maps of the area carry the numbers.

Follow FR 080 to the left, between alder and willow branches that sometimes meet above the roadbed. The route is clearly apparent at ground level, even when enthusiastic tree growth obscures the track. Spring flowers, including bleeding heart, yellow violets, and wild ginger brighten the narrow road's shoulders.

About 0.3 mile from the turn onto FR 080, there is a large clearing on the right side of the road. It has always seemed a likely spot for a building, but no historical use has been discovered.

The next switchback in the road stands at the top of a distinctive spur ridge running south from Dusk Peak. This corner is a popular camping spot, and there are several ways to clamber down to an old roadbed that follows the ridge a short distance downhill. The Neby Lookout Tree site was reported as a half-mile down this ridge from Dusk Point, but an easier route will be found on the return trip downhill.

The view across the Satsop River Valley from the Neby Lookout Tree site.

After this corner, the road reverses from a counterclockwise spiral to clockwise. The route is approaching the summit but requires a full rotation to reach the top. At one corner, there are views of the three "C peaks" of the south Olympics: Capitol, Church, and Chapel.

Emerging on the flat summit of Dusk Point, attention goes to the panoramic view of distant Cascade peaks; Mount St. Helens, Mount Adams, and Mount Rainier can all be seen on a clear day. The towers on the two peaks of South Mountain and the glint of Puget Sound's waters appear in the middle distance.

The only significant artifact near the summit can be found under the trees and down a short slope on the southeast edge of the clearing. It is a 3×4-foot hole, about 4-feet-deep, that is easy to interpret as an outhouse hole in the rocky ground. There are a few pieces of lumber fastened with nails lying at the bottom. It doesn't go far to prove Dusk Point was an active fire lookout station, but loggers and hunters don't dig similar holes, and outhouses are often located a short distance downhill from lookout stations.

On the return trip from the summit, you can stop at a long-abandoned forest track, partway down FR 2364, to explore for the Neby Lookout Tree. Leave the west side of the gravel road at 47.4083°, -123.4636°. Clamber over or around two low berms and ditches and follow the narrow track cross-country, one-third mile southwest, to a clearing filling with young Douglas firs and hemlocks. Continue southwest through a final cluster of trees and shrubbery to a rocky viewpoint at 47.4054°, -123.4701°, and a 2770-foot elevation. In 2021, this point was graced with a thick, rotting stump with a grand view of forested slopes as far as the eye could see. This is the best candidate for the Neby Lookout Tree discovered to date.

WILLAPA HILLS

Hikes on state and private forestlands
west of Interstate 5 from the Capitol State Forest
and the Pacific Ocean to the Columbia River.

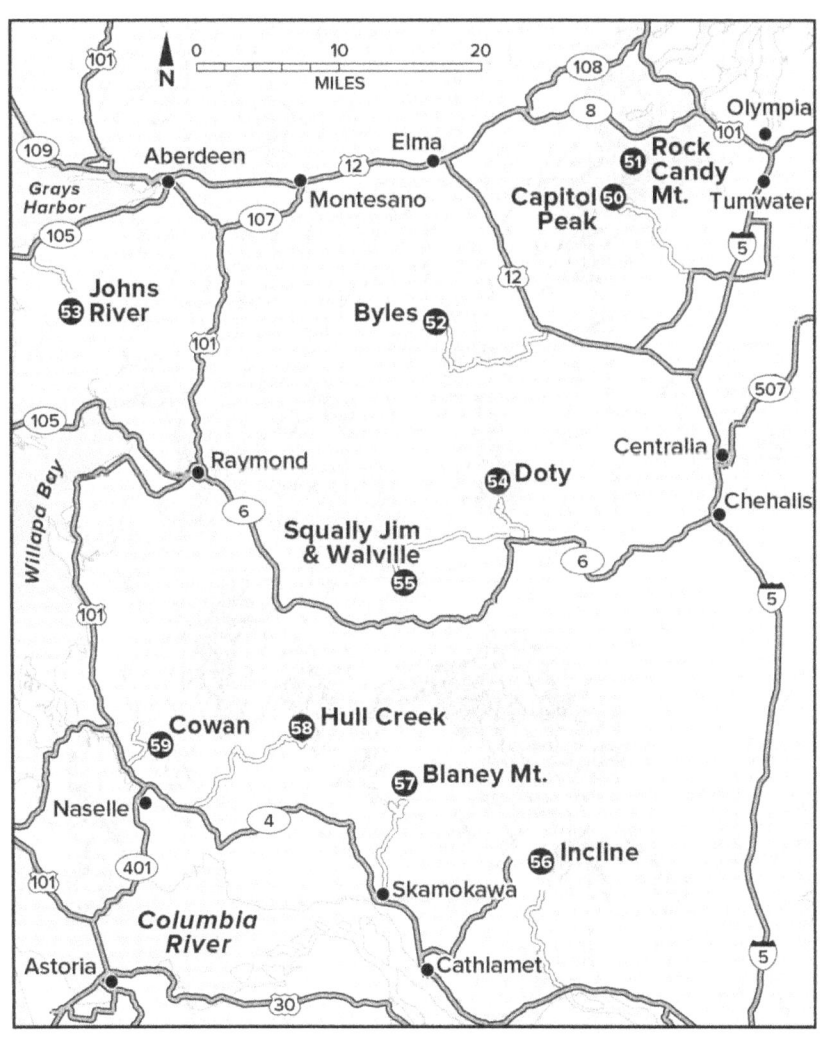

50. CAPITOL PEAK LOOKOUT

RT Distance: 8.2 miles
High Point: 2658 feet
Elevation Gain: 1850 feet
Season: Apr-Nov
A Discover Pass is required.

History

The private Washington Forest Fire Association built the first fire lookout tower on Capitol Peak in 1929 in cooperation with the state's Department of Conservation and Development's Division of Forestry. The initial building was unique—and very tall. Trees still covered the mountain's broad, flat peak, so a tower was needed to assure a clear view. Four live trees were topped and braced, and a platform built at 84 feet with a trapdoor to allow access for fire watchers. A 30-foot tripod tower rose from the platform, taking the height of the small viewing cabin to 114 feet. Lookout staff used a bosun's chair with a counterbalance to ascend to the platform, and a ladder from there to the top. A tent and stove were provided for shelter on the ground.[1]

The Capitol Peak Lookout tower, 1935. (Courtesy of the Washington Digital Archives.)

Within a year, this lookout and another nearby reported almost simultaneously on an unusual and challenging fire. The blaze was started by "supposed sportsmen," according to a press report, to smoke out a wild beehive. The fire smoldered and broke out later. The Minot Peak and Capitol Peak lookouts worked together to identify the location and the response was prompt. Unfortunately, "the difficulties of the country, wind and weather hampered the fire crew, and a considerable acreage of virgin timber was killed and destroyed."[2]

---

[1] Washington Forest Fire Association, *Twenty-Second Annual Report*, 1929, [2, 13-14]; *Twenty-Seventh Annual Report*, 1934, 15.
[2] Washington Forest Fire Association, *Twenty-Third Annual Report*, 1930, [18].

50. CAPITOL PEAK LOOKOUT

The Capitol Peak Lookout was rebuilt four times after its first makeshift construction, indicating the importance of its location above the state capitol. Its panoramic views stretched from the Pacific to the Cascades and Olympic Mountains to central-southwestern Washington.

The original tower was replaced with a 100-foot structure of pressure-creosoted Douglas fir timbers in 1935.[3] Ray Kresek's *Fire Lookouts of the Northwest* reports the US Army took down the 100-foot tower in 1942 to build a World War II radar station on the site. The tower was replaced in 1943.[4] That one came down in a 1946 windstorm and was rebuilt in 1947—as a 68-foot tower with a live-in cabin on top. It fell down in 1954, and the last lookout tower there was built the same year. It lasted until the Department of Natural Resources decided it was a hazard on the popular hilltop and brought it down in August 1968.[5] From the three photos published in the DNR monthly magazine, it appears guy wires were released on one side of the tower and tightened on the other, producing a graceful descent for the abandoned structure.

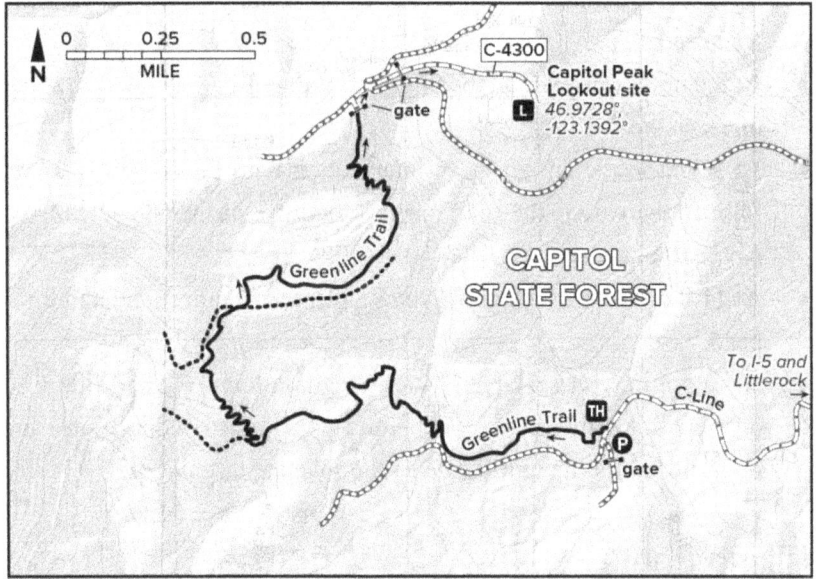

---

[3] Washington Division of Forestry, "Capitol State Forest and Nursery," *Thirty-First and Thirty-Second Annual Reports for the Period Commencing December 1, 1934, and Ending November 30, 1936*, 7. The date is established by a photo on http://willhiteweb.com/washington_fire_lookouts/capitol_peak/larch_mountain_420.htm

[4] Kresek, *1998*, 114.

[5] Washington Department of Natural Resources, *Totem*, vol. 10, no.9. September 1968.

Hike Summary

Hike a usually well-maintained trail with territorial views for much of its route and 360-degree panoramas on the summit. The landscape is managed for timber harvests and recreation, so healthy forest and tree nurseries alternate as you ascend toward Capitol Peak.

Getting There

- Drive Interstate 5 to Exit 95 in central Thurston County. Follow the exit west, toward Littlerock.
- Drive 2.9 miles west to the stop sign at the intersection of 128th Street and Littlerock Road. Continue straight on 128th Street.
- At 3.8 miles from Interstate 5, turn right at a T on Waddell Creek Road.
- At 6.1 miles, enter the Capitol State Forest and pass a Discover Pass Required sign.
- At 8.0 miles, turn left on the Sherman Valley Road, labeled on some maps as the C-Line.
- At 9.3 miles, keep left at an intersection with the Noschka Road. Shortly thereafter, the road narrows and the surface changes from paved to oiled.
- At 11.8 miles, pass a sign for the Fall Creek Campground and trailhead.
- At 12.5 miles, pass a Green Line #6 sign. Pull into a gated side road on the left. Park without blocking the gate. Return to the Green Line #6 trailhead on the uphill side of the road to start hiking.

Hiking Route

Start uphill in tall trees with a healthy understory. The trail is bordered with a procession of spring and summer flowers that starts with open-faced trilliums and yellow violets in April. After a short distance, emerge into a young tree farm and the first view across broad valleys patched in shades of green—hinting at the maturity of the trees in each section of the forest. After 0.6 mile, reenter the forest and head downhill toward a pretty, metal-framed wooden bridge crossing exuberant Fall Creek.

Ascend out of the creek valley, turn a corner, and follow a quiet creek through the forest to a wetland featuring a grove of devil's club at 1.2 miles. Emerge from those trees to cross a road into a younger tree plantation. A hillock among the young trees is crossed with a steep bike path—an alternate to the footpath that circles the little hill. At 1.65 miles, come to a trail junction with routes to Wedekind and Porter Creek. One sign claims Capitol Peak is only 2.1 miles ahead.

The trail starts winding short switchbacks through tall, slender trees, a sure sign of more serious elevation gain. But the views expand as you ascend—Mount St. Helens to the southeast; Mount Rainier, due east; and, Mount Adams in between. Smaller snowy peaks between Mounts St. Helens and Adams are the Goat Rocks; even smaller white peaks in the distance beyond these major Washington peaks are Mounts Hood and Jefferson in Oregon.

Denser forest on the next ridge features wild ginger at trailside, with leathery, heart-shaped leaves hiding exotic maroon blooms in May. Cross another road at 2.3 miles and 2010-foot elevation. In a short distance, enter a young plantation established after mature trees were harvested in early 2018. The trail will have been fully restored and new trees planted by the time you read this. The trail winds steadily uphill around saved-tree islands, ending at a gated side road a few hundred feet higher.

Before turning right toward Capitol Peak, turn around and enjoy the view. Mount Adams, Goat Rocks, and Mount St. Helen will have expanded on the horizon as you have gained elevation. Mount Rainier has temporarily disappeared around the corner to the left.

Between you and Capitol Peak's best views is a 0.5 mile of gravel road popular with beer-can-tossing motorized recreationalists. Fortunately, the route has another gate to help keep roaring vehicles at bay. Of the three roads ahead, follow the only one climbing a hill. Its yellow gate is buttressed with thick concrete barriers and broad root balls with stumps, and currently manages to withstand all motorized traffic. Hikers can step over the gate or around the sturdy gate posts.

Continue up the hill, gaining views to the west and north as you go. A half-dozen communication towers, block buildings, remains of former communication towers, and a variety of fences occupy the notably broad hilltop. A slightly taller broad green ridge stands between Capitol Peak and the Olympics. It is Larch Mountain, the highest peak in the Capitol State Forest, still fully forested in 2018.

In the center of the clearing are the remains of the last fire lookout tower to stand watch over this section of the region's forests. A few footing blocks with broken galvanized iron posts sit on a slightly raised area. A few others can be found in the underbrush nearby. The main attraction of the site remains as it always has been—spectacular views in all directions.

If you would like more information to support further site exploration, three sets of National Geodetic Survey markers were located on Capitol Peak, starting in 1911. Here are the web addresses for those US Geodetic Survey datasheets with their histories:

https://www.ngs.noaa.gov/cgi-bin/ds_mark.prl?PidBox=SC1580,
https://www.ngs.noaa.gov/cgi-bin/ds_mark.prl?PidBox=SC1581,
https://www.ngs.noaa.gov/cgi-bin/ds_mark.prl?PidBox=SC1583.

At some time in its history, each survey marker had its distance from its contemporary Capitol Fire Lookout Tower measured. One benchmark was even labeled "Capitol LOT" for Look Out Tower. With careful reading and measurement, you may find more survey markers or lookout tower artifacts in obscure locations on this summit. Happy exploration!

51. ROCK CANDY MOUNTAIN LOOKOUT

RT Distance: 6.5 miles
High Point: 2364 feet
Elevation Gain: 1800 feet
Season: All Year – Best: Apr
A Discover Pass is required.

History

For a fire lookout with a name as enticing as this, little of its history has been recorded. Its location was a modest knoll in the Capitol State Forest, a few miles south of State Route 8 and Summit Lake. The Kresek lookout inventory includes buildings in its description: "1930s: tower, cabin. [Aban'd]"[1] Eric Willhite found a series of three of the Osborne panoramic photographs taken from Rock Candy Mountain, October 5, 1934. Unlike the origin of some Osborne panoramic photos, there is no indication the photographer stood on a tower to take the images.[2]

The only other suggestion that this lookout station had a structure is the inclusion of Rock Candy Mountain on a list of state lookout stations submitted for consideration by the Aircraft Warning Service in summer 1942. The Rock Candy Mountain Lookout was categorized as a "Ground Type" building on that list.[3]

There have also been two sets of US Geodetic Survey station markers here, installed in 1937 and 1974. The datasheets for these benchmarks do not mention a fire lookout cabin or tower, despite the earlier set of marker discs being installed when a lookout building would most likely have stood on Rock Candy Mountain.[4]

The name itself, Rock Candy Mountain, draws us in. There was a memorable childhood song that could well have inspired the name of this third highest point in the state forest. The later twentieth century song was a sanitized version of a folk song released in

---

[1] Kresek, *1998*, 115.
[2] The Osborne images taken on Rock Candy Mountain are posted at: http://www.willhiteweb.com/puget_sound_hiking/rock_candy_mountain/capitol_forest/black_hills_313.htm.
[3] [State] "List of Lookout Towers, received August 10, 1942," p.2. Image of the document is posted on https://willhiteweb.com/washington_fire_lookouts/aircraft_warning_service/state_lookout_towers/aws_274.htm.
[4] US National Geodetic Survey, "Data Sheet PID SY1789 ROCK CANDY USE 1937"; https://www.ngs.noaa.gov/cgi-bin/ds_mark.prl?PidBox=SY1789.

1928, romanticizing a hobo life of an even earlier period.[5] While the original talked about cigarette trees and handouts that grow on bushes, later versions emphasized easy rhymes and lines about lemonade springs and peppermint trees.[6] The timing of the original recording allows us to at least speculate on a link between the song and the naming of the peak and its lookout.

On the other hand, hiking this trail when ice and frost are on the ground is reminiscent of the old-fashioned candy that shares the peak's name. The confection is white, translucent, and clear, just like the ice that forms on Capitol State Forest trails on frosty winter days.

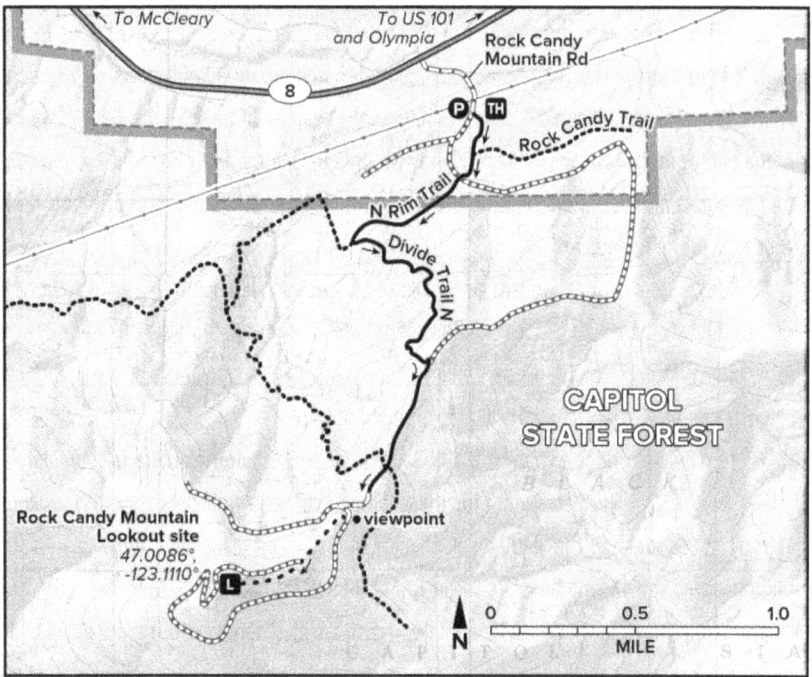

Hike Summary

This is a good example of hikes in the Capitol State Forest. There are several ways to reach the destination; each involves numerous junctions and a few road crossings. Trail conditions come and go, as do the well-intended trail signs. The trails to Rock Candy Mountain are shared with

---

[5] The lyrics are posted at: https://genius.com/Harry-mcclintock-big-rock-candy-mountain-lyrics.
[6] The original version for children is generally credited to Burl Ives, 1949.

bicycles all year and motorized bikes during May through October. Despite these drawbacks, the views of snow-topped Cascade and Olympic peaks can be wonderful, and sections of the forest are truly beautiful. The convenience of the hike to the state capitol area cannot be beat.

Getting There

- From Interstate 5 in Olympia, take Exit 104 to US Highway 101 northbound.
- Drive west 5.8 miles and keep left on State Route 8, where US Highway 101 turns north.
- Pass milepost 17. Get in the left lane to exit left.
- A road sign indicates a left turn to the Rock Candy Mountain Road and a right turn to Summit Lake. Pull into the median left turn lane and cross the two eastbound lanes to enter the Capitol State Forest.
- Drive a short distance and park in the parking lot on the right, or adjacent to it during the winter season when the lot is gated.
- The trailhead is across the road from the parking lot.

Hiking Route

Cross the road to a clearly marked trailhead for the Rock Candy and North Rim #1 trails. Do not let the trail names draw you in. The route that starts with the North Rim #1 Trail offers the most direct hiking path to Rock Candy Mountain. The route of the Rock Candy Trail is more than 2 miles longer and goes to the same destination. The 0.1-mile trail shared by the two routes briefly crosses open land before entering the forest. The trail splits under the trees, with the Rock Candy Trail crossing an attractive bridge and heading east. The North Rim #1 Trail heads south into a mixed forest without any enticements beyond a well-maintained walking surface. The route's first road crossing appears at 0.33 mile with a big X sign (present in 2016, absent since 2018), Capitol State Forest's standard warning of a road with possible crossing traffic, ahead. A brown sign here reaffirms you are on the North Rim #1 Trail.

At 0.8 mile, turn left (east) at a 3-way intersection. The sign here in 2020 said that North Rim Trail continued east and west. Maps indicate the North Rim Trail continues west from this point, not continuing toward Rock Candy Mountain. In 0.1 mile, the trail turns south and passes an area of young trees that provides views of the south Olympics and western Capitol State Forest. This part of the route ends on another section of old forest road whose use is now reserved for two-wheeled, horse, and hiking traffic. You have come about 1.65 miles and now enter what was in the past the prettiest section of trail to the Rock Candy Mountain Lookout site as it ascends the west slope of the peak.[7] In the next mile, the route climbs the hill in moderately steep zigzags, with more and more of the Olympic Mountains appearing as you ascend. The evergreens have been tall here, making them subject to a series of harvest projects starting in 2018. Where it remains, the forest contains a mixture of conifers and low shrubs, with hedges of Oregon grape, sword ferns, and a mixture of other native flowering and evergreen plants often bordering the trail.

A view of the Olympic Mountains from the trail to Rock Candy Mountain.

At 2.65 miles, the trail reaches the ridge that runs northeast from the Rock Candy Mountain summit and intersects the longer Rock Candy Mountain Trail route to the top. The elevation is about 1700 feet, indicating that most of the elevation gain for the hike has been completed. Turn right and discover a major junction of forest trails. The sign for the trail you have just completed identifies that route as the Rim Trail.

---

[7] Sections of the Capitol State Forest surrounding the upper trail have been identified for harvest since 2018. Different parcels are shorn each year, opening views, disrupting trails, and displacing trail signs. In conversations, the Capitol Forest Recreation manager has indicated a lack of staff to keep up with needed trail maintenance.

The wide forest path you have joined is the Divide North Trail. Two additional wooden signs name the destinations of a downhill side trail, Waddell Creek and Porter Creek.

Continue on the broader, flatter trail as it gradually becomes steeper, turns right, then left onto a road that opens onto a grand viewpoint offering Mount Rainier, Mount Adams, and Mount St. Helens to the east, and forested landscape in all directions at your feet.

After admiring the view from the road edge, cross the gravel to a fairly steep bank marked with informal trails. In 2021, several former trails had resolved into one shared by hikers, bikers, and dirt bikes. Ten-to-twelve feet above the road this informal way-trail levels out and wanders through open forest. The route ascends very gradually at first, becoming steeper after 0.25 mile, when it approaches an area with sky visible above young trees. The clearing is a road end; the road continues the gradual elevation increase for another 0.15 mile. When the road you are hiking veers to the right, take the trail opening in tall salal on the left side of the road, continuing the straight route. Follow the trail through salal and forest for little more than a 0.1 mile, where it emerges at a hilltop road end.

This is the top of Rock Candy Mountain and the site of its fire lookout. The curiously named hill offers panoramic views west and north over many miles of forest to the Olympics and possible glimpses of the southern bays of Puget Sound. Most of the timbered acreage between here and the Pacific Ocean, and south to the Columbia River, is privately owned. There are only eight publicly accessible fire lookout sites outside of Capitol State Forest in the Willapa Hills. Almost all you can see is commercial timber—private tree farms—grown to be harvested repeatedly with little regard for ecosystem health or wildlife.[8]

---

[8] This opinion echoes that of Robert Michael Pyle in his award-winning book about the Willapa Hills, *Wintergreen, Listening to the Land's Heart*, New York, Charles Scribner's Sons, 1986.

52. BYLES LOOKOUT

RT Distance: 9.0 miles
High Point: 970 feet
Elevation Gain: 1000 feet
Season: All Year
A Discover Pass is not currently required for this hike.

History

A 70-foot-tall wooden forest fire lookout tower was built on a low hill in private forestland southeast of Minot Peak and southwest of the Capitol State Forest in the 1940s. The staff had only a 7×7-foot cabin at the top of the tower for shelter when they watched for wildfires. A photograph of that tower was included in a 1991 booklet celebrating the 50th anniversary of the Weyerhaeuser Clemons Tree Farm.[1] Fortunately for hikers, the Weyerhaeuser Company and the Department of Natural Resources (DNR) exchanged some land parcels in this area in 1986.[2] As a result, the Byles Lookout site is now in the Lower Chehalis State Forest and readily available for public access.

The Byles Lookout tower. (Undated Ken Brown photograph, courtesy of the Forest History Society, Durham, NC.)

    Treated lumber remnants and galvanized steel rods remain spread over the landscape, suggesting the building was abandoned and fell where it had stood. US National Geodetic Survey audits of the Byles Lookout survey station reported the bronze marker was under the center of the lookout tower in 1952. The tower was gone in 1960.[3] The survey markers have not been found.

---

[1] *A Celebration for Generations to Come*. A 16-page booklet distributed at the Clemons Tree Farm celebration; Kresek, *2015*, 22.
[2] The Department of Natural Resources Library provided a digital copy of "The History of the Lower Chehalis State Forest" in 2018. The text was published on an undated map of the Capitol and Lower Chehalis State Forests.
[3] US National Geodetic Survey, "Data Sheet PID SC1603 BYLES LOOKOUT"; https://www.ngs.noaa.gov/cgi-bin/ds_mark.prl?PidBox=SC1603.

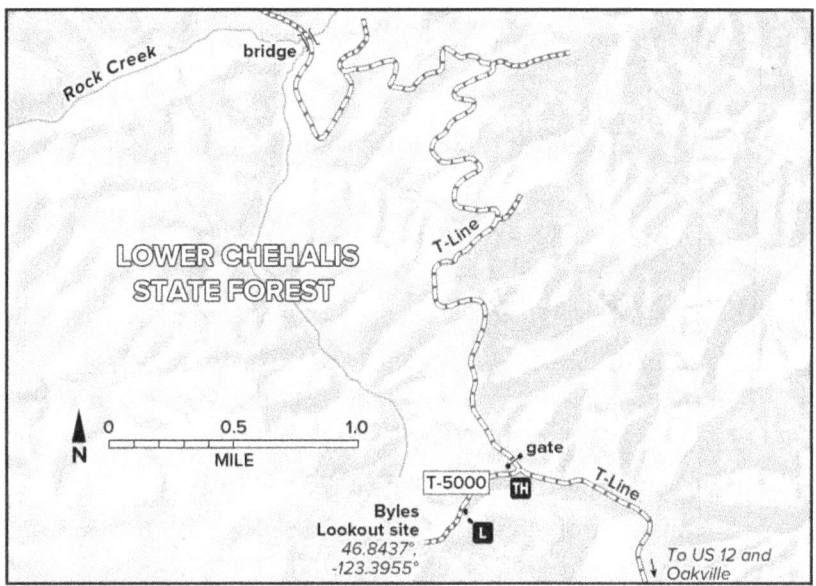

Hike Summary

This lookout site sits 0.3 mile from the parking spot in the little-known Lower Chehalis State Forest on the eastern border of Grays Harbor County. Rather than walk directly to the Byles site, my preference is to hike down to pretty Rock Creek on the border between the state forest and Weyerhaeuser's Twin Harbors Tree Farm, then return to the starting point and the lookout site nearby. The area surrounding the historic site is scheduled for timber harvest between 2021 and 2023, making the short, off-road visit to the lookout site an unknown adventure at this time.[4] Where forest remains, it is a beautiful mixture of evergreen and deciduous trees, shrubs, ferns, lichen, and moss, with vistas of lowland forests and distant mountains provided by expanding clearcuts.

---

[4] Visit the author's website, www.leslieromer.com, for an update.

Getting There

- Drive Interstate 5 to Exit 88 in southern Thurston County. Drive west on US Highway 12, passing the traffic light in Rochester in 4.7 miles.
- Pass signs for turns to the Lucky Eagle Casino and the Chehalis Tribal Center.
- At 11.2 miles from Interstate 5, enter Oakville, and turn left on State Street with the US Post Office on the corner on your left.
- The street's name changes to South Bank Road when it curves to the right. Cross the Chehalis River Bridge at 13 miles from the Interstate and immediately turn left on Garrard Creek Road.
- At 16.5 miles from Interstate 5, Garrard Creek Road turns left and the Oakville-Brooklyn Road goes straight. Take the Oakville-Brooklyn Road and continue traveling west.
- The pavement ends at 19.7 miles from Interstate 5.
- At 20.7 miles, enter a short stretch of one-lane road that has a "Single Lane Road" sign.
- The one-lane road is followed by a sharp right turn, 20.9 miles from Interstate 5. Take the unsigned road on the right. You are entering the Lower Chehalis State Forest on the T-Line forest road.
- The parking spot for this hike is 4.5 miles up the T-Line. The road surface is usually in good condition, but it does have a few narrow stretches with steep drop-offs. I have never met a logging truck on this road, but it is wise to check with the Department of Natural Resources office to see if there are current logging or road construction activities using the road. The DNR Castle Rock office manages the Lower Chehalis State Forest: 360-577-2025.
- There are few side roads to distract you from the T-Line, but at 4 miles from the entry into the state forest, a two-lane road continues north while the now one-lane T-Line goes northwest (left). Continue on the T-Line.
- Just past milepost 4.5 (about 25.4 miles from Interstate 5), there is a gate (usually closed) on the T-Line. A wildlife protection area

sign is posted on a tree on the left behind the gate. Parking space for a couple of cars is available at the junction with Road T-5000, left of the gate.

Hiking Route

Tree harvesting in the Lower Chehalis State Forest resumed in earnest sometime in the second decade of the twenty-first century. Few hikers will find recent clearcuts attractive, but the soil in this forest is rich, and recovery will happen. I anticipate the landscape will eventually return to its characteristically lush mixture of conifer and deciduous trees, with a healthy understory of shrubs and wildflowers, mosses, and lichen.

Rock Creek beside the Byles Lookout hike route.

The T-Line behind the wildlife gate is a well-maintained gravel road, which takes more than 4 miles to reach Rock Creek and the State Forest boundary, 2 aerial miles away. The old road zigs and zags its way north, curving around steep hills on its right and above little canyons and creek headwaters on its left. Keep track of progress for most of the distance with the yellow mile markers on the trees. 4.5 is posted near the gate and the signs continue in 0.5-mile increments until milepost 7. After hiking 1.5 miles, the 6-mile marker stands beside a junction in a broad field of young trees, offering a clear view of the Cascades. After admiring the eastern prospect, turn left and continue slightly downhill. Forest and clearcut areas alternate, offering more views of young trees and distant green hills. There are two more left turns on the route. A few huge, ancient cedar stumps can be spotted in the still forested areas, while harvests in 2018 to 2019 left 4-foot-wide maple stumps beside the roadway.

The last section of road leads through thick forest with increasing sounds of a busy creek on the left. Rock Creek comes into view in the center of a narrow valley with open forest on both sides of its little floodplain. Cedar trees dominate the downhill slope between the road and the creek. The hike route ends at the wooden plank bridge crossing the gently flowing Rock Creek. The only indication of a forest boundary is a "Discover Pass Required" sign that faces traffic coming from the Weyerhaeuser Tree Farm to the west.

But where is the lookout site? Retrace your steps to the T-Line gate. The side road leading south is T-5000. It leads in a short distance to the Byles Lookout site. Hike 0.3 mile to a widening of the ridge on the left. Now look at the large trees on your right (west). One has a rectangular yellow sign with the number 2 on its south side. The short cross-country route to the lookout site is across the road.

This area is scheduled for harvest in the 2020s. The Byles Lookout site is in a Save Tree grove that will remain, at the top of the low ridge. Find your way carefully through whatever dense vegetation or logging debris covers the 100 yards between the road and the reserved forested area at the lookout site.

There, you will find sturdy wooden beams bolted to each other at right angles lying on the mossy ground. There are also a few metal plates bolted to the beams, but low vegetation is eager to conceal all the remnants of the once tall tower. A little farther northeast are galvanized steel rods and angles protruding from four concrete bases hidden under shallow duff. The metal protrusions suggest these concrete blocks supported a tower, but they are too close together for it to have been 70 feet tall. Are they footing blocks that have been moved, or did they have a different purpose entirely?

It appears the spread of the artifacts equals the 70-foot height of the original tower. It is possible that other remains are hidden under the rich vegetation, including a bronze benchmark that once stood under the center of the Byles Lookout structure. If you find anything interesting, please let me know.

53. JOHNS RIVER LOOKOUT

RT Distance: 3 miles or more
High Point: 410 feet
Elevation Gain: 300 feet
Season: All Year
No pass or permit is required.

History

The existence of this fire lookout was seemingly forgotten sometime in the twentieth century. A fellow lookout hunter found clues to its history in the World War II Aircraft Warning Service (AWS) archives in 2017 and offered me the opportunity to see what I could find on the ground.

In Seattle National Archive documents, Eric Willhite found several tables listing Markum, Markham, and Johns River Lookout at the same location near the Johns River, between Westport and Aberdeen in Grays Harbor County. A series of memos discussing the names of AWS stations around western Washington show the name went quickly from Markum in September to Markham in October and permanently to Johns River in November 1942.[1] Concern about assigning the same name to multiple AWS stations caused the changes.

In 1944, a document considering the disposition of AWS stations after their two-year service for the war identified the Johns River Lookout as located on private land with a 14×32-foot, reconditioned cabin. As AWS observation posts were staffed year-round, while fire lookouts were only used during the driest months, it is likely the cabin constructed for winter shelter was stronger and more durable than those built only for summer use. The report recommended the State Division of Forestry retain the building as a fire lookout.[2] The building is certainly gone now.

---

[1] These memos are posted at: http://willhiteweb.com/washington_fire_lookouts/johns_river_lookout/markham_157.htm.
[2] Washington Division of Forestry, Memo for File: A.W.S. Posts Retained for Use by State Under Cooperative Agreement with the U.S. Forest Service, [June, 1944].

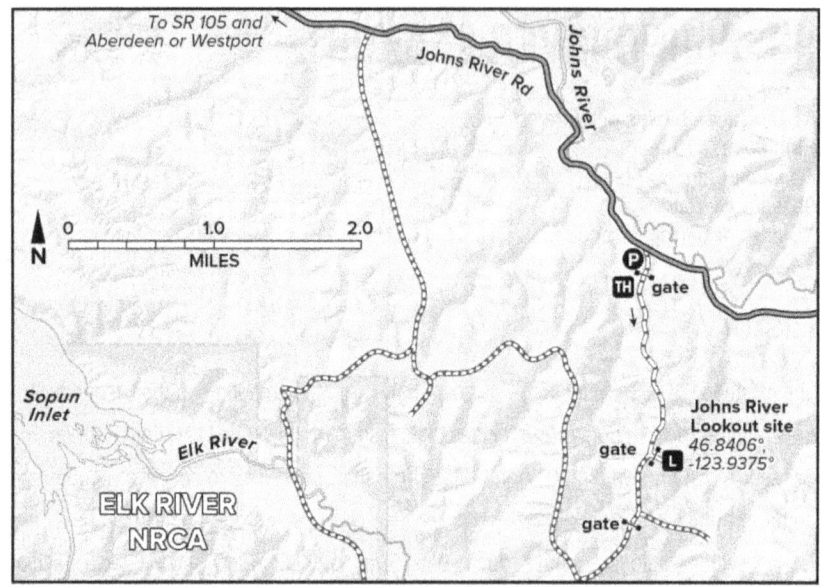

Hike Summary

This is a short road hike on private forestland with little elevation gain to an ill-defined fire lookout location. There are few known hikes in this area of Washington's coastal forests, so take the opportunity to explore the adjacent roads and land and enjoy views over the low hills to the saltwater of Grays Harbor and the uplands beyond.

Getting There

- From the center of Aberdeen, turn south on US Highway 101 toward Raymond and Westport.
- Cross the bridge over the Chehalis River; immediately turn right on State Route 105 toward Westport. Reset your trip meter to 0.
- Pass signs for the Stafford Creek Correctional Center. The most noticeable signs instruct: Do Not Pick Up Hitchhikers.
- Pass the big, square Ocean Spray building on the right, then cross the Johns River Bridge, about 11.9 miles from the turn onto State Route 105.

- After crossing the bridge, get in the left turn lane and turn left on Johns River Road.
- Drive the paved Johns River Road as it passes the Johns River Wildlife Area on the left. Cross Atwood Creek and watch for a gravel road on the right with a stop sign at its junction with the Johns River Road. This intersection is about 4.8 miles from State Highway 105. The Johns River Road is paved for only a short distance after this junction—do not continue east on the gravel road.
- Turn right on the unsigned gravel road with the back of a stop sign facing the main road. Park outside the yellow gate, a few hundred yards uphill from Johns River Road. The sign beside the gate identifies Campbell Global as manager of the road and surrounding land. Non-motorized visitors are welcome when no extreme wildfire hazard or active logging is present.

Hiking Route

This hike starts in a section of the tree farm where large, old stumps are obvious among young trees. The variety in the height, size, and age of the stumps is unusual. A few are very old, tall, and wide, with crumbling, reddish wood fiber. A fair number have the fairly standard 2-foot tall, 2-foot diameter of trees harvested in the twenty-first century. Less common, but well-represented here, are wide stumps of multi-trunked trees, cut at multiple heights, forming steps, seats, or shelves of varying heights. These are the remains of nurse stumps, which sprouted new shoots that grew into substantial trees harvested in their turn. In early summer, foxgloves, daisies, and occasional ocean spray brighten the landscape.

The open fields narrow as the route enters the forest, gaining a little elevation. After 0.5 mile, the forest thickens on both sides of the road. Hemlock, spruce, and fir crowd together, allowing space for salal, sword ferns, and Oregon grape, only at the road edge. Occasionally, space between the trees has been opened with commercial thinning:

slim, young, undesirable trees—usually deciduous species—have been sliced off about a foot above the ground. They have been left to return to the soil where they fall.

There are a few inconsequential side roads branching away along the 1.5-mile route to the lookout site. As the high point on the road is approached, a drivable side road to the right is followed by a gated road on the left. What we know about this lookout station supports its location at the top of the ridge on the left.

The track to the left continues to rise from the main road's elevation, suggesting it leads to a reasonable location for a lookout cabin. From its high point, branch roads head downhill. The clearing at the junction is broad enough to site a 14×32-foot cabin. The GPS records 410-foot elevation, the highest on the hill. But no nails, window glass, or even dimensioned lumber have been found here to support the theory of a fire lookout site. Searching the surrounding forest and the gravel tracks west of the main road offers no better location for a fire lookout cabin.

"Mushroom man"—a gift from nature discovered beside the route to Johns River Lookout site, December 2019.

To see a different forest management regime, continue south on the road for another 0.5 mile. A sign at a gate lets us know we are entering Grays Harbor County Timberlands. Here, too, non-motorized visitors are welcome. The county forest has a different character than the private tree farm. The sections of the woodland not yet harvested contain larger trees, including cedar, not present on the private forestland. This more mature forest has more space for a variety of plants and shrubs under its big trees.

Ascend the first knoll for its views. The wooded ridge to the west glimpsed earlier is now a green wall blocking any coastal panorama. To the northwest is a clear vista of Grays Harbor's broad bay and the land rising beyond it. The road we have been hiking continues southwest, descending the next valley, and turns north, then west. The map indicates it splits, leading north and southwest. The southerly branch leads to the Elk River Natural Resources Conservation Area and "the largest, highest quality estuarine system remaining in Washington or Oregon."[3] Turning north provides a return route to the narrow Johns River Road, 3-miles northwest of the parking area and trailhead.

One of the "stair step stumps" beside the route to the Johns River Lookout site.

---

[3] Washington Department of Natural Resources, "Elk River Natural Resources Conservation Area" at https://www.dnr.wa.gov/elk-river-natural-resources-conservation-area, accessed October 2020.

54. DOTY LOOKOUT

RT Distance: 6 miles
High Point: 2081 feet
Elevation Gain: 950 feet
Season: Apr-Nov
No Discover Pass is currently required in this state forestland.

History

The Doty forest fire lookout was on a ridge, a few miles north of a hamlet in western Lewis County with the same name. The little community was named for C. A. Doty, who built a sawmill at the townsite in 1900.[1] In 1942, the Washington State Division of Forestry built a pole tower on the viewpoint, with a 7×7-foot observation cabin on top. A small house was built at the same time,[2] as the roofed viewing platform was not big enough to shelter the staff. Fire watchers climbed a ladder to reach their station, which a 1953 National Geodetic Survey report mentions as 25 feet north of the cabin.[3]

In 1954, Centralia's *Daily Chronicle* published several updates on JoAnn Hadaller and Marilee Step's summer jobs on the Doty Lookout. Newspaper articles announced their arrival July 21, reported harassment by male visitors at the lookout that required a sheriff's response July 30, and shared an August goodbye party for one of their visitors who was moving to California.[4] This level of press coverage of fire lookout staff is unusual, suggesting close ties between the state forestry office and a local reporter. The same paper

The Doty Lookout, 1953. (Courtesy of the Washington Digital Archives.)

---

[1] Phillips, 41.
[2] Kresek, *2015*, 27.
[3] US National Geodetic Survey, "Datasheet PID SC1589 DOTY"; https://www.ngs.noaa.gov/cgi-bin/ds_mark.prl?Pid Box=SC1589.
[4] These newspaper articles are quoted in https://washingtonlookouts.weebly.com/doty.html.

reported vandalism to the lookout building several times in the 1950s and '60s. Windows in the tower observation post and cabin were broken repeatedly and cable and copper tubing were stolen in 1964. The station was destroyed in 1966.[5]

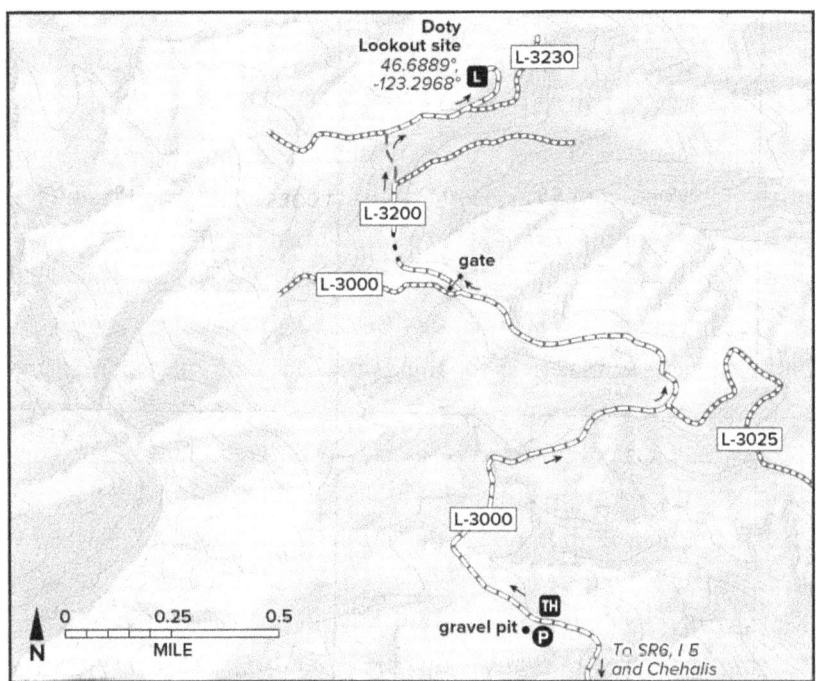

Hike Summary

This is a pleasant hike on state forest roads with a short scramble up a bank to bypass a washout. Enjoy panoramic views of major Cascade peaks along the route, as well as roadside beds of wildflowers in spring and summer.

Getting There

- Take Exit 77 from Interstate 5, turning west on State Route 6 toward Pe Ell.
- Between mileposts 35 and 34, turn right on Chandler Road. Follow Chandler Road to milepost 2.

---

[5] Kresek, *2015*, 27.

- Drive an addition 0.1 mile; turn right on Forest Road L-3000, passing through its open yellow gate.
- Drive L-3000 for 3.3 miles and park at the mouth of a small gravel pit on the left.

Hiking Route

The hike starts on a one-and-a-half-lane gravel road with a healthy mixed forest on both sides. Douglas fir, alder, and bigleaf maple offer a shady track for the first mile. The undisturbed road shoulders support a surprising variety of wildflowers, including Oregon iris rarely seen west of Interstate 5 in Washington. Birds sing their hearts out; woodpeckers noisily inspect trees for bugs, and even an owl may sit roadside, watching for unwary grouse chicks in late spring.

The route curves to the right, passing over three small streams that have helped form steep little valleys, sloping downhill beside the road. At 1 mile, the hillside forest to the left has been selectively harvested since 2010, leaving deciduous trees and young conifers on the slope while a reserve of tall firs remains on the ridgetop.

In another 0.1 mile, turn left at a T-intersection in a clearcut area. The road curves around a high point and opens to panoramic views. Below is the broad farm and forest land of the Chehalis River Valley in northwestern Lewis County. To the right, Mounts Rainier, Adams, and St. Helens stand tall, even with haze in the lowlands. The route now follows a ridge above the west branch of Dunn Creek. There are three separate hilltops to the northwest. The Doty Lookout site is on the forested center knob. Shortly after the view of the three snow-topped Cascade peaks to the east, a pass between ridges to the northwest allows glimpses of Olympic Mountains, too. It is hard to begrudge loggers the trees when their work reveals such wonderful views, hidden for decades.

Stay on the mainline road for 1.75 miles. Where a grassy side track on the right offers a L-3200 road sign, turn toward its old yellow gate. In early summer, this section of the route is colored with bright flowers on tall stalks: pink and lavender foxgloves, pink and bluish corydalis, white yarrow, and pretty pink hedge nettle.

A little more than 0.25 mile past the gate, a series of earthen berms and ditches intersect the closed road. The traditional route to Doty Lookout suffered a major slump in 2015. Another gravel track was built from the north that comes close to meeting the lower section of the old road, but it has not been connected with the upper part of the route to Doty Lookout, about 20 feet uphill. Hike over the berms and new road until parallel with an abandoned culvert hanging from the old road on the ridge to the left. There are several game and hiker trails going up the bank. Choose one to ascend the steep rise, avoiding the grove of devil's club about 50 feet beyond the culvert.

The original road to Doty resumes at the top of this short scramble. Before getting to a drivable gravel road in about 0.25 mile, cross another set of berms and ditches. Then, turn right and pass a small, abandoned gravel pit on the left before reaching a Y with a road sign, L-3230, just past its junction. Take the left branch and follow the winding path up to the clearing at the road end. In 2004, a bronze benchmark and a metal rod set in concrete stood in a logged area, near the right edge of the open space. There was a pile of old wooden beams and lumber here, as well. A few years later, we found a Washington State survey marker witness post, but the bronze National Geodetic Survey marker had disappeared. In 2017, tall trees hung over the clearing and a vigorous understory of salal, evergreen huckleberries, and blackberries were doing their best to conceal any remains of fire lookout buildings. A pile of thick, wooden beams and lumber now sat among the vegetation, some with galvanized bolts holding them together. Among the wood were beams with a shiny creosote coating, looking much newer than my recollection of our discoveries here in 2004. Despite the road washout on the hiking route, drivable roads led to the lookout site in the not-too-distant past. My strong suspicion is that debris has been added to the site since my first visits here early in this century. Take a look and decide for yourself.

55. SQUALLY JIM AND WALVILLE PEAK LOOKOUTS

RT Distance: 6.0 miles
High Point: 2417 feet
Elevation Gain: 1300 feet
Season: All Year
No pass or permit is required.

History

These two fire lookout sites, located on state forestland in eastern Pacific County, have an intertwined history. They are both on the P and E Ridge,[1] southwest of the village of Doty. Walville Peak is the high point on the ridge, and indeed the highest elevation in the county, at 2417 feet. Squally Jim Hill, about a mile to the west, is only 2071 feet. Walville Peak was named for a mill town on what is now State Route 6, near the western edge of Lewis County. In 1903, the town got its name from the lumber mill there, Wallworth and Neville.[2] A couple of sources have said Squally Jim Hill was named for a member of the Chehalis Tribe, but the details are not clear.[3]

The lookout tower built on Squally Jim Hill, 1955. (Photograph by Alta Bailey Moore, courtesy of the Alta Bailey Moore Collection.)

---

[1] The P and E Ridge likely got its name from the Pacific and Eastern Logging and Railroad, which left tracks through Pacific County. The railroad appears in photos at the Pacific County Historical Society Museum, South Bend.
[2] Tacoma Public Library. Northwest Collection. Washington Place Names: https://cdm17061.contentdm.oclc.org/cdm/search/collection/p17061coll4/searchterm/Walville/.
[3] I first visited this site with a hiking friend, Rosalie Gittings. She talked about bringing a friend who was a member of the Chehalis tribe here, because Squally Jim Hill and Lookout were named for one of the friend's relatives. On his website, Eric Willhite suggests Chehalis tribal member Jim Sanders (1830-1903) was Squally Jim and the Lookout was named for him or his son (also Jim Sanders). See http://www.willhiteweb.com/washington_fire_lookouts/squally_jim/walville_peak_393.htm.

55. SQUALLY JIM AND WALVILLE PEAK LOOKOUTS

The first mention of a fire lookout at either location was a June 1927 article in the *Chehalis Bee-Nugget* that mentioned "a new phone line was built from Walville to Walville lookout station 5.5 miles distant."[4] A 1929 article in the same newspaper named a group of "Lewis County field men, including Oral Weese of Pe Ell, in charge of Walville lookout."[5]

The Washington Forest Fire Association included the first mention of a building on either site in their 1941 annual report. It was called Squally Jim Lookout, but its location matches Walville Peak: Section 27 in Township 13 North Range 6 West. It was a two-story building, 10×10-foot square and 16-foot tall, with large windows on the second floor. The report said the building would be used for six years or more, when a site about a mile to the west, presumably Squally Jim Hill, would be cleared and a more permanent lookout building constructed.[6] The federal Aircraft Warning Service (AWS) used the 1941 building from 1942 to 1944, with AWS adding a 12×20-foot garage to support the year-round monitoring they required.[7] The lookout station was retained for use by the State Forestry Division at the end of the AWS program.[8]

Photo labeled "Old Squally Jim Lookout." (Photographer unknown, courtesy of the Alta Bailey Moore Collection.)

By 1952, the fire lookout station on P and E Ridge was definitely at the Squally Jim site. It was either moved there or a new building built without mention in either the state Division of Forestry or Washington Forest Fire Association annual reports. US Geodetic Survey reports document a building at the Squally Jim site. The federal agency installed a survey station at the coordinates of Squally

---

[4] The newspaper article is quoted in https://washingtonlookouts.weebly.com/squally-jim.html.
[5] The newspaper article is quoted in https://washingtonlookouts.weebly.com/squally-jim.html.
[6] Washington Forest Fire Association, *Thirty-Fourth Annual Report, 1941*, 14-15.
[7] [US Forest Service] Region 6, "Report of Aircraft Warning Service Stations," May 1, 1944, Sheet #2.
[8] *Memo for Files – A.W.S. Posts Retained for Use by State under Cooperative Agreement with U.S. Forest Service*, Washington State Archives, Olympia.

Jim Hill: 46.5884°, -123.4430°. One of its reference marks, RM 1, was located on the "peak of roof of cupola of LOH [Look Out House]."[9]

The Division of Forestry replaced the old building with a 40-foot timber tower with a 14×14-foot cabin on top in the 1954 to 1956 biennium.[10] Alta Bailey Moore was assigned to the new Squally Jim Lookout, to finish the fire season in late summer, 1955. She has photos of both lookout buildings used on the Squally Jim Hill in 1955, but she only worked in the tower.[11]

The massive Columbus Day Storm in October 1962 brought high-powered winds to the Willapa Hills, destroying the tower.[12] It was rebuilt one more time during the 1962 to 1964 biennium.[13]

One of the last people to staff the tower was "Mrs. Roy Thompson of Lebam [who] gave a talk about her five summers in the Squally Jim Lookout at a luncheon gathering in January 1966."[14] The state Department of Natural Resources (DNR) removed the building in 1968.

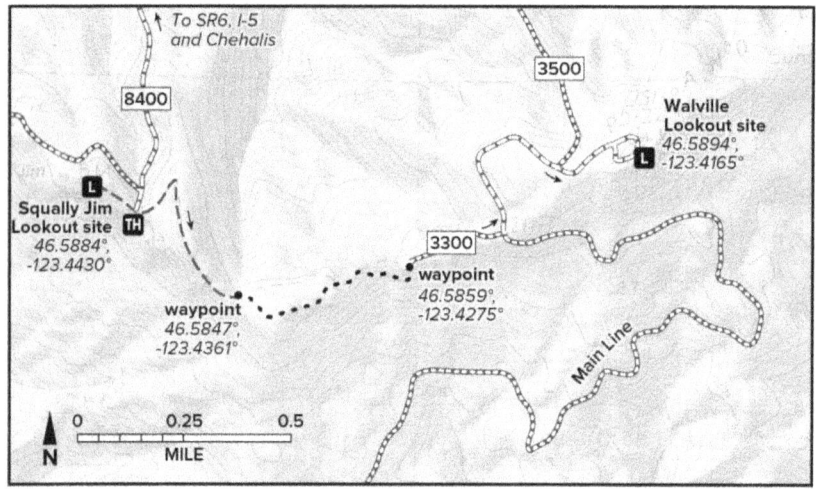

---

[9] US National Geodetic Survey, "Datasheet SC1597 Squally Jim"; https://www.ngs.noaa.gov/cgi-bin/ds_mark.prl?PidBox=SC1597.
[10] Washington Division of Forestry, *Fifty-first and Fifty-Second Annual Reports*, July 1, 1954 - June 30, 1956, 35.
[11] Conversations with Alta Bailey Moore and Clarence Moore, March 2021. Clarence Moore remembered the footing blocks for the old building were beside the feet of the new tower, confirming both buildings' locations.
[12] Kresek, *2015*, 24.
[13] Washington Department of Natural Resources, *Fourth Biennial Report*, 1962-64, 13.
[14] *Centralia Daily Chronicle*, January 26, 1966 article quoted in:
https://washingtonlookouts.weebly.com/squally-jim.html.

Hike Summary

The adventure hike route between the two sites is a combination of little-used forest roads and an amazingly lush game trail that takes a fairly direct route over the high points of the P and E Ridge between Squally Jim Hill and the top of Walville Peak. A careful search of the wooded peak reveals an interesting variety of artifacts, while twenty-first century timber harvests have improved views but left little of historical interest on Squally Jim Hill.

Getting There

- Leave Interstate 5 at Exit 77, State Route 6.
- Turn west, toward Pe Ell and Rainbow Falls State Park.
- Between mileposts 34 and 33, and 18.4 miles from Interstate 5, turn right on Stevens Road toward Doty.
- At 18.8 miles, turn left on Elk Creek Road. The speed limit drops to 30 mph for 2 miles, then the county road and the pavement end.
- At 22.1 miles, a large sign announces the Weyerhaeuser MacDonald Tree Farm and a small sign identifies the main road as 7000.
- At 23.5 miles, stay left at a Y, on Forest Road 8000. The signs for 7000 and 8000 may be obscured by brush here. Pass two side roads, 8200 and 8300.
- At 27.6 miles, go left on 8400 at the junction.
- In another mile, pass a gravel pit on the right. To start the hike near Squally Jim Hill, continue another mile and drive up a short, steep spur road where 8400 turns right. Park at the upper junction.

Hiking Route

The area immediately north of Squally Jim Hill was clearcut in 2015. Pause before you walk toward the lookout site and enjoy the broad views over forested hills to the north. This shows why the location was selected as a lookout site after logging in the 1940s.

From the parking spot, it is a short distance on the rocky road to the lookout site to the west. From the top of the hill, a grassy track disappears into the forest, continuing west. Old maps show a "BM" for benchmark at the highpoint, but the bronze discs intended as permanent survey stations have been missing from Squally Jim Hill for decades. Prior to the 2015 tree harvest, the roof of a collapsed building served as a picnic table on Squally Jim Hill. More recent searches have found only a likely outhouse hole, old mason jars, and a rusted metal basin.

After re-examining the Squally Jim site for clues of its history, I am always curious about conditions on the route to Walville Peak. The nature of hiking in a working forest is to expect change. Road development and logging in the last few years have brought transformations requiring route adjustments, as will future timberland activities.

The harvest that occurred close to Squally Jim Hill did not have much effect on the roadless ridge between Squally Jim and Walville, a beautiful forest landscape when this was written. To approach that forest, look east from the high point of Squally Jim. A few hundred yards beyond the cleared Squally Jim spur road, the forest forms a seemingly solid wall of trees—except for one opening, close to the high point to the south. Going east, cross the road used to ascend Squally Jim Hill and walk the new spur angling to the northeast. Near its end, turn a sharp right and ascend a cat track[15] running southeast toward the opening in the trees. When you reach the trees, the environment immediately changes.

The route is now a mossy, abandoned forest road, surrounded by tall trees, with oxalis and ferns underfoot. Follow this for about 0.25 mile, until it heads northeast to an open area of young tree growth. This attractive path continues for a while but does not connect with the roads needed to reach Walville Peak, so it is best to leave it here. At coordinates 46.5847°, -123.4361° and 2016-foot elevation, follow a game trail cross-country. The hill is moderately steep here, suggesting the trail was left by the agile elk. It takes a zigzag route through the open forest, rounding

---

[15] A two-track path, left by a vehicle with a continuous tread.

trees to avoid the occasional downed trunk or to hike an easier slope. Its initial destination is the broad top of the first rise on the ridge, elevation 2129 feet. From there, the route heads northeast and gradually downhill. There may be numerous trails on the hill, so watch for the reappearance of the old roadbed on lower slopes on the north side of the hillock. This leads to a logging landing at coordinates 46.5859°, -123.4275° at 2053-foot elevation. It has a south-facing, open slope overlooking an amazingly broad forest landscape. That hillside was vividly blooming with violet and white foxgloves when visited in July, an unusually large area to be covered so densely with these lovely, tall blossoms.

After enjoying the view, follow the spur road (HM-3300) uphill about 0.2 mile to a junction with the gravel road DNR labels HM Mainline on its maps. Turn left and follow its spiral toward the top of Walville Peak. Pass a junction with HM-3500 on the left and consider the varied forest landscape as the road ascends. Wildflowers—Oregon iris as well as yellow violets and other spring flowers—brighten the understory during early summer. About halfway to the top, an unusual square post stands beside the road. It is painted white with black letters: "10 mile." The natural question arises: Ten miles to (or from) what?

At the top, a circular road leads to artifacts from several different structures. Turning right, the first clearing on the right contains a wooden, boxlike frame, a remnant of a communication tower at least partially constructed here at the start of this century. It appeared abandoned in 2004 and was almost completely gone a decade later. Continue uphill, exploring the right side of the road and the top of the hillside in that direction. More than one 3-foot-tall concrete footing block has been found pushed over the edge, but there is no documentation of a fire lookout tower that would have used large footing blocks at this location, only the two-story wooden lookout house. Having the size and shape of standard supports for tall towers, they probably served a communication tower here. Near the high point on the hill are two "Walville 1953" benchmarks set in concrete, about 20 feet apart. The one closest to the road has old lightweight lumber fastened together in a 30-inch square that has remained near the benchmark through the years. The original function of the wood is unknown, but it appears now as a frame around the benchmark, which otherwise hides among low plants in the shadows of tall trees.

There are many signs of different human activities on these two hills and the ridge between them. While returning to the trailhead, enjoy the natural landscape and notice how well the forest continues to recover after more than 140 years of repeated timber harvests here.

The abandoned road section of the route between the Squally Jim and Walville Lookout sites.

56. INCLINE LOOKOUT

RT Distance: 7.8 miles
High Point: 2291 feet
Elevation Gain: 1250 feet
Season: Apr-Nov
A Discover Pass is recommended.

History

The Civilian Conservation Corps built a 40-foot tower with a live-in cabin on Incline Mountain, close to the border between Cowlitz and Wahkiakum counties, for the State Division of Forestry in 1938.[1]

In the early 1940s, the tower became an Aircraft Warning Service (AWS) station. Because AWS observation was a year-round operation, the Service management appreciated that firewood was available on the site, and a water supply was only a mile away. In 1942, observers improved the station with a two-room shake cabin and a toilet near the tower.[2] At the end of the war, all the facilities were transferred back to the Washington Division of Forestry for continued fire lookout use.[3]

Incline Lookout. (Bill Paflin photograph, courtesy of the Alta Bailey Moore Collection.)

The National Geodetic Survey (NGS) placed three of their bronze reference marks on concrete footings of the tower in 1952.[4] The fire lookout buildings were removed in 1967.[5]

---

[1] Washington Division of Forestry, *Annual Report for 1938*, quoted in https://washingtonlookouts.weebly.com/incline-mountain.html.
[2] August 1942 report from an AWS Engineering Inspector quoted in http://willhiteweb.com/washington_fire_lookouts/incline-mountain/wahkiakum-county_133.htm.
[3] Washington Division of Forestry, Memo to File: A.W.S. Posts Retained for Use by State under Cooperative Agreement with US Forest Service [1944].
[4] US National Geodetic Survey. "Data Sheet PID SC1614: INCLINE LOT"; https://www.ngs.noaa.gov/cgi-bin/ds_mark.prl?PidBox=SC1614.
[5] Kresek, *2015*, 23.

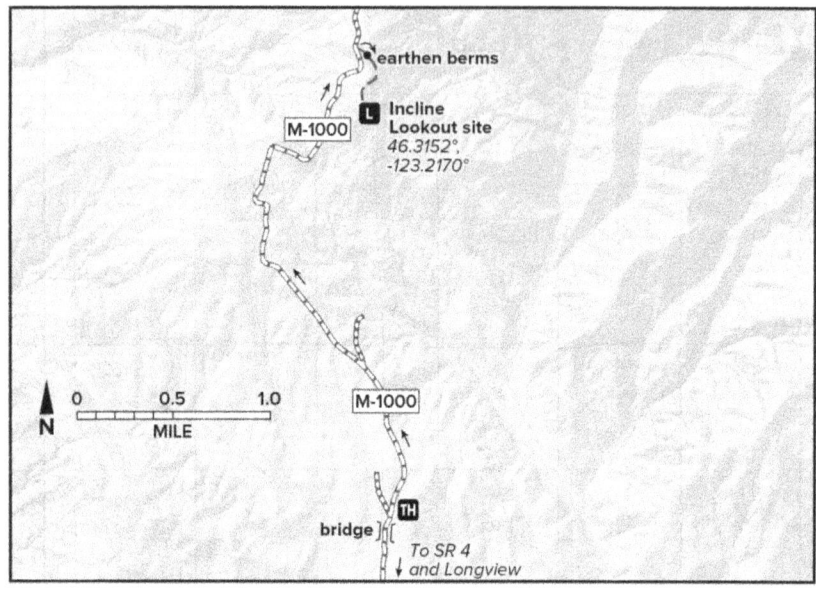

Hike Summary

The hiking route to Incline Mountain gets steeper as it approaches the intriguing short trail to the top of the peak. Park near the distinctive bridge about 3.4 miles from the lookout site to enjoy a variety of views while passing the deep Abernathy Creek basin on the way to the mountain.

Getting There

- From State Route 4, turn north on Mill Creek Road between mileposts 47 and 48.
- Drive 3.15 miles on paved road with pretty Mill Creek on the left side of the route.
- Leave the pavement at a Y, keeping right on Road M-1000. Follow the main road as it continues to gain elevation.
- At 7.2 miles, turn right where 1400 is painted vertically on a 6-inch-diameter tree stub at a T-intersection.
- Drive another 1.95 miles to a bridge beside a small pond and wetland, followed by a branch road leading west. The state forest west

of this junction has many recreational routes for ATVs and motor bikes. The weekend trail riders on the Bradley ORV Trail seem to have little interest in the roads and trails to the north in the direction of Incline Mountain. Park on the wide shoulder beyond the bridge and hike north from here. While no signs in the area currently indicate a Discover Pass is required, this is a popular recreation area, and expectations may change. To carry and display one on your dashboard is prudent.

Hiking Route

The first 0.25 mile has thick forest on both sides, offering an opportunity to take a closer look at the variety of trees and shrubs that have flitted past the car windows. Fir and hemlock stand tall above salal, red huckleberry, and elderberry. The buzz of wide-tired bikes fades as bird songs dominate.

The views become longer as thick forest transitions to young tree farm and the rolling landscape is revealed. At 0.8 mile from the hike start, pass a side road that leads into the forest on the right. The map shows that route leads down to Abernathy Creek, which parallels the hiking route until it passes the creek's headwaters in another mile.

The slope between our two-lane gravel track and the creek gets steeper as the route continues north. After the last tall trees on our side of the water are passed, the broad Abernathy Valley comes into view. Large areas of the forest in the basin have been harvested and replanted early in this century. On the east side of the valley is a tall, mile-long ridge with a distinctive saddle in the middle. Some of the southern knob appeared recently logged when the route was scouted in 2017, but most of the ridge was still heavily wooded at that time. The peak of Incline Mountain is on the northerly knob.

Continue ascending the road as it curves around the northern end of the Abernathy basin and heads east. Several stub roads head into a gravel pit on the north side of the road. The pit's walls and forest remnant conceal views to the north, but the map indicates another river valley lies in that direction, with the potential of forested ridges beyond ridges there, too.

Past the gravel pit, side roads angle southeast into the Abernathy basin and its tree plantation. The hike route turns north into a shady forest. The next 0.5 mile of roadside has not been harvested for many years and tall trees rise on both sides. Pass a forest clearing made attractive by wildflowers and its grassy track. The final approach to the Incline Lookout site is close; investigation of the opening will need to come later.

At 3 miles from the car, turn a corner to the right and notice a one-lane track headed uphill to the right. The first 0.1 mile of this old road has been "decommissioned" within an inch of its life: a dozen or more 4-foot-tall earthen berms cross the track to discourage any wheeled vehicle coming this way. A narrow foot trail skirts the right edge of the first berm. Enough hikers and game have persisted to prevent vegetation from completely obscuring the route and keep the way passable.

After a steep 0.25 mile, the track flattens and widens, curving across the top of the wooded ridge to its 2291-foot grassy summit. A small open area at the top offers views down into the Ordway Creek Valley to the east.

A careful look around the perimeter reveals 2-foot concrete footing blocks lying on their sides under a large fir tree. The top side of each block has a galvanized metal angle beam protruding, the remains of the support system for the old wooden tower. There are no signs of bronze survey markers on these footing blocks. Nor have visitors to the site reported finding the missing blocks or benchmarks. If you find either bronze markers or more concrete blocks, please let me know.

57. BLANEY MOUNTAIN LOOKOUT

RT Distance: 2.5 miles or more
High Point: 2546 feet
Elevation Gain: 350 feet or more
Season: Apr-Nov
A Discover Pass is required.

History

Washington's Division of Forestry built an 84-foot tower with a 14×14-foot cabin on top of this local high point in 1950. Other lookouts in the southwest corner of western Washington were constructed in the 1930s and '40s. It is likely that roads and tree harvesting came later to this remote area in the southeastern corner of coastal Pacific County, and the need for a fire watch station came with them.

The fire lookout inventories published in the 1980s reported that no Blaney Lookout buildings remained, but gave no dates for their removal.[1] Other state fire lookouts in the area were removed in 1967 to 1969, which is a reasonable guess for the end of Blaney's service as well.

Blaney Lookout. (Florence Bailey photograph, courtesy of the Alta Bailey Moore Collection.)

Hike Summary

The approach to Blaney Mountain is on drivable state forest roads in Wahkiakum County. The lookout site is little more than a mile across the county line in Pacific County on Hancock Forest Management land. Park your car in the state forest and enjoy a hike through beautiful landscape on your way to the tree farm that now surrounds Blaney

---
[1] Kresek, *1998*, 114; Spring and Fish, 200.

Mountain. The last 0.25 mile to the high point requires navigation on old routes replanted with obliteration in mind. The summit hosts a grove of spruce trees planted long after the 84-foot tower was built to provide views far beyond.

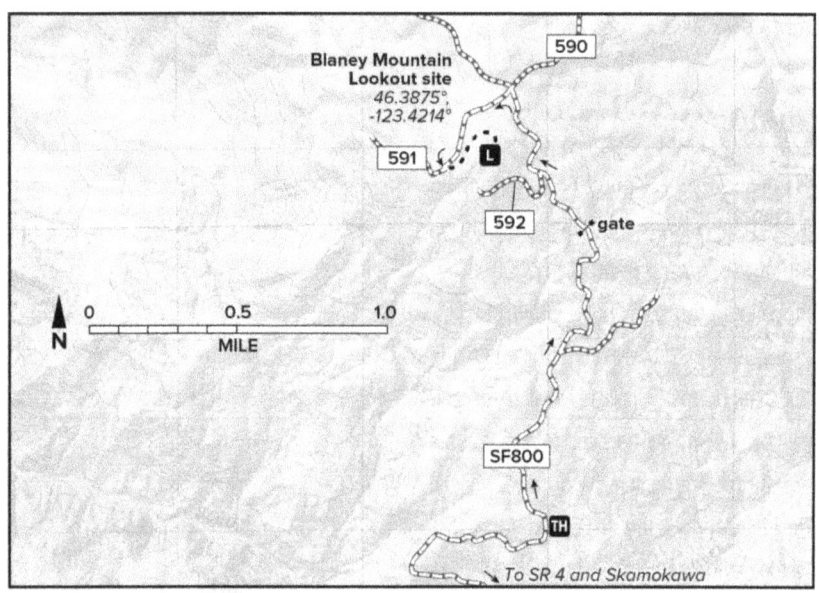

Getting There

- Start in Skamokawa on State Route 4. In the center of town, turn north on the Skamokawa Valley Road.
- At 1.25 miles, take the left branch at a Y, onto the Middle Valley Road, which follows the Middle Fork of the Skamokawa River north.
- Follow this road to the end of pavement, about 4 miles from State Route 4.
- A sign on a tree identifies the main road, now two-lane gravel, as 1000. Follow this road 4.3 miles to a junction with road LF800.
- The junction is at the top of a bluff. Take the right fork of LF800, following the road about 2.2 miles, angling down the bluff and across the river bottom to cross the old green metal bridge with

wooden planks over the Grays River. Keep your tires on the raised boards. (Hike from here for 8 miles RT and 1680-foot gain.)
- The road becomes SF800 after the bridge and works northeastward. After 1.4 miles, the main road turns a corner to the left and north. (Hike from here for 5.2 miles RT and 1000-foot gain.)
- While I recommend parking and hiking the road to enjoy the plant life, bird song, and landscape, the road is usually drivable to the white Hancock Timber Management gate near the Wahkiakum-Pacific County line. State forests continue to the county line, but the road numbering system changes to a 590 series about 0.5 mile before the border.
- The Hancock gate is 10.3 miles from Skamokawa. Starting at the gate, the lookout site is 2.5 miles roundtrip with 350-foot elevation gain.

Hiking Route

The state forest in this part of the region appears well-managed, with healthy stands of mixed conifer and deciduous trees supporting a variety of wildlife. Road edges are adorned with wildflowers in late spring and summer, and bird songs attest their approval of the vegetation and clear, flowing water. The lengthy warble of the western wren and whistle of the varied thrush compete with the babble of creeks near the roadway. About 0.33 mile before the Hancock gate, a side road on the right leads to a logging landing on a bluff, offering views of the eastern reaches of the Grays River Valley.

In another 0.2-mile, a sign on a tall tree to the left announces a Hancock Forest Management gate ahead: *May be locked at any time. No dumping. No campfires.* Timber near the gate was harvested in 2010. Hemlocks planted since then have been doing their best to fill the air space.

In a short distance, walk past the Hancock gate. The sign above the gate is old enough to be blank, beyond the company name. Both signs agree on the company's reputation for welcoming visitors on foot or bicycle in the Willapa Hills. Permits are not required.

The remaining 1.25 miles to the lookout site is well-marked with road signs—as far as there is a one-lane track to follow. Beyond the gate, hike Road 590 to a junction with 591. Along the way, pass 592 on the left as it heads into a mixed, mature forest. Road 592 curls around the south side of Blaney Mountain but ends before it meets 591 on the west side of the short ridge.

The Blaney Lookout site is on the top of this replanted hill.

Between the junctions of 590 with 592 and 591, a long section of young forest on the left appears to offer a passible route to Blaney's summit. If you especially like cross-country travel, this could be a feasible route. The old roadbeds and tree growth patterns on the other side of the ridge strongly suggest the historical route to the lookout was there. For that reason, I recommend circling Blaney and approaching the peak from the southwest.

From the junction with 592, continue north to the old road's high point at 2400 feet, then downhill to a four-way junction, with well-maintained routes in all directions. Continue the spiral on Blaney Mountain by turning left on Forest Road 591. It splits after 100 yards, with 591A heading downhill, while 591 hugs the peak on the left and continues ascending. Proceed uphill around Blaney's southwest corner. The old road peters out, with only a minimal grassy track heading north toward the peak.

It is soon clear the roadbed underfoot was included in the replanting that followed the 2010 harvest. Pines and hemlock crowd the path, making route-finding a challenge. Follow the slightly depressed track along the west side of the peak, turning east when a patch of clear roadbed appears under larger trees, some of which are prickly spruce.

Find your way to the high point on Blaney Mountain. There are several narrow trails through the spruce grove, despite its efforts to merge individual trees' broad skirts in an impenetrable hedge.

Without a tower or a tree to climb, there were no panoramic views from the summit when last visited. An open glade with a 20-foot diameter remained, with very few signs of human development. At the end of a lengthy search of the area and a leisurely lunch in the clearing, we realized the sparkles catching the sunlight at our feet were small pieces of window glass. They are possibly the only remains of the proud tower that once stood here, guardian of the broad Grays River forest acreage.

58. HULL CREEK LOOKOUT

RT Distance: 4 miles
High Point: 2042 feet
Elevation Gain: 1050 feet
Season: Apr-Nov
Display a Discover Pass when you park in this state forest.

History

During the 1930s, the Civilian Conservation Corps built a road that ended about 2 miles from this state forest site. Until a cat road[1] was completed to the lookout site and a cabin built in 1942, Aircraft Warning Service observers were expected to camp on the hilltop to watch for enemy planes approaching from the mouth of the Columbia River or southern Willapa Bay.[2]

At the end of the war, the lookout site was returned to the Washington Division of Forestry[3] and used as a fire lookout site until it was abandoned in 1962. Historical photographs show a two-story cabin with small windows on the first floor and cedar-shake siding. The upper level had large windows on all four sides.

Hull Creek Lookout. (Photographer unknown, courtesy of the Alta Bailey Moore Collection.)

---

[1] A cat road is a two-track path, left by a vehicle with a continuous tread.
[2] Image of an excerpt from a March 1942 memo to files titled "Hull (Creek) Lookout," accessed at http://willhiteweb.com/washington_fire_lookouts/hull_creek_lookout/aws_183.htm.
[3] [US Forest Service] Region 6, "Report of Aircraft Warning Service Stations," May 1, 1944, Sheet #II; and a September 6, 1962, *Longview Daily News* article, quoted in http://washingtonlookouts.weebly.com/hull-creek.html.

58. HULL CREEK LOOKOUT

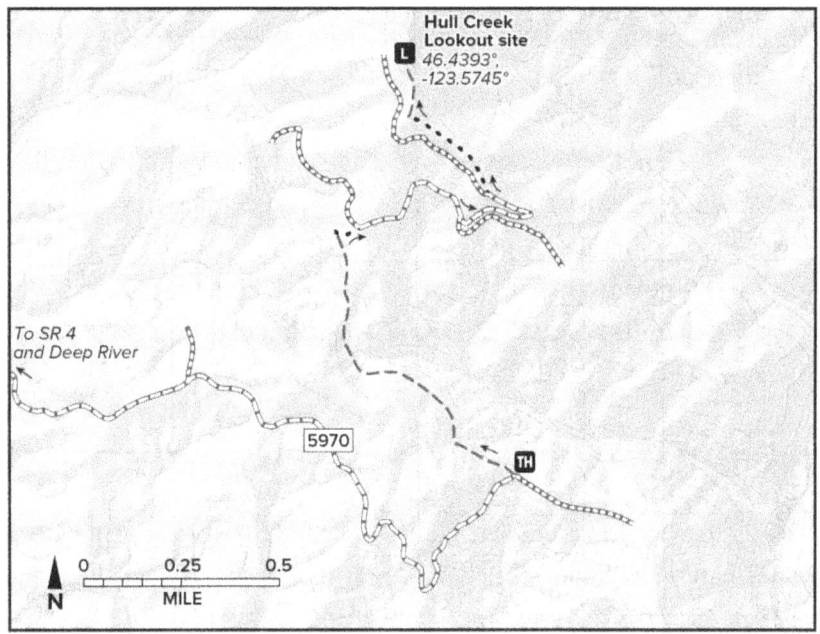

Hike Summary

This is a fairly short adventure hike on abandoned roads in state forestlands, with briefly challenging hill climbs on informal trails. When scouted in 2018, the first section of the route was one of the prettiest moss-covered old roads I have hiked anywhere.

Getting There

- Start on State Route 4, between Deep River and the junction with State Route 401 south. Just east of milepost 8, turn north on Salmon Creek Road. On a sunny day, this is a beautiful drive beside a burbling, tree-lined stream.
- The first 7 miles are paved; the rest of the 14-mile drive is on good gravel. Forest Road (FR) 5900 begins at the end of the paved county road. At 8.1 miles from State Route 4, pass a sign for FR 3000 on the left.

- At 9.7 miles, cross a wooden bridge over Salmon Creek. Shortly afterward, turn right onto FR 5970, through an old yellow gate standing open.
- At 11.5 miles, road number 5973 is painted on a tree to the left where a major road goes north. In another 0.3 mile, cross a bridge with wooden side-rails.
- At 13.2 miles, go left uphill at a Y with no signs.
- At 14.0 miles, park on the left at a junction with a narrow, grassy road. This is the trailhead.

Hiking Route

The first mile of this route is on an abandoned forest road with a deep valley barely discernable beside the path. The route is thickly carpeted with moss and soft grasses, providing an unusually soft tread underfoot. Deer and elk leave their prints in bare soil, helping to maintain a trail down the middle of the revegetated roadbed. Humans apparently pass by once in a while; occasional downed trees have been sawn to provide a clear route. Spring visitors will encounter whatever tree limbs and trunks winter storms deposit, as well as seasonal blossoms. Shamrock-like oxalis offer large patches of green with shy white flowers; yellow woodland violets, trilliums, hot pink salmonberry, and violet-pink bleeding hearts brighten the shady trail.

The route first curves to the right, and then the left, as it passes the headwaters of creeks rushing down from both sides of the ridge. At the junction of the two curves, the relics of early-twentieth-century logging stand sentinel beside the trail: two 8- to10-foot cedar stumps stand as gate posts on either side of the path, while a scan of the nearby forest brings their contemporaries into view.

This enchanting trail abruptly ends about one-third mile after the two giant stumps. Sometime early in this century, someone decided to do a proper job of closing the other end of the abandoned road. They took a common road-closing practice to an extreme: they stacked bulldozed stumps with fans of roots attached in a pile about 10 feet tall, blocking the access of our route to a drivable forest road. When I first visited the area in May 2010, we bushwhacked our way through thick brush up to the road, then continued our exploratory trip. Revisiting 7 years later, there was a well-established trail zigzagging up the short, steep, and still brushy slope. It is only 0.1 mile to the top, but the change from the mossy path at the bottom of the hill is startling.

Emerge at a gravel forest road beside a clearing probably used as a logging landing or a road construction equipment storage site. The vegetation is slowly returning, but the changes in soil structure will probably keep it sparsely covered for a long time. Turn right and follow the road with a high bare bank on the left and thick forest below the road on the right. Around the next corner, the steep left hillside releases lots of water. A dripping wall about 10-feet wide appears first, supporting very thick moss and small, water-loving plants. Then, two narrow cascades stream down, each producing its own bright patch of green.

Continue uphill, taking the left branch of the Y at the next corner (1.6 miles from the trailhead). This branch road offers great views as it approaches the high Hull Creek ridge. Through the trees on the right can be seen communication towers on K.O. Point, an old fire lookout site across Grays River to the north. Only purchasers of Weyerhaeuser recreation permits can visit that historic site now.

The broad Columbia River comes into sight through the trees on the left. The bay at Astoria, Oregon, hosts ocean freighters waiting their turn to enter ports farther upriver. Even the outline of the saddle on Saddle Mountain, farther south into Oregon, is visible on a clear day.

The road continues around the Hull Creek summit, but this hike does not. A drivable route once wound up to the summit of the hill to the right. A more recent road-cut amputated that route at a height of about 12 feet above the current roadbed. To intersect the old route without carving footholds in the steep roadside or using technical climbing maneuvers, step onto the hillside on the right while it is only a foot above the road. Follow one of several faint trails that parallel the road for a hundred yards, then head more steeply uphill to meet the old summit route as it turns a corner at the end of Hull Creek ridge. This cross-country adventure covers about 0.1 mile.

Henry Romer, dwarfed by the giant stumps beside the trail to the Hull Creek Lookout site.

Once on the old, tree-lined road, follow the grassy track uphill a short distance to the wide clearing on top. Timber harvesting on the lower slopes between 2000 and 2010 allows broad views to the west through tall conifers. Wildflowers, Oregon grape, and other low shrubs grow under the canopy on the high point. A careful search of the hilltop in 2010 found an old stovepipe, jars, and a few dishes. These may be remains from the lookout cabin abandoned in the 1960s—or not. If you find them, please leave them for others to discover and consider the stories they may tell.

59. COWAN LOOKOUT

RT Distance: 6.5 miles
High Point: 1940 feet
Elevation Gain: 1500 feet
Season: Apr-Nov
A Discover Pass is required.

History

Cowan Lookout. (Photographer unknown, courtesy of the Alta Bailey Moore Collection.)

This fire lookout tower, a few miles north and uphill from Naselle, was the forest watch station closest to the southwestern corner of Washington state. A 20-foot wooden viewing platform was built here in 1947. After it accidentally burned, a 40-foot tower with a live-in cabin on top replaced it in 1952.[1] The State Division of Forestry, the private Washington Forest Fire Association, and the Weyerhaeuser Company, owner of most of the private forestland in the Willapa Hills at that time, cooperatively managed the lookout. The replacement tower was named Cowan Peak in honor of Major C. S. Cowan, manager of the Washington Forest Fire Association for several decades,[2] and an internationally known forester.[3] The building was abandoned in 1967,[4] when air patrols became more popular than lookout towers for fire monitoring in western Washington.

Interestingly, the name selected for the tower in 1952 does not appear on any maps. The opposite (west) end of the ridge is known throughout the region as "Radar Hill" for

---

[1] Kresek, *2015*, 22.
[2] World Forestry Center, "Biographical portrait: Charles S. Cowan (1887-1969)" in *Forest History Today*, Spring 2012.
[3] Quotes from June 1952 articles in the [Centralia] *Daily Chronicle* and the *Issaquah Press*, reporting on the recent dedication of the tower, in: http://washingtonlookouts.weebly.com/cowan-point.html.
[4] Kresek, *2015*, 22.

the tower that still stands there, but official maps have no label on the mile-long, 1900-foot-high ridge.

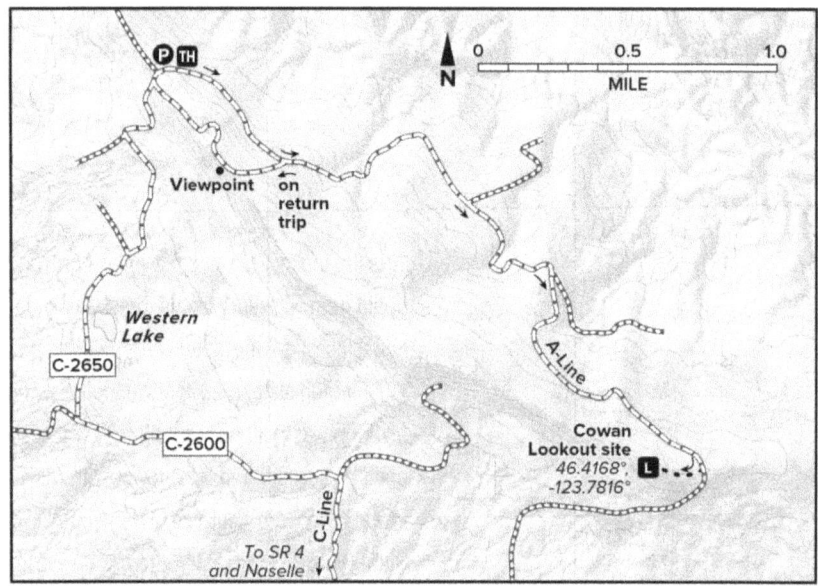

Hike Summary

Several routes on forest roads can take you close to the remains of the Cowan Lookout. I prefer hiking the summit ridge for panoramic views north and south. Reaching the lookout site requires adventurous off-road travel for the last quarter mile. The ascent to the high point was fully forested and the old road obscure when scouted in 2017. Exercise patience to find the interesting variety of artifacts remaining there. On the return trip, take a side road to hike the south side of the ridge for great views of the Naselle River's pastoral landscape.

Getting There

- Start at milepost 3 on State Route 4, 1.65 miles west of its junction with State Route 401. Drive north on a usually well-maintained gravel road that passes the entrance to the Naselle Youth Camp

close to the highway. A small roadside sign identifies the route as the C-Line, the main road in this state forest.
- At 2.5 miles, take the branch road to the left. Department of Natural Resources directions to recreation sites identify this as the C-2600 Road, while the map provided on the same website labels it C-2000. This is the route around the Radar Hill Ponds, a popular fishing area with two small campgrounds. The continuation of the C-Line leads to a radio tower on the western summit of this state forest's high ridge.
- At 3.5 miles from State Route 4, turn right on the unsigned road that DNR driving directions identify as C-2650 (it is labeled C Line on the website map). This route soon passes an outhouse and one of the Radar Hill Ponds, Western Lake, which stand on the right.
- Continue driving north and uphill, passing two side roads on the left. At 4.75 miles from the highway, reach the high point of the driving route at a junction with three other roads. Bypass the one coming from the left and immediately park on the wide left shoulder on the north side of the ridge for a 6.5-mile hike.

Hiking Route

The starting elevation at this high point on the ridge is 1510 feet, while the height at the destination is only 1940 feet, despite a promised elevation gain of 1500 feet. As the numbers suggest, the route crosses several ridges and shallow valleys along the way. The initial section of the forest road disappears abruptly, a hundred yards from the start of the hike. Fortunately, the first descent is not as steep as its loss from view suggests. The forested Willapa Hills fill the horizon north and east with range upon range of close-to-parallel ridges. They are not uniformly green; straight-edged brown patches indicate recent timber harvests; light-green and tan suggest evergreen saplings in plantations. The darkest green patches are the forest patriarchs, remnants of the original tree stock that sustained native Americans and welcomed explorers Robert Gray, Meriwether Lewis, and William Clark.

This view is replaced by trees beside the northern road edge after the first 0.25 mile. At 0.6 mile, another road merges into the hike route from the right. This is the branch recommended for the return trip, for surprisingly different views.

Continue on the route circling the north side of the ridge, a gravel road with wide shoulders hosting young conifers and wildflowers. Coltsfoot, trilliums, and yellow violets are the earliest spring flowers here, followed by salmonberry, elderberry, and May lilies. There are lots of red huckleberries and foxgloves in summer, too.

The little-traveled road gains elevation cumulatively, with slightly greater ascents than descents on the rolling terrain. The increasing height allows views of Willapa Bay to the northwest, spreading blue beyond the sea of green forest. At 1.8 miles, a side route heads off to the left. Our hiking track is now the A Line, the main road on the east side of this state forest. Beyond the junction, our route curves south around a minor promontory of almost 1700 feet.

The hike route's elevation rises more steeply in the next mile, reaching 1850 feet at 3.0 miles. The landscape is more open here, with a swath of land on either side of the road harvested and replanted in the first decade of this century. At this point, an abandoned one-lane track leaves the gravel road on the right, curving westward into the forest. This is the historic route to the Cowan Lookout.

The lookout site on top of the hill is just 0.25 mile away. The grassy roadbed, which was an easy walk when visited in 2010, offered the challenges of new vegetation and fallen trees in 2017. The track circles the end of the ridge to the left before rising steeply to the top. Follow the track as long as feasible, then pause and look around. A number of lookout hunters have come this way and left clues better than breadcrumbs. Some have sawn-off branches, making narrow trails through the open forest. Others have tied survey tape at eye level in colors originally bright but still noticeable when faded.

An old outhouse at the high point identifies the top of the hill. There are also four short concrete footing blocks with rebar protruding from their tops, 10-to-20-feet south of the outhouse. A 2-foot-tall, galvanized metal eyebolt stands near the footing blocks. Early in the twenty-first century, a flattened plywood building lay a short distance southeast of the concrete blocks. The remnants of that abandoned building seemed like a treasure trove then, but there may be even more concealed under the spreading branches of the growing forest.

Take the left branch in the road on the return trip to your parking spot. It climbs the final ridge and navigates around a gravel pit being carved into its south side. The immediate scenery is admittedly unattractive, but the high point of the ridge's south side provides views unmatched anywhere on the route. As the road shifts direction from south to west about 0.25 mile from the last junction, the panorama of an unexpectedly broad Naselle River comes into view. The tidal waters have sculpted sinuous contours in the verdant marshy banks, while thick stands of trees darken the hillside above. To the right, a low bridge crosses the river, short vertical pilings supporting a low horizontal line of deck to punctuate the landscape at the river mouth. I found this one of the most lovely and unusual views offered on any fire lookout hike. Come prepared to record the scene in your favorite media.

APPENDIX ONE: FIRE LOOKOUT SITES NO LONGER ACCESSIBLE

NAME	REASON			
	PRIVATE LAND REQUIRING FEES[1]	MILITARY BASE OR PROTECTED WATERSHED	INDIAN NATION LAND[2]	PHYSICAL CHALLENGES
Abernathy	Weyerhaeuser			
Artic/Arctic	Rayonier			
Bangor		Naval Base Kitsap		
Bawfaw/Boistfort	Weyerhaeuser			
Blue Mountain/South	Weyerhaeuser			
Brittain	Rayonier			
Burma Point	Rayonier			
Burnt Mountain	Rayonier			
Burt	Weyerhaeuser			
Clearwater North	Rayonier			
Clearwater South	Rayonier			
Constance, Mount				Undefined site; likely a technical climb[3]
Cook Creek Spar Tree			Quinault	
Dayton Peak	Green Diamond			
Deep Creek	Rayonier			
Elk Creek			Quinault	
Gobbler Knob			Quinault	
Gunderson	Rayonier			
Hobi	Weyerhaeuser			

[1] The forest lands of the timber companies listed here were all freely accessible to hikers until 2010, when these major timberland owners gradually established programs to charge for entry to their properties. In 2021, most Green Diamond timberlands may still be hiked without an access permit. The other companies listed here offer no free public access to the lands for which they receive tax deductions as open space.

[2] These Indian nation lands were closed to the public in 2020-21. Visit their websites for current information: http://makah.com/makah-tribal-info, www.quinaultindiannation.com/

[3] A technical climb is one that requires a climber to use more than their hands and feet to ascend safely.

NAME	REASON			
	PRIVATE LAND REQUIRING FEES[1]	MILITARY BASE OR PROTECTED WATERSHED	INDIAN NATION LAND[2]	PHYSICAL CHALLENGES
Hoh/Oil City	Rayonier			
Jupiter, Mount (19 miles)				Lack of water supply
K O Point	Weyerhaeuser			
Kitsap		Bremerton Watershed		
Lem	Weyerhaeuser			
Lightning, Mount				Technical climb
Lincoln, Mount				Technical climb
Lone Mountain			Quinault	
McAfee Hill	Rayonier			
Minot Peak	Weyerhaeuser			
Moclips			Quinault	
Neah Bay			Makah	
North Bay	Rayonier			
Packsack	Weyerhaeuser			
Palix	American Forest Management			
Point Grenville			Quinault	
Prices Peak	Weyerhaeuser			
Pysht	Merrill-Rings			
Raft (River)			Quinault	
Salmon River			Quinault	
Scar Hill	Weyerhaeuser			
Sekiu	Rayonier			
Sooes Peak			Makah	
Trap Creek	Rayonier			
Vesta	Weyerhaeuser			
Weikswood	Weyerhaeuser			
White Star	Green Diamond			

APPENDIX TWO: SEKIU FIRE LOOKOUT AT THE FORKS TIMBER MUSEUM

Throughout Washington state there are several museums and parks where old fire lookout cabins can be visited without a hike. The Forks Timber Museum's outdoor displays include a replica Sekiu Fire Lookout cabin on a second-story tower. The museum is located on the east side of US Highway 101, at 1421 S. Forks Avenue, as the highway is known as it passes through the town of Forks. The museum is open daily, with a $3 entrance fee. Contact the museum: forkstimbermuseum.org or (360) 374-9663 for the latest information.

The Sekiu Lookout can be viewed from the ground or its catwalk, which can be visited from the second floor of the Forks Timber Museum.

History

In 1964, the Washington Department of Natural Resources built a 40-foot tower with a cabin on top at Sekiu Mountain, 8 miles southwest of the fishing village with the same name on the Strait of Juan de Fuca. The name is said to come from a Native American word meaning "calm water."[1] An August 1965 newspaper article reported the "new cabin-on-stilts" was first staffed by Mrs. Della Turner of Forks, wife of a DNR fire warden. She had views of "more than 700 square miles of valuable private and state-owned timberland" as logging roads gave access, and harvested forestland provided panoramic views from

---

[1] Phillips, 128.

the summit.² Documents at the Forks Timber Museum show the Sekiu Lookout was kept in service until the mid-1980s.

The final chapter of this fire watch station's history is known among Northwest Washington forest historians, but the details have not been previously published. In 1988, there was a community project to build a museum of local forestry in Forks, which included bringing the lookout cabin down from the tower and setting it up beside the brand new museum. Two work parties from the county jail had roles in the project. The first crew brought the tower down to the ground as planned. The tower legs were put in a burn pile and the sections of the deconstructed cabin were stacked in a second pile. The next day, the second crew arrived and either burned the wrong pile, or burned them both.

Fortunately for the museum, that was not the end of the story. The Washington Department of Natural Resources had another cabin available for the museum's use. The very similar Deming fire lookout cabin, sited on a similar tower 2 miles north of Deming in Whatcom County, was brought to Forks and erected beside the Forks Timber Museum. Manuals and equipment from the Sekiu Mountain Lookout building are now displayed inside the cabin standing on second-story stilts at the museum.³

---

² The August 26, 1965, *Port Angeles Evening News* article was quoted in http://washingtonlookouts.weebly.com/sekiu-mountain.html.
³ Ray Kresek provided the first clue to this story in his inventories listed in this book's Bibliography. It has been confirmed and expanded in conversations with Forks Logging Museum staff, DNR staff, and a northwest forestry historian.

GLOSSARY AND ABBREVIATIONS

Blaze: a mark made on a tree trunk by removing a section of bark using a hatchet. Its principal purpose has been to mark a trail route.

Boot path or track: a trail about 2 boot-widths wide.

Borrow pit: a construction term for a hole, pit, or excavation created for the purpose of removing gravel, clay, or sand, usually for a nearby project, such as a forest road.

Braided river or trail: a network of intertwining river channels or footpaths. Braided river channels are separated by small islands, tidelands, or marshland. Braided trails are usually separated by trees or sturdy shrubs that discourage merging of the narrow footpaths.

Cat track: A two-track path, left by a vehicle with a continuous tread.

Clearcut: a timber harvest practice that removes all or almost all trees from the tract being cut. It results in the patchwork forests common throughout the Pacific Northwest, with the trees in each patch a similar height. When replanted with only one tree species, it can result in a monoculture forest.

Key exchange: two parties of hikers start from different trailheads, meet on the trail they are hiking in different directions, and exchange their vehicle keys, intending to meet and return vehicles to their owners later.

Landing: the wide end of a forest road created to receive recently harvested logs.

Lookout: both a building and a job title.

Osborne firefinder: a device invented in 1911 by USFS forester William C. Osborne Jr. in Oregon. Its round iron baseplate holds an area topographic map and supports a rotating sighting mechanism that allows accurate identification of the location of smoke or a fire.

Spar Tree: a topped tree used as the main support for block and tackle and cables for moving cut logs in a harvesting operation.

Talus: geologically, the rock rubble brought downslope by earth movement or freeze-and-thaw activity.

Abbreviations

AWS: Aircraft Warning Service: a federal program to staff aircraft monitoring sites year-round, active in Washington state from late 1941 through May 1944.

CCC: Civilian Conservation Corps, 1933 to 1942.

DNR: The Washington Department of Natural Resources. Established in 1957, it replaced the Division of Forestry, which was in the Department of Conservation and Development.

FR: A forest road.

ONF: Olympic National Forest, established 1907.

ONP: Olympic National Park, established 1938.

RM: Reference mark: a secondary survey marker.

USFS: United States Forest Service.

USC&GS: United States Coast and Geodetic Survey. The federal agency that installed most of the survey markers on prominent locations to provide permanent benchmarks as a basis for local surveying. Established in 1807 to survey the US coast, it was expanded in 1817 to include land. The United States Coast and Geodetic Survey became part of the National Oceanic and Atmospheric Administration (NOAA) when that agency was formed in 1970. Its name was then changed to National Geodetic Survey.

WFFA: The Washington Forest Fire Association, an organization of private forest owners, reorganized in 1957 as the Washington Forest Protection Association.

ACKNOWLEDGMENTS

It took more than a village to write this book. Hikers, historians, rangers, foresters, archivists, librarians, and fellow writers have all contributed. *Lookouts: Firewatchers of the Cascades and Olympics* by Ira Spring and Byron Fish helped me realize the feasibility of exploring for lost fire lookout sites in the first place. The Tuesday Trotters and The Olympians Hiking Club were the two hiking clubs that welcomed me on their hikes to regional fire lookout sites. Olive Hull, Rosalie Gittings, Priscilla Pryor, and Harold Lloyd led the early twenty-first century hikes that got me hooked. Ray Kresek's more comprehensive lookout books and inventories expanded my horizons. National forest maps, Washington Department of Natural Resources quadrangle maps, and tree farm hunting maps supported my exploration for additional lookout sites.

Outstanding among the hikers who shared and supported my explorations in the Olympics and the Willapa Hills are Nancy Adams, Barb Agee, Susie Knight, Kerry Lowry, Linda Stretz, and Gordon Wiggerhaus. I especially appreciate the willingness of Jennifer Weldon and Henry Romer to come on recent lookout hikes while I rechecked my notes on routes and conditions.

The trail notes of the late Olive Hull got me thinking about writing a hiking guide with historical notes. She considered writing a guidebook for the fire lookouts and sites she had hiked to, but other priorities got in the way. I planned to write a hiking guidebook with brief historical notes, based on the work of Ray Kresek, Ira Spring, and Byron Fish, and Ron Kemnow. Weekly reviews by the Olympia Writers Critique Group urged me to liven the histories with the stories of fire lookout staff.

I fortunately met Keith Hoofnagle, 1960s' staff at Weatherwax Lookout, at a Forest Fire Lookout Association (FFLA) western conference. He told me about *"Ten-Eight,"* as he called it, the informal newsletter of the Washington DNR fire lookout staff, where they shared their stories.

While I was writing, Eric Willhite was expanding his travel website to focus on fire lookout buildings and sites, digging deeply into the National Archives in Seattle. His initial focus there was on the Aircraft Warning Service (AWS) of World War II, and the Osborne panoramic photographs taken at fire lookout stations in the mid-1930s. Eric has been very generous with the documents, photographs, information, and insight he gained through his research. We have also shared information on fire lookout stations discovered through our individual research efforts.

Ray Kresek gave my research a warm welcome at the Fire Lookout Museum in Spokane. He provided access to important documents there, and both access to, and information about, obscure historical fire lookout photographs.

Oregon fire lookout historian Ron Kemnow and I met at several FFLA conferences before I discovered his collection of quotes about, and photos of, individual fire lookouts on his lookout web pages. I appreciate his prompt responses whenever I email questions about his postings.

Irene Potter shared her valuable maps and photos from her explorations for the elusive Kelly and Byles fire lookout sites, making my efforts much easier.

Individual Olympic National Forest rangers and staff, active and retired, have been key to finding maps and documents that revealed little-known lookout station locations and histories. Molly Erickson and Deborah McConnell retrieved old fire management maps that confirmed the existence of questionable lookouts. Early in his retirement, Steve Ricketts organized a highly valuable collection of fire management maps, documents, and photographs, among a broad collection of other Olympic National Forest documents. With his help, I was able to access them at the National Archives in Seattle. Retired ranger Stan Graham has always found time to answer my questions and discuss interpretations of documents I have found. Former lookout staff Sandy Floe cleared up the confusing history of two Humptulips fire lookouts and an AWS station.

Washington Department of Natural Resources staff, from a regional manager to numerous local foresters, have provided a great deal of information on road and forest conditions as I planned field visits.

I spent long days in the National Archives in Seattle, the Olympic National Park Archives, the Washington State Archives, the Jefferson County Historical Society Research Center, and the Washington Department of Natural Resources Library. Each of these institutions has amazing professional staff who provided significant research assistance, which I greatly appreciate. Matthew DuBeau at the Olympic National Park Archives provided particular help when I was starting my institutional research in 2016, and gracefully responded to my follow-up questions.

Over the last several years, my drafts have been polished and the form of this book molded by the questions and support of the Olympia Writers Critique Group. The recommendations and assistance provided by Amanda Lowrence, Lindsay Pierce, Dave Weber, Ian Ferguson, Paul Pickett, Rick Taylor, Lance Brender, and Daisha Versaw have helped make this book possible and are hugely appreciated.

BIBLIOGRAPHY

Archival Records

Jefferson County Historical Society Research Center, Port Townsend. Newspaper articles and photographs related to fire lookouts on the Olympic Peninsula.

National Archives in Seattle. Records of the US Forest Service, Olympic National Forest. Maps—Seen area, Maps—Fire, and Maps—Lookout [and related documents].

Olympic National Park Archives, Port Angeles. Historical photographs, clippings and documents.

Washington State Archives, Olympia. AR9-0-12: Natural Resources Department, Forestry Division, Miscellaneous Fiscal Records.

Books

Amundson, Mavis. *The Great Forks Fire*. Port Angeles: Western Gull Publishing, c 2003.

Chriswell, Harold C. *Memoirs*. [Bellingham, WA: 1989.]

Dictionary of the Chinook Jargon; or Indian Trade Language of the North Pacific Coast. Seattle: The Shorey Book Store, Facsimile Reproduction, 1964.

Evans, Gail. *Olympic National Park Historic Resources Study*. 1983. Chapter 4. Wild and Quiet Places: Recreational Development; Chapter 5. Putting the Unemployed to Work: Depression Years and Federal Relief Programs; Chapter 6. Mobilized for War: World War II Military Involvement. Accessed 2016-2021 at www.nps.gov/parkhistory/online_books/olym/hrs/chap4.htm; chap5.htm; chap6.htm.

Felt, Margaret Elley. *Capitol Forest: The Forest That Came Back*. Olympia: Washington State Department of Natural Resources, 1975.

Krenmayr, Janice. *Footloose around Puget Sound*. Seattle: The Mountaineers, 1969.

Kresek, Ray. *Fire Lookouts of Oregon and Washington.* Fairfield, WA: Ye Galleon Press, [c1985].

Kresek, Ray. *Fire Lookouts of the Northwest*. Revised 3rd edition, 1988. Spokane: Historic Lookout Project. [First edition Sept. 1984.]

Kresek, Ray. *Fire Lookouts of the Northwest. Lookout Inventory. Revised 2015.* [Spokane: Fire Lookout Museum, 2015].

Manning, Harvey. *Footsore 4*. Seattle: Mountaineer Books, 1979.

Morgenroth, Chris. *Footprints in the Olympics: An Autobiography*, edited by Katherine Morgenroth Flaherty. Fairfield, WA: Ye Galleon Press, 1991.

Olympic National Park. *Historic Resource Study*. National Park Service, 2009. Accessed at www.nps.gov/parkhistory/online_books/olym/hrs/chap3.htm.

Olympic National Park. *Historic Resource Study*. Appendix A: A Chronology of the Public Domain. Accessed at www.nps.gov/parkhistory/online_books/olym/hrs/appa.htm

Parratt, Smitty. *Gods and Goblins: A Field Guide to Place Names of Olympic National Park.* Second Edition, edited by Gary L. Peterson and Glynda Peterson Schaad. Forks: Poseidon Peak Publishing, 2009.

Peterson, Gary L. and Glynda Peterson Schaad. *High Divide: Minnie Peterson's Olympic Mountain Adventures.* Forks: Olympic Graphic Arts, 2005.

Phillips, James W. *Washington State Place Names.* Seattle: University of Washington Press, 1971: 5th printing, 1985.

Rooney, J. R. *Frontier Legacy: History of the Olympic National Forest, 1897–1960.* Seattle: Northwest Interpretive Association, 1997.

Shaw, George C. *The Chinook Jargon and How to Use it.* Seattle: Rainier Printing Company, 1909. Facimile reproduction, Seattle: Shorey Publications, [1983].

Spring, Ira and Byron Fish. *Lookouts: Firewatchers of the Cascades and Olympics*, 2nd edition. Seattle: The Mountaineers, 1996.

Sterling, E. M. *Trips and Trails, 1; Family Camps, Short Hikes and View Roads in the North Cascades and Olympics*. Seattle: The Mountaineers, c1967.

Thomas, Edward Harper. *Chinook: A History and Dictionary of the Northwest Coast Trade Jargon*, 2nd edition. Portland: Binfords and Mort, c.1970.

Wood, Robert L. *Olympic Mountains Trail Guide: National Park and National Forest*. Seattle: The Mountaineers, 1984; 3rd edition, 2000.

Wood, Robert L. *Wilderness Trails of the Olympic National Park*. [Seattle: The Mountaineers, 1970].

Magazines

Olympia District's Ten-Eight, 1962–66. (The monthly newsletter of the Department of Natural Resources' fire lookout staff, compiled and distributed by Olga Hughett, May through September during its years of publication.)

The Totem, v.1–13, May 1958–December 1971, viewed at the Department of Natural Resources Library, Olympia.

Websites

www.ngs.noaa.gov/NGSDataExplorer

http://washingtonlookouts.weebly.com

http://willhiteweb.com/washington/fire_lookouts/olympics/list_460.htm

http://willhiteweb.com/washington_fire_lookouts/aircraft_warning_service/locations_091.htm

ABOUT THE AUTHOR

Photo by Lynn Murphy, courtesy of the photographer.

Leslie Romer grew up on a barrier island off New Jersey, with sand dunes the high points on the landscape. First hiking Olympic forest trails in her mid-twenties, she acquired a fascination with forest fire lookouts from her hiking companions and has now visited over 500 lookout sites in the Pacific Northwest and beyond. In this hike-and-history book about the forest fire lookouts in Washington's coastal region, she has brought together old-timers' memories and forgotten historical records to solve some of the mysteries surrounding the iconic fire watch sites.

Leslie now lives in Olympia, Washington, and loves dividing her time between hiking and writing about it.

AUTHOR'S NOTE

In her text, the author recognizes that questions remain—the answers not found in archives, or hidden in the salal at a fire lookout site. If you make discoveries, she asks that you share them with a comment to her website, www.LeslieRomer.com, or a post on the *Fire Lookouts of Washington* Facebook page.

The hike information in this text is the result of two decades of exploring these trails. Road, trail, and weather conditions change. Property ownership and use regulations change. When Leslie gains new information about the lookout sites in this region, she posts on her website, usually with a summary message on the *Fire Lookouts of Washington* Facebook page.

INDEX

Aircraft Warning Service (AWS), 18, 27, 38, 42, 47-48, 58, 66, 84, 98, 102, 126, 135, 144-145, 151, 165, 170, 177, 182, 188, 192, 198, 210, 214, 234, 242, 252, 271, 281, 291, 306, 322, 324, 328

Anderson Butte Lookout, 14, 186, 233, 252-258

Beeman, R. M., 42, 120, 134, 219, 229-230, 247, 259

Bethel, Jim, 47, 88-89

Big Quilcene Lookout, 12, 94-96

Blaney Mountain Lookout, 14, 301-305

Blue Mountain Lookout, 14, 22, 25, 26-29, 42

Blyn Lookout, 11, 18-21, 78, 94

Bogachiel Mountain Lookout, 11, 52, 57-64

Bulchis, Robert, 88, 98

Byles Lookout, 14, 276-280, 324

Capitol Peak Lookout, 14, 266-270

Capitol State Forest, 265, 268, 270-276

Chester Ridge Lookout 12, 170-172

Chriswell, Harold C. (Chris), 101-102, 211, 214, 252-253, 326

Civilian Conservation Corps, 18, 26, 42, 88, 97, 109-112, 198, 252-253, 297, 306, 322

Clearwater State Forest, See Hoh-Clearwater State Forest

Colonel Bob Lookout, 13, 149, 173-176, 186

Columbia River, 265, 275, 306, 309

Cowan Lookout, 14, 311-315

Crowsnest Lookout, 12, 130-133

Deer Park, 22, 25-29, 42

Dennie Ahl Lookout, 13, 210-213, 214

Doty Lookout, 14, 286-289

Dow Mountain Lookout, 12, 119-123, 124

Drake Lookout, 13, 242-246

Dusk Point Lookout, 14, 259-264

Ellis Lookout, 11, 71-75

Finley Peak Lookout, 12, 156-161

Foothills Lookout, 11, 34-37

Forest history, 1-2

Geodetic Hill Lookout, 12, 134-139

Gold Mountain Lookouts, 13, 203-208

Grays Harbor County Timberlands, 183, 185, 284

Green Diamond Resource Company, 6, 183-184, 189, 215-216, 219-220, 224-226, 230-232, 239-240, 242-244, 249-250, 317-318

Green Mountain Lookout, 13, 197-202

Green Mountain State Forest, 106, 197-205

Grisdale Hill Lookout, 13, 210, 213-218

Hamma Hamma Guard Station Lookout 12, 109-113

Harner, Wes and Winona, 162, 170

Higley Peak Lookout, 12, 162-164

Hoh-Clearwater State Forest, 142, 144, 150-151

Hoofnagle, Keith Lundy, 239, 247-48, 323

Hughett, Olga, 18-19, 78, 84, 94, 102, 327

Hull Creek Lookout, 14, 306-310

Humptulips AWS station, 165-166, 177

Humptulips Auxiliary Lookout, 13, 166, 177-181

Humptulips Ridge Lookout, 12, 165-169, 177-178

Hurricane Hill Lookout, 11, 38-42

Hyas Lookout, 12, 126-130

Incline Lookout, 14, 297-300

Jefferson Ridge Lookout, 12, 114-118

Johns River Lookout, 14, 281-285

Kelly Lookout, 13, 229-233, 324

Kitsap Peninsula, 13, 187

Kloshe Nanich Lookout, 11, 42, 65-70

Kloochman Rock Lookout, 12, 149, 150-155

Lost Lake Lookout, 13, 234-238

Lower Chehalis State Forest, 276-77

Mason Lake Lookout, 13, 188-191

Mealey, Robert H., 22-23, 30, 34, 101, 120

Mobray Lookout, 13, 239-241

Morgenroth, Chris, 52, 57-58, 140, 326

INDEX · 331

Mount Baker, views of, 32, 39, 45-46, 50, 78, 85, 92, 204

Mount Octopus Lookout, 12, 140-143, 149

Mount Pleasant Lookout, 11, 30-33

Mount Rainier, views of, 92, 100, 176, 189, 191, 202, 206, 211, 218, 227, 233, 245, 249-50, 269

Mount Townsend Lookout, 12, 81, 88-93

Mount Walker Lookouts, 12, 81, 97-100

Mount Zion Lookout, 12, 83-87

Neby Lookout Tree, 14, 259-264

Ned Hill Lookout, 11, 22-25

North Point Lookout, 11, 65-70

Olympic National Forest, contact information, 5, 116, 157

Olympic National Park, contact information, 5, 33, 49, 157

Olympic Peninsula East, 12, 77

Olympic Peninsula North, 11, 17

Olympic Peninsula South, 13-14, 209

Olympic Peninsula West, 12-13, 125

Owl Mountain Lookouts, 12, 144-149

Peterson, Minnie, 47, 58-59, 327

Pyramid Mountain Lookout, 11, 47-51, 58

Rock Candy Mountain Lookout, 14, 271-275

Safety, ii, 6-10, 50, 151, 154

Sekiu Lookout, 318, 319-320

Skidder Hill Lookout, 12, 78-82

Simpson Lookout, 13, 219-223, 224, 229-230

Simpson Timber Company, 214-215, 219, 230, 242, 250

Sol Duc Lookout, 11, 52-56

Sol Duc River, 52, 55, 61, 65-66, 68

South Mountain, 216, 219, 233, 263

South Mountain Lookout, 13, 219, 224-228

Squally Jim Lookout, 14, 290-296

Strait of Juan de Fuca, views of, 22, 27, 29, 31, 43, 50-51, 66, 75, 79, 93

Striped Peak Lookout, 11, 42-46

Tahuya Lookout, 13, 192-196

Twin Peak Lookout, 13, 182-186

Walville Lookout, 14, 290-296

Weatherwax Lookout, 13, 233, 239, 244, 247-251, 323

Webb Mountain Lookouts, 12, 101-108

Willapa Hills, 14, 265

www.ingramcontent.com/pod-product-compliance
Lightning Source LLC
Chambersburg PA
CBHW070906030426
42336CB00014BA/2313